SIMONE WEIL

Twentieth-Century Political Thinkers
General Editors: Kenneth L. Deutsch and Jean Bethke Elshtain

Raymond Aron: The Recovery of the Political
  by Brian C. Anderson, American Enterprise Institute
Jacques Maritain: The Philosopher in Society
  by James V. Schall, Georgetown University
Martin Buber: The Hidden Dialogue
  by Dan Avnon, Hebrew University of Jerusalem
John Dewey: America's Philosopher of Democracy
  by David Fott, University of Nevada
Simone Weil: The Way of Justice as Compassion
  by Richard H. Bell, The College of Wooster

SIMONE WEIL

The Way of Justice as Compassion

RICHARD H. BELL

ROWMAN & LITTLEFIELD PUBLISHERS, INC.
Lanham • Boulder • New York • Oxford

ROWMAN & LITTLEFIELD PUBLISHERS, INC.

Published in the United States of America
by Rowman & Littlefield Publishers, Inc.
4720 Boston Way, Lanham, Maryland 20706

12 Hid's Copse Road
Cumnor Hill, Oxford OX2 9JJ, England

British Library of Cataloguing in Publication Information Available

Library of Congress Cataloging-in-Publication Data
Bell, Richard H.
    Simone Weil : the way of justice as compassion / Richard H. Bell.
        p.   cm. — (Twentieth-century political thinkers)
    Includes bibliographical references and index.
    ISBN 0-8476-9079-2 (cloth : alk. paper). — ISBN 0-8476-9080-6
(pbk. : alk. paper)
    1. Weil, Simone, 1909–1943.   I. Title.   II. Series.
B2430-W474B434   1998
194—dc21   98-17453
                                                                                    CIP

Printed in the United States of America

♾ ™ The paper used in this publication meets the minimum requirements of
American National Standard for Information Sciences—Permanence of Paper
for Printed Library Materials, ANSI Z39.48–1984.

Dedicated to an inspired teacher,
Philip P. Hallie,
whose passionate life reminds us
how to live "truly" and "madly"
through the darkest hours of an age.

CONTENTS

Abbreviations for Simone Weil's Works Cited in Text — *ix*

Preface — *xi*

Acknowledgments — *xvii*

1   How Simone Weil Thinks: Time, Method, and Morality — *1*

2   "The Secret of the Human Condition": Power, Oppression, Work, and Liberty—A Brief Retrospective — *21*

3   Rethinking Justice and Rights — *33*

4   A New Virtue of Justice: Love, Friendship, and "Madness" — *57*

5   The Way of Justice as Compassion — *77*

6   Civil Society and the Law — *103*

7   Community and Politics: Human Needs and Social Obligations — *123*

8   Education and Civilization — *147*

9   Simone Weil, Post-Holocaust Judaism, and the Way of Compassion — *165*

10   Simone Weil's Way toward a "Worthy" Civilization: A Legacy for Moral and Political Practice — *191*

Appendix: "The Spirit of Simone Weil's Law"   *217*
    Ronald K. L. Collins and Finn E. Nielsen

Selected Bibliography   *243*

Index   *251*

About the Author   *259*

ABBREVIATIONS FOR SIMONE WEIL'S WORKS CITED IN TEXT

EL   *Ecrits de Londres et Derniéres Lettres.* Paris: Gallimard, Coll. Espoir, 1957.

ER   "Essay on the Notion of Reading." Translated by Rebecca Fine Rose and Timothy Tessin. *Philosophical Investigations* 13:4 (October 1990). Originally published as *"Essay sur la notion de lecture." Etudes Philosophiques* (Marseilles), N.S. 1 (January–March 1946): 13–19.

FLN   *First and Last Notebooks.* Translated by Richard Rees. London: Oxford University Press, 1970.

FW   *Formative Writings: 1929–1941.* Edited and translated by Dorothy Tuck McFarland and Wilhelmina Van Ness. Amherst: University of Massachusetts Press, 1987.

FWK   "Factory Work" in *The Simone Weil Reader.* Edited by George A. Panichas. Wakefield, R.I.: Moyer Bell Limited, 1977. (Second printing, 1994)

GG   *Gravity and Grace.* Translated by Emma Craufurd. London: Routledge & Kegan Paul, 1972.

IC   *Intimations of Christianity among the Ancient Greeks.* Translated by E. C. Geissbuhler. London: Routledge & Kegan Paul, 1957.

IL   *The Iliad or The Poem of Force.* Translated by Mary McCarthy. Wallingford, Pa.: Pendle Hill Pamphlet, no. 91, 1981. This essay is also in IC in a different translation.

IP   *Intuitions Pré-chrétiennes.* Paris: La Colombe, 1951.

LP   *Lectures on Philosophy.* Translated by H. Price with an introduction by Peter Winch. Cambridge: Cambridge University Press, 1978.

LPG   "The Legitimacy of the Provisional Government." Translated by Peter Winch. *Philosophical Investigations* 53 (April 1987).

LTP   *Letter to a Priest.* London: Routledge & Kegan Paul, 1953. op.

N   *Notebooks.* Translated by Arthur Wills. London: Routledge & Kegan Paul, 2 vols., 1956. op.

NR   *The Need for Roots.* Translated by Arthur Wills with a preface by T. S. Eliot. New York: Harper Colophon Books, 1971.

OL   *Oppression and Liberty.* Translated by Arthur Wills and John Petrie. Amherst: University of Massachusetts Press, 1973.

SE   *Selected Essays: 1934–1943.* Translated by Richard Rees. Oxford: Oxford University Press, 1962. op.

SJ   "Are We Struggling for Justice?" Translated by Marina Barabas. *Philosophical Investigations* 53 (January 1987).

SL   *Seventy Letters.* Translated by Richard Rees. London: Oxford University Press, 1970.

SNLG *Science, Necessity and the Love of God.* Translated by Richard Rees. London: Oxford University Press, 1968.

WG   *Waiting for God.* Translated by Emma Craufurd. New York: Harper Colophon Books, 1951.

Note: None of Simone Weil's translated texts quoted was changed to reflect gender inclusive language. For example, "man" and masculine pronouns are regularly used by her, and translations are consistent with that usage. Given her philosophical views, they would imply inclusion of *all* human beings.

op: out of print.

PREFACE

M any of the writers and actors covered in this Twentieth Century
Political Thinkers series are better known to English-speaking
audiences than is Simone Weil. Although not exactly "household
names," Reinhold Niebuhr, John Dewey, Mahatma Gandhi, Albert
Camus and Simone de Beauvoir are more easily recognized as having
effected some change either in our actual world or in how we think
about our world. Others in the series have influenced the theoretical
debates of political philosophy in many important and visible ways (e.g.,
John Rawls, Hannah Arendt, Leo Strauss, Martin Heidegger, and Jürgen
Habermas). Simone Weil, however, deserves greater visibility for the
originality of her thinking and for the potential ways in which her
thought can influence, even radically change, the way we think about
issues of justice, human community, friendship, education, and the law
as we enter a new and uncertain millennium.

The challenge of reading Simone Weil is to render her extraordinary thoughts and language into an ordinary idiom and to connect her
uncommon insights to our common life. To do this requires being serious students of her work. Most readers of Simone Weil, however, tend
to be like Lao Tzu's "average" or "worst" students of "the way"—they
are either "one moment there and gone the next" or "laugh out loud"
at proposals that seem incongruous with today's "enlightened" thinking.
If, however, there were none who "laughed," or scoffed, thought Lao
Tzu, "It would be unworthy of being the way." The way of Simone
Weil's moral and political thought is difficult and has both its skeptics
and its scoffers. This book is primarily for the skeptical readers and those
who wish to be "better" readers of her thought, as well as for those who

may even come to believe that "assiduous practice" of her way could benefit both personal and public life.

Simone Weil did not go unnoticed during her brief life (born February 3, 1909, and died August 24, 1943, at age 34),[1] and her life and thought did influence a number of important thinkers in our twentieth century. Maurice Schumann, classmate of Simone Weil and subsequent foreign minister of France under Charles de Gaulle, said that since her death there was hardly a day that the thought of her life did not positively influence his own and serve as a moral guide.[2] Both Albert Camus and André Gide referred to her as the most important spiritual writer of the century. Camus had Simone Weil in mind as "the very prototype of the *Révoltés* so vividly portrayed in . . . *The Rebel*," and in the early 1960s two successive Popes, John XXIII and Paul VI, found Weil to be among the most important influences in their intellectual development. Angelo Roncalli, the future John XXIII, once exclaimed to Maurice Schumann, "O yes, I love this soul!"[3] Even as a schoolgirl her reputation went ahead of her. Simone de Beauvoir wrote of Simone Weil: "Her intelligence, her asceticism, her total commitment, and her sheer courage—all these filled me with admiration; though I knew that, had she met me, she would have been far from reciprocating my attitude. I could not absorb her into my universe, and this seemed to constitute a vague threat to me." Of their first meeting in 1927 (both just eighteen years old), Simone de Beauvoir wrote: "I envied her for having a heart that could beat right across the world."[4] Other well-known literary and political figures of the twentieth century have testified to the powerful influence that Simone Weil had on their thinking and their lives. Such testimony comes from T. S. Eliot, Flannery O'Connor, Dwight McDonald, Mary McCarthy, Susan Sontag, Adrienne Rich, and Iris Murdoch, among others.

There are three books that serve as inherited background to this one. They are the intellectual biography of Simone Weil by David McLellan, *Simone Weil: Utopian Pessimist* (1989); the study of Simone Weil's philosophical ideas and their development by Peter Winch, *Simone Weil: "The Just Balance"* (1989)[5]; and the collection of essays, which I edited, by thirteen Simone Weil scholars focusing on the central ideas of her thought and how they relate to contemporary culture, *Simone Weil's Philosophy of Culture* (1993)[6]. What follows does not presuppose that the reader is familiar with any of these background books.

These books do, however, along with the works of Weil herself, locate the author's point of view and inheritance in approaching such a complex thinker in our century. The particular interpretation here is faithful to Simone Weil's texts and also shows how compelling her thought is in helping us develop a compassion-based moral philosophy that centers around what she calls "the supernatural virtue of justice." A continuing current in this book brings Simone Weil's thought about justice as compassion into the mainstream of contemporary moral and political thinking and extends her vision to important public policy issues.

Simone Weil makes us acutely aware of human abuse of power and the resulting instability and fragile nature of our civic order; she reminds us of the suffering and injustice that accompany our having abandoned any spiritual roots that may have earlier informed our moral and political thinking. Some fifty years after Simone Weil's death, Václav Havel, writer and president of the Czech Republic, laments our loss of a spiritual language in which to frame our political discourse. We have all but destroyed our ability to talk of politics and public policy in any transcendent idiom. "God," says Simone Weil, "was out of fashion" (OL 172).[7] Simone Weil, along with some contemporary thinkers like Havel, provides us with a new, broadly spiritual way of casting our moral and political discourse as it impinges on policy and on daily life. It is this reformulation of moral and political discourse and action in a spiritual framework that distinguishes Simone Weil's writing from others (with the exception perhaps of Gandhi) in this series.

Simone Weil's biographer, Simone Pétrement, said of her that "she felt that there should not be the slightest discrepancy between one's beliefs and one's way of life."[8] Although there are few discrepancies between her beliefs and her life, there are numerous discrepancies in ways of reading and interpreting her thought and life. The most contentious dispute among interpreters has to do with her religious integrity, particularly in her understanding, or lack thereof, of her Jewishness and her relationship with the Catholic Church. Was she a "self-hating" Jew or a self-proclaimed Christian? How one reads this controversy is very important to how one understands her meaning of compassion as we shall see. Was she more of the mystic and "saint" or the rebel and countercultural heroine? There is controversy over her death: Was it foolish or principled? Were her political schemes utopian and naive, or can they inform our sense of civic order and moral reform?

These controversies and more will be taken up in the course of this book. They are not, however, at this book's core. To understand justice as compassion is the moral core of her thought; it is what drives her political ideas and what weaves together her love of early Greek thought with her philosophical reflections. These, along with an intense experience with the incarnational center of Christianity and with "Oriental wisdom" in the latter years of her short life, led her to an understanding of justice linked with what she called a spiritual way of life. Contrary to Marx and other "liberal views," she believed that justice may be *in* this world by virtue of the supernatural, but that justice is not *of* this world (OL 176). There is for her an infinitely small, supernatural, paradoxical, secret core found "here on earth" that cuts across religious and cultural boundaries that lie at the root of all meaningful conceptions of justice (OL 174f.).

In her final London writings, Simone Weil says that the first duty of education is to remind its children, "ceaselessly," to be attentive "in order to be just." Attention is primarily an individual act, while justice necessarily involves human relationships—social relationships that involve varying levels of order and responsibility among their members. Her ceaseless, unrelenting reminder about *attending* and *being just* in all circumstances of human life is the legacy she leaves us—her "average" and "best" readers. But why should we care about *this* legacy? Because in our rapid-paced, digitized, commercialized society, our capacity for attention seems to have greatly diminished. In our haste we have all but lost the art of listening and attending to one another, and justice and the quality of our civic life are victims of this diminishment. Attention is one of Simone Weil's hallmarks; it manifests itself in compassion, which in turn evolves toward a new virtue of justice.

The structure of this book reflects a movement from understanding the evolution of her idea of justice to its application in broader moral and political thinking. Chapters 1 and 2 focus on her method as a philosopher and central themes from her literature and life that are formative for her moral and political thought. Chapters 3, 4, and 5 probe the crucial texts in Simone Weil's work that give shape to her unusually rich concept of justice as compassion and her compassion-based morality. Then, in chapters 6 through 9, we examine how her concept of justice as compassion applies to our thinking about issues of the law and civic order, community and politics, education, and to her understanding of how love and justice may be expressed to all human beings who suffer from cruelty and affliction in our world. All the while her thought is brought into dialogue with that of other philosophers, political actors, and traditions, ancient and contemporary—Socrates, Antigone, Taoism, contemporary feminism, Václav Havel and Paolo Freire, among others—to show its concreteness and importance for thinking through similar issues for ourselves. In these latter chapters (especially in chapter 9) we also try to understand how we are to balance the "religious" or "spiritual" features of her life with her more precise philosophical way of thinking. The last chapter recapitulates a number of themes discussed throughout the book that help us focus on the present human condition and how we might reconceive that condition with the help of *thinking with Simone Weil.*

Camus wrote: "The spirit of rebellion can exist only in a society where a theoretical equality conceals great inequalities. The problem of rebellion, therefore, has no meaning except within our own Western society."[9] As we approach Simone Weil, we meet "the spirit of rebellion"—a spirit that, in Camus' words, understands that the theoretical equality expressed in Western democracies "conceals great factual inequalities." Part of her rebellion is to seek remedies for such inequalities from outside ourselves and from cultures other than our own. Furthermore, Camus says, "Rebellion indefatigably confronts evil."[10] The evil of injustice and suffering will always be with us, and Simone Weil forces us, with Ivan Karamazov, to listen to the cry of each suffering child.

In Simone Weil's life and thought we are, as Iris Murdoch said, "reminded of a standard"—a standard of moral purity and austerity, intellectual integrity and political intensity. From all these things it is our hope that we may find some measures with which to analyze and understand our current human condition, and find a way toward a more humane civic order.

NOTES

1. Controversy surrounds the interpretation of her death. The basic facts are that she died of malnutrition after being hospitalized in Kent, Canterbury, England, for tuberculosis and either being unable or refusing to take more nourish-

ment than was being rationed to her compatriots in occupied France. Later, more will be said about understanding her death.

2. This was said by Schumann in an interview in the documentary *Simone Weil: Utopian Pessimist*, written by David McLellan and produced and directed by John Mair (A Mair Golden Moments Production for Channel 4, Great Britain, 1989).

3. See David McLellan, *Simone Weil: Utopian Pessimist* (London: Macmillan, 1989), 268f.; and Gabriella Fiori, *Simone Weil: An Intellectual Biography*, trans. Joseph R. Berrigan (Athens and London: University of Georgia Press, 1989), 309. These two biographies along with the indispensable work of Simone Pétrement, *Simone Weil: A Life* (New York: Pantheon Books, 1976), provide richly comprehensive and diverse pictures of the life and thought of Simone Weil. Readers who wish these more personal glimpses and the larger narrative of her life are referred to these works.

4. As found in McLellan, *Simone Weil,* 1 and 18. See also Pétrement, *Simone Weil,* 51.

5. Rowan Williams in a "Critical Notice" of Peter Winch, *Simone Weil: "The Just Balance"* (Cambridge: Cambridge University Press, 1989), notes that the main purpose of Winch's book "is to make us think *with* Weil, and in so doing to recognize her as a philosopher," and hails it as "the harbinger of a new generation of Weil scholarship." See R. Williams' review in *Philosophical Investigations* 14 (April 1991): 155–71.

6. This book—Richard H. Bell, ed., *Simone Weil's Philosophy of Culture* (Cambridge: Cambridge University Press, 1993)—resulted from three consultations in 1990 and 1991 held in Cambridge, England; Princeton, New Jersey; and Wooster, Ohio, where fifteen to twenty Simone Weil scholars from Europe and North America came together with the aim of focusing on her philosophical contribution for understanding culture. Portions of chapters three and four of this book are revisions of my essay "Reading Simone Weil on Rights, Justice and Love," taken from chapter nine in *Simone Weil's Philosophy of Culture*. These consultations were funded through a grant from the National Endowment for the Humanities and The College of Wooster.

7. The eighteenth century had a moral discourse rooted in deism, and the nineteenth century's "romantic turn" surrounded political discourse with a poetry of spirit. But in the twentieth century, Marxist and capitalist rhetoric had no transcendent voice, and in the wake of the mood of positivism and skepticism there is no dominant discourse of the spirit. Simone Weil understands this historical development clearly in her discussion of Marx in "Is There a Marxist Doctrine?" (see OL 171–74).

8. Pétrement, *Simone Weil,* 44.

9. Albert Camus, *The Rebel* (New York: Vantage Books, 1958), 20

10. Camus, *The Rebel,* 303.

ACKNOWLEDGMENTS

Three people brought me closer to Simone Weil. Sue Meinke Walters, as one of my students in 1972, persuaded me to read and discuss several Simone Weil works with her for an undergraduate independent study project. This was my first encounter with Simone Weil. Thank you, Sue. My former teacher Philip P. Hallie taught me how to think about the morality of good and evil, especially through his book *Lest Innocent Blood be Shed* and through his passionate life and teaching. Philip died on August 7, 1994. Peter Winch is mentor to a new generation of Simone Weil scholars who are coming to know her better as "philosopher." His book on Simone Weil showed the subtle, but clearly philosophical, maneuvers made in her thought and the attention she gave to the importance of language. Peter died suddenly on May 5, 1997.

With respect to shaping this particular book, I am grateful to Eric O. Springsted, who as President of the American Weil Society has hosted and supported a number of conferences on Simone Weil that have facilitated exchange among many scholars from different disciplines and between two continents. His good sense and insight into Simone Weil kept many from straying too far from where her thought may lead a reader. Eric's comments on an early draft of this book forced a number of new thoughts and refinements. Christine Ann Evans gave generously of her time in reading an earlier draft and called my attention to a number of important narrative examples of Simone Weil I may have otherwise overlooked. Remarks by Ronald K. L. Collins have been deeply appreciated—especially in suggested revisions on chapter seven. Sigrid Renner, a "master teacher" at University City High School in Missouri and a long-time friend, read an early draft knowing nothing of Simone

Weil. This provided me with an invaluable gauge as to how clear and engaging I was being for a more general audience. Thank you, Sigrid; your comments were very helpful.

I owe a debt to several students in a seminar titled "Simone Weil: Justice and Spirituality," which I taught at The College of Wooster in the spring of 1997. They showed unusual maturity and insight related to the ideas at the center of this book and were not afraid of trying to be the "best" students of her "way" of justice as compassion. One of those students, Rebecca Barnes, has also ably assisted me in creating the bibliography and with other important editing tasks. The College of Wooster, through a grant from its Henry Luce III Fund for Distinguished Scholars, freed me from teaching responsibilities during the fall semester 1997 in order to complete this book. Heidi Haverkamp was a great help in producing the index.

My wife, Barbara, was a continual inspiration as she was completing her own very different book begun only a year before I started writing this one. It was more than three times larger than my undertaking and a model of technical precision I held before me. She and our son and daughter, Jonathan and Rebecca, are continual joys in my life.

The Sisters of the Ecumenical Monastery of St. Benedict in Madison, Wisconsin, provided me with the freedom and solitude necessary to think hard about Simone Weil's often impenetrable writings and ideas and with a hospitable environment where I could discuss her ideas with a thoughtful and interested community. Much of the first draft of this book was crafted in the quiet woods at Courtney House on the monastery grounds during the summer of 1996. The book was completed in the same setting in the fall of 1997.

Wooster, Ohio
December 1997

When the best student hears about the way
He practices it assiduously;
When the average student hears about the way
It seems to him one moment there and gone the next;
When the worst student hears about the way
He laughs out loud.
If he did not laugh
It would be unworthy of being the way.

Tao Te Ching, Lao Tzu

1

HOW SIMONE WEIL THINKS:
TIME, METHOD, AND MORALITY

My relation to time forms the tissue of my life.

Simone Weil, *Notebooks*

"BATTLES AGAINST WINDMILLS"

The tissue of all humans' lives is bound up in their relationship to time: to the everyday concrete struggles of survival, of loves and hopes, fears and discouragements. The tissue of anyone's life is not only bound to time, to passage in our physical world, but also to other human beings. My life is formed in my relationships in communities—communities of play, work, worship, family, and society. Of course, time embraces both "me" as an individual and "my" relationships; the tissue of my private and public life unfolds in time. It is not easy to unpack the terse remarks of Simone Weil, especially as they appear unconnected in her notebooks. It is clear, however, that our lives are given their meaning in "our time," the time "we" receive and in turn shape through "our" actions. In Simone Weil's remark about time we have, in the words of Ludwig Wittgenstein, "A whole cloud of philosophy condensed into a drop of grammar."[1]

Simone Weil's conception of doing philosophy, like Socrates', is to see it as a remedial task—as preparing us to see things for which we may be otherwise blinded. Philosophy forces questions more than it gives clear answers. Simone Weil's philosophy is one of interrogation and contemplation of our culture; it makes us aware of our lack of attention to words and empty ideologies, to human suffering, to the indignity of work, to our excessive use of power, to religious dogmatisms—it relocates us in time. Rather than set out a system of ideas (like a theory of Justice or a theory of the Good), Simone Weil uses her philosophical reflections to show us how to think about work and oppression, freedom and the good, necessity and power, love and justice—even how to think about, or not think about, God. God, too, is in time insofar as God is part of the tissue of one's life. In this way we are asked to examine the temporal human condition and learn to discern a way through it.

In her essay, "The Power of Words" (1937), we gain some insight into how Simone Weil thinks. She writes: "When a word is properly defined it loses its capital letter and can no longer serve either as a banner or as a hostile slogan; it becomes simply a sign, helping us to grasp some concrete reality, or concrete objective, or method of activity. To clarify thought, to discredit the intrinsically meaningless words, and to define the use of others by precise analysis—to do this, strange though it may appear, might be a way of saving human lives" (SE 156). How could one restate the Socratic agenda more clearly? It is not just, as Socrates might say, that clarifying thought, discrediting meaningless words, and defining the use of terms by precise analysis may improve one's moral life, even one's community, but Simone Weil takes us a step further to say that this may be a way of "saving human lives." This is so because of the "Capital" abuses in the name of power and self-interest we experience so pervasively in our century. Simone Weil is specifically attacking what she calls "vacuous abstractions" that "stupify the mind" and "make us forget the value of life" (SE 170). In "our political and social vocabulary: nation, security, capitalism, communism, fascism, order, authority, property, democracy . . . we make these words mean anything whatsoever" (SE 157). And she concludes this thought, giving substance to her remark about our "relation to time form[ing] the tissue of [our] life," by saying:

> Our lives are lived, in actual fact, among changing, varying realities, subject to the casual play of eternal necessities, and modifying themselves according to specific conditions within specific limits; and yet we act and strive and sacrifice ourselves and others by reference to fixed and isolated abstractions which cannot possibly be related either to one another or to any concrete facts. In this so-called age of technicians, the only battles we know how to fight are battles against windmills. (SE 157)

This last thought of hers points to one of the most striking features in her philosophy. She always turns our focus to the concrete, the changing and varying realities in our lives, and the specific circumstances that affected them. This is often done through her use of historical and literary examples and in retelling short narratives from ordinary life. Each example presupposes a surrounding—a connectedness with a culture or concrete situation. Through them we are brought to the edge of new discoveries in our self and raised to new levels of insight. Christine Ann Evans notes that Simone Weil's examples suggest new readings of situations, and "with condensed energy and power they blast the reader into another reality newly configured over the course of a few words and sentences."[2] This philosophical/literary strategy gives her writings a pragmatic edge; it keeps surprise alive and prompts our "seeing" things once obscured by numerous ideological masks or otherwise myopic self-centered pursuits.

The "windmills" are the fixed ideologies that deflect us from time, from changing realities and the concrete facts of our day-to-day lives. The fixed ideologies—the Capital letter abstractions—mean whatever serves our interests, personally or politically. Let us look at two examples she gives us: first her assessment of the meaning of "national prestige" and "national security" when those become "capitalized," and second, how she characterizes the "murderous absurdity" in "the opposition between *fascism* and *communism*." These are 1936 observations of the raging ideological debates in Europe.

She notes that a nation's interests seem to serve the end of making war more than they serve the people's well-being—"petrol is much more likely than wheat to be a cause of international conflict" (SE 158). National prestige is oriented more toward "demoralizing other nations" than upbuilding one's own. And national security, she says, "is an imaginary state of affairs in which one would retain the capacity to make war while depriving all other countries of it" (SE 158f.). She concludes with this revealing question and answer: "But why is it so essential to be able to make war? No one knows, any more than the Trojans knew why it was necessary for them to keep Helen. That is why the good intentions of peace-loving statesmen are so ineffectual" (SE 159).

Simone Weil's analysis would apply to current (or at least pre-1989) textbook realpolitik rhetoric, and what was called the Cold War only heightened such rhetoric. Her analysis applies equally well to our stubborn nuclear predicament where mutually assured destruction (MAD) and détente also keep our capacity to make war, or extinction of humankind, a live option.

A second example about fascism and communism speaks for itself. She can hardly contain herself in describing how the two "isms" are "almost identical political and social conceptions" and yet people in France and Germany are about to go to civil war over them (in Spain they already had). Not to notice their similarities was, she believed, a sympton of "intellectual atrophy." She writes:

> In each of them the State seizes control of almost every department of individual and social life; in each there is the same frenzied militarization, and the same artificial unanimity, obtained by coercion, in favor of a single party which identifies itself with the State and derives its character from this false identification, and finally there is the same serfdom imposed upon the working masses in place of the ordinary wage system. No two nations are more similar in structure than Germany [Third Reich] and Russia [Stalin's regime], each threatening an international crusade against the other and each pretending to see the other as the Beast of the Apocalypse. Therefore one can safely assert that the opposition between fascism and communism is strictly meaningless. (SE 159)

Simone Weil observed while in Berlin the summer of 1932 that communists and fascists, while arguing loudly in the public squares, usually grew puzzled as it "became clear to both disputants that they were defending exactly the same program" (SE 160). Again drawing a parallel with the Trojan War, she says:

> That was four and a half years ago; the Nazis are still torturing German communists in the concentration camps today, and it is possible that France is threatened with a war of extermination between anti-fascists and anti-communists. If such a war took place it would make the Trojan War look perfectly reasonable by comparison; for even if the Greek poet was wrong who said that there was only Helen's phantom at Troy, a phantom Helen is a substantial reality compared to the distinction between fascism and communism. (SE 160)

She goes on to show how a "real opposition" exists between the concepts of "dictatorship" and "democracy" related to "order" and "freedom." But here too we must avoid capitalizing "Freedom" and "Democracy" lest they become "a thing-in-itself" devoid of specific reference to concrete social situations. At the very end of her life, in a manuscript that literally breaks off in the middle of a sentence, she said that much of philosophy is surrounded "with metaphysical clouds which, after one has looked at them fixedly for a certain length of time, become transparent, but reveal themselves to be empty" (OL 170; she thought this to be true of "Marxist doctrine").

Her very "philosophical procedure," Peter Winch notes, "is to root the concepts which are most important to her in actual, very concrete, features of human life."[3] She starts with specific circumstances of life that give rise to more abstract theoretical considerations. This feature quickly becomes clear in all of her essays, early and late. She turns us again and again to the "tissue" of life, to its circumstances that give rise to the many specific concepts in order, possibly, to "save lives." Speaking of Simone Weil's method of thought, J. P. Little says, "Every idea, to be real, has to find its incarnation. . . . We start in our experience of the world, and our perceptions are at the root of concepts about it."[4] Whatever our ideas about the world are, whether they be matters concerning our knowledge of the natural order or moral and political matters concerning rights and justice, love and hatred, war and peace, and how we use concepts to express our ideas, we start from where we are, with our perceptions and reactions, making concrete those ideas—"incarnating" them into our lives. "Our *perception* of the external world," Simone Weil says, "constitutes the essential relation between us and what is outside us, a relation which consists in a *reaction*, a reflex. The simple perception of nature is a sort of dance; this dance is the source of our perceiving" (LP 52).

Our approach to Simone Weil sees her thinking with and about concepts. This is an extension of her concern for "precise analysis" and the clarification of thought. Although a reader should not think of these concepts as isolated in her thinking (for they are highly interrelated as will become clear), it is useful to turn them over and interrogate how they are used by her. In doing so we reveal nuances in their meaning that might otherwise be missed. So in this book attention is focused on the concepts of "rootedness," "work," "rights," "justice," "love," "consent," "compassion," "law," "obligation," "education," and "community." Through these and related concepts a larger picture of Simone Weil's complex moral and political worldview emerges.

Simone Weil was a woman who always thought ahead of herself, who acted *with* her thoughts and who demanded no less of her contemporaries and those who might read her sometimes unconnected and condensed thoughts. Her writings, like her life, ended prematurely. They were as a whole incomplete. But in part because of their incompleteness, they invite readers to complete them through themselves—through the appropriation of her many insights applicable to their own lives. The reader is forced to "read" his or her *self* relative to the very specific circumstances in which he or she lives or relative to concrete actions that are being undertaken. This, too, is a fundamental Socratic characteristic: we should examine ourselves continually in our seach for truth and justice. Thus, it could be said, "This book is a reading of *myself* as one who stands at the juncture of two centuries in a time of great moral, philosophical and political ambiguity and transition in our human world, trying to clarify my own thought and understand my world."

Although it is often argued that Simone Weil's social philosophy reflects an "uncompromisingly individualistic point of view," stemming from her early anarchistic political outlook as well as a persistent epistemology that places obstacles in the way of realizing any meaningful knowledge of the other,[5] this interpretation is misleading. To emphasize her individualistic point of view causes a reader to overlook how Simone Weil understands the very concept of the individual as connected to a culture—as formed in a context by language, traditions, moral and religious practices, and more. Mary Dietz, for example, gives only a few pages to Simone Weil's discussion of "rights" and "justice," two concepts that necessarily involve relationships in social settings. Justice, as we shall see, always involves knowledge of and compassion for the other. The distinction between "rights" and "justice" will be shown to be pivotal for understanding Weil's moral and political thought in subsequent chapters of our study. As we unpack her meaning and use of justice, we will see that it leads us to a particular kind of moral practice *in* the public realm. Dietz sees Weil's thought to be centered on individual liberty over a person's moral role in the public sphere.[6] Our interpretive framework is very different. We will continually look at Simone Weil as a philosopher struggling to understand the nature of human language and action in time and view this struggle through the meaning of her central moral and political concepts as these are embedded in a largely "hostile" human world.

This latter point is clearly and convincingly shown in Winch's book. There we glimpse the evolution of this philosophical struggle through her writing. He reveals the movement in her thought from a Cartesian starting point to a more social view of language. He writes at the end of his chapter on "Language":

> Here the emphasis is on the role of language in the kinds of life people lead: the handing down of traditions, the uniting in action and feeling of those distant from each other, the intimacies of friends and lovers; the discourse of the soul with itself. Language is part of the essential constitution, so the suggestion seems to be, of certain distinctive patterns of human life: patterns formed in the intercourse of people with each other and in their attempts to see, or give form to their own lives as individuals.[7]

Winch is sure that these ideas were in place, in an embryonic form at least, in Simone Weil's *Lectures on Philosophy* (from 1933–34), and they are clearly developed in her later writings.

What Winch goes on to do in his book, and which is of particular importance to this book, is to set forward an approach to her thought from which there seems no turning back—an approach again that is best understood by keeping Socrates and his interrogative mode, rather than Plato, before our eyes as the model philosopher.

In Winch's reading, Simone Weil is giving us a kind of "geometry of human life" as the central feature of her later thought. This "geometry of human life" seeks an equilibrium between human beings and the natural order in which they live, or "a just balance" between the two and among human beings in the world. This balance requires several things, all of which are reflected in our argument: consent, the power to refuse, attention to the different readings that human beings give to the world and to one another, and an active "waiting" before God in order to "draw God down" into the arena of time and human action. This latter point shows how equilibrium is sought between what Simone Weil calls the natural and the supernatural.

As some equilibrium is approached, what is revealed is that the moral life should be, by choice, built upon obligations and compassion linked with supernatural sources toward the other and not upon the protection of an individual's "rights." This will be a central theme when discussing justice, love, and the law and again when *The Need for Roots* comes back into view.

Simone Weil's philosophy is one that continually asks whether we are truly "struggling for justice." Her works passionately and persistently call for a more humane sense of community and civic order, a revised legal and educational system, and a civilization that might overcome the gravitational weight of human power and arrogance. As was noted in the preface, when Simone Weil is read today—as would be true of any political writer who used terms like affliction, gravity, compassion, love, and supernatural virtue—she speaks to an audience largely unfamiliar with her language. But her language cannot be easily written off. She has credibility as a major social critic of European culture between the wars and as a serious activist for the oppressed. Increasingly, however, her language does make particular sense in our time. It challenges the empty rhetoric of a morally bankrupt enlightenment thought and matches a new tolerance—even searching—for a more spiritually connected or rooted life, especially since her spirituality, as we shall argue, is not tied to a particular set of doctrines or a single religious tradition.[8]

We must pause for a moment and step back to view some biographical features in her life that survey the moral and political landscape in which she found herself and try to understand her philosophical and personal approach toward the world in which she lived—a world that is also recognizable as part of our own.

ON BEING INSIDE THE FRAY

Simone Weil is best known for the intensity and single-mindedness of her life—a life that she said made "it impossible to take a position outside the fray." Being "in the fray" meant "shar[ing] the misfortunes of the workers and not the victory of the oppressors, even where the issue is one of sure defeat."[9] The focus of her early political concerns was that of the French workers. Not only did she write on behalf of trade unionism but she participated in strike action, gave night classes to miners in Saint-Etienne, and even organized a strike of unemployed street sweepers in Le Puy. She was active in the left political developments in the 1920s and 1930s in France and Germany, not as a communist but as an anarcho-syndicalist, and, in spite of her professed pacifism, exposed herself to the dangers of war by volunteering with the Spanish Popular Front in 1936 during its civil war. Even near the end of her life, while briefly "out of the fray" in New York City in 1942, she writes her friend Maurice Schumann, who is working with the French resistance in London, to save her "from being wasted by sterile chagrin" and get her back to Europe nearer the "frontlines." In her letter she says: "Suffering all over the world obsesses and overwhelms me to the point of annihilating my faculties and the only way I can revive them and release myself from the obsession is by getting for myself a large share of danger and hardship. That is a necessary condition before I can exert my capacity for work" (SL 156). She soon made it back to London. Beyond this intensity for political involvement was a philosopher who honed like a laser beam on how human power rules our public life and how we have diminished a quality of the spiritual in our life. It was that latter quality that she was determined to restore to thinking about the human condition and an individual's public role in it.

In December 1934 through July 1935 she plunged herself into manual labor at three factories in Paris. She found the factory experience both physically exhausting and spiritually humiliating. She kept a journal on this work that was a turning point for widening her concerns from primarily oppressed workers to the poor and oppressed found everywhere in our human condition. This wider concern was deepened by observing a village religious ceremony in Portugal in 1935 while convalescing and seeing for the first time that the power and attractiveness of the Christian religion lay in its being "a religion of slaves." At this time she did not see herself as a particularly religious person and certainly not a Christian believer. Over the next three years her moral and political ideas were slowly transformed by a series of religious experiences[10] and intense reflection on the relationship of God to the human condition and to the natural order of the world. In her seminal essay "Reflections Concerning the Causes of Liberty and Social Oppression," finished in autumn 1934 and collected in her book of essays *Oppression and Liberty,* she summarizes her perspective on workers and work, on the individual and the collective, on technology, on totalitarian regimes and the dangers of fascism, and on free market capitalism and communism in developing an adequate social and political philosophy.

After 1935 her social and political outlook is increasingly informed by a new spiritual development in her life. Political and moral reflection become inseparable from spiritual reflection. The latter reflection, as we shall see in subsequent chapters, had its own course of development that interfaces with classical Greek thought, Christianity, Platonism, her own Jewish background, and finally with Eastern (Hindu and Chinese) and North African traditions. What had been concerns for the liberation of the individual in *Oppression and Liberty* gives way to a more abstracted "human creature" and reflections on an ideal society without oppression. Such an ideal society must acknowledge not just human "rights" but "obligations," rooted in a new awareness of suffering and affliction and the pervasiveness of "injustices," where all humans may aspire for some good to come to them and struggle to avoid harm and where justice is reconfigured as a recreation of God's love where acts of love and compassion for all human creatures become its central moving force.

Her final statement on the building of society comes in her last and most ambitious work, *The Need for Roots: Prelude to a Declaration of Duties Toward Humankind*—a work commissioned by the Free French, headquartered in London, and completed in 1943 shortly before her death. In this work, says McLellan, "what was distinctive . . . was not so much her specific suggestions as the lucid and uncompromising expression of the philosophico-religious background from which she sought to justify them."[11] We will look more at the "philosophico-religious background" and the content of this work throughout this book and see, contrary to McLellan's conclusion, that many of "her specific suggestions" were equally distinctive to its style and background. Camus was to write of this work that "it seemed to him impossible to imagine the rebirth of Europe without taking into consideration the suggestions outlined in it by Simone Weil."[12] The rebirth of Europe after the war, of course, ignored her suggestions and on the one hand, pursued a frenetic free market strategy (Western Europe and Japan under American influence—a scenario she warned sternly against in her essay "Thoughts on the Colonial Problem") and, on the other hand, continued in a totalitarian path (Eastern Europe under Soviet control) and found itself once again poised to morally self-destruct. Perhaps the time is ripe once again, especially after the collapse of fascism and communism, to consider some of her radical suggestions.

"In her four months she spent working for the Free French," writes

McLellan, "she produced what amounts to about eight hundred pages of printed material. Writing very little in her notebooks now, she poured forth her thoughts in a series of essays and papers in an assured, lucid and compact style."[13] This material along with her essay on *The Iliad* (1940), "Reflections on the Right Use of School Studies with a View to the Love of God" (1942), and her Marseilles and New York *Notebooks* (1941–42) form the bulk of her most mature political, moral, and spiritual writings—three areas that can no longer be separated but form a philosophical whole and from which the major themes of this book are developed. In these we are given a new prism through which to read the human condition. These works reflect on twentieth-century culture and human nature from a moral perspective informed by a spirituality that embraces Greek classical thought, her selective absorption in and critical interpretation of the Christian religion, and what she called "Oriental wisdom." This moral perspective forces a radical reorientation on our understanding of such concepts as "rights," "justice," "love," "human obligation," "community," "law," and "education." Before we focus attention on this later group of writings and their major moral and political themes, we will make one last observation on how Simone Weil thinks—on her method and her moral point of view.

PHILOSOPHY FROM A COMPASSIONATE POINT OF VIEW

We must ask what difference there may be when reflecting on the human moral and social order with a woman thinker. Although this is a precarious path to set out on, it does seem clear that different concerns are taken up with different emphases and from a different point of view when a woman does the reflecting. The human condition, of course, is neither male nor female. It is both, in complex and interwoven ways. We have come to know it, however, in philosophy and political theory predominantly from a male point of view. And "power" as a social and political concept has "male" written all over it. So to see the human condition through Simone Weil's eyes may teach us some things that are very fresh and new. We believe that to be true, and accept Adrienne Rich's challenge that Simone Weil's thought must be examined in the light of her being a woman. Rich writes: "Her life and thought will only come clear to us when we begin to ask what it meant to be a woman of her genius and disposition. Her stunning insights into domination and oppression, her self-derogation, her asceticism, her efforts at self-creation, her final self-destruction—all have to be examined in this light."[14]

Questions in philosophy and society cannot be adequately answered from a single point of view; they take place "in the matrix of human relations and traditions"—in the "tissue" of people's lives, in continual telling and retelling from many perspectives. And the perspective we have been given by male moral and political philosophers has simply not told the whole story with respect to understanding how we know and value our world or about the human self and divinity.[15] Simone Weil provides another perspective on understanding these issues—one that stands on its own two feet epistemologically, logically, morally, and spiritually in her time and in ours.

Simone Weil clearly writes her self into her texts and into the world and history in a manner that is both personally dramatic and philosophically profound. She does this with such bold declarations in her notebooks as "*Je ne suis pas féministe*" [I am not a feminist]. This is not unlike her having said in another context, "I am not a Jew." But where do such seemingly uncompromising declarations take us? In both these cases she wishes to diminish the "I" (ego) of the human self. Gender, like race and class and religion, designates artificial qualities of a human being, peripheral to what is essentially human. There is an important difference, however, in her denial of being a feminist and being a Jew. (We will explore this latter denial in detail in chapter 9.) To hear her say that qualities of our "personality" are artificial may, in itself, give us pause. How could Simone Weil put herself into a text simply as a human being and not as a *specific* human being—as a woman, French, and intellectual of a particular time? If, as she says in the late 1930s, "I am more French than Jew," we can more easily see *her* as "*she*" and not as merely "human"—"she" is Simone Weil and not Simone de Beauvoir. So it is "her"—all of her—and not someone else who is in her texts. *While denying being a feminist she, at the same time, sees and develops virtually every aspect of her thought with the eyes that proceed or originate from a particular woman's experience.* We should not lose sight of this.

Simone Weil frequently focuses on women's needs. In her factory journal she becomes an oral historian for her coworkers—anonymous, forgotten, exploited women. She gives voice to oppressed and silenced groups in society—to her women co-factory workers, to prostitutes, to vagrants, the crippled, to violated women. She condemns the "commerce" of the "white slave traffic" (OL 183). Simone Weil gives names to all who are humiliated and stripped of power.[16] Also specific women are, for her, moral heroines for both men and women: Antigone, Electra, Joan of Arc, Rosa Luxemburg, and George Sand. Rarely in Western political and philosophical literature are women lifted up as moral models (we hear only of a few "saints" and their saintliness is based in part on perceived "miraculous" or pious behavior, not ordinary moral qualities).

Way ahead of current discussions in moral philosophy, Simone Weil teaches us a capacity to care. She, in Clare Fischer's words, analyzes "the fragility of the human spirit" and "refines an ethic of care."[17] Simone Weil explores the human condition, and in particular her notion of justice, with this particular sensibility in a manner not unlike that of Nel Noddings in her relational ethics of caring.[18] Noddings places "caring" as a motivation for our being moral: it is the way we strive for the good. We will develop the implications of the notion of an "ethic of care" with Noddings and others in chapter 5 in connection with our discussion of Simone Weil's "compassion-based" morality.

Finally, Simone Weil gives us an epistemology that focuses on action linked to the "bodiliness of human beings," increasingly drawing away from and rejecting Descartes' mind—body dualism, and seeing the world from the perspective of one's "lived-body." Thinking is extended through our bodies, our perceptions, like one's thoughts are "carried to the end of the pen" (ER 298). This, of course, is not to be thought of as a "feminist epistemology." It is an idea consistent with other contemporaries of Simone Weil such as phenomenologists Maurice Merleau-Ponty and Martin Heidegger (though there is no evidence that she borrowed any of this from them). It is an idea, however, about how we know and relate to our world that is lifted up by many feminist philosophers a generation after its development in thinkers like Weil, Merleau-Ponty, and Heidegger. The very notion of our bodies being involved in knowing relates to Simone Weil's belief that every idea must find its incarnation—of our simple perceptions being "a sort of dance." Emphasizing our bodies even more she says: "the body classifies things in the world before there is any thought. (Example: the chick leaving the egg distinguishes between what is to be pecked and what is not.) So, for the very fact that we have a body, the world is ordered for it; it is arranged in order in relation to the body's reactions" (LP 30f.); "Everything that we see suggests some kind of movement, however imperceptible. (A chair suggests sitting down, stairs, climbing up, etc.)" (LP 31); and "There is already, then, an elementary geometry in perception. . . . It is this . . . which moves us in [seeing] a cathedral spire or in [hearing] a symphony" (LP 51f.). She ties the beauty of the world to "carnal love": "We want to love the beauty of the world in a human being—not beauty of the world in general, but the specific beauty which the world offers to each man and which corresponds exactly to the state of his body and his soul" (FLN 84). Her very point of departure in how we experience the world is centered in seeing, feeling, responding to her surroundings. This "fleshing out" of our thinking, carrying it into how we know and constitute our world, is what she calls "reading."[19] This may not be "feminist" in the way we understand that word today, but it is in this case clearly thinking from a woman's (Simone Weil's) point of view.

Near the end of her intellectual biography of Weil, Gabriella Fiori provides us with still another perspective on her point of view as a woman. Fiori says: "Simone Weil is *genius-woman*. She is a moral genius in the orbit of ethics, a genius of immense revolutionary range."[20] The character of this "genius" will become clear as we see how she treats the concepts of justice and love and how her ethical concern moves us out of our individualism to a particular other and to obligations we have in a civic order. Fiori also says Simone Weil is a woman with

> characteristics of spiritual fruitfulness: the importance of nurturing, of tending, of protecting . . . ; attention to preservation . . . ; the prevalence of weakness over force; the importance of words, of language that communicates; . . . the emphasis placed upon the practical application of wisdom for the greatest possible happiness . . . on earth.[21]

Although Fiori may be too unbridled in her praise, the qualities she points to can all be found in Simone Weil's work, albeit in often indirect allusions. Part of our job is to remove the veil from some of these allusions and reveal the energy of this woman's voice.

CONCLUDING REMARKS ON METHOD

"Philosophy (including problems of cognition, etc.)," says Simone Weil, "is *exclusively* an affair of action and practice. That is why it is so difficult to write about it. Difficult in the same way as a treatise on tennis or running, but much more so" (FLN 362). Whether our philosophical problems are about cognition, or about the moral life, or about our public political lives, they are matters of action and practice and not of *theory* for Simone Weil. This difference with respect to her moral and political thought will become clear as each chapter unfolds. Striving for the good, avoiding harm, combating harm-doing are all things people do, and they all take place in time and in social contexts. Simone Weil never skirts this fact. To be a human being is a practice. It requires that we learn which moves in each game we play yield the most humane and practical results and create the most decent and desirable world.

Late in Ludwig Wittgenstein's life he remarked: "When you are philosophizing you have to descend into primeval chaos and feel at home there."[22] One could hardly find a more accurate description of Simone Weil's "philosophizing." Along with many "stops and starts" in making sense of her ideas, one always accompanies her in a "descent" into some form of "primeval chaos." In these descents there are sufficient moments when her way of putting something or her way of taking you through a difficult thought makes you feel at home—when you are given a sudden "aha!" when "the penny drops," when the human order suddenly becomes perspicuous or, as noted above, you are "blasted" into "another reality newly configured over the course of a few words and sentences." That happens, however, *because* you descend deeply into a "primeval chaos" and resurface with some new clarity or a deeper human puzzle to resolve. Simone Weil, like Wittgenstein, wanted to dispel the "metaphysical clouds" and move us back to, as Wittgenstein said, "the rough ground"—the terrain of action and practice.

Rush Rhees, reflecting on Weil's writings in the early 1960s remarked: "On a great number of questions I have found remarks of hers which are more illuminating than any others I know." Rhees finds some ideas "barren," some "wonderful." He believed, for example, that "her religious observations go deeper than Kierkegaard's." "She is an example," continues Rhees, "of a writer whose greatness of soul comes out in frequent remarks—which makes the difficulties or shortcomings of her more theoretical observations seem of no importance at all."[23]

The "primeval chaos" of Simone Weil's world is the world of Greek poetry and tragedy and Greek philosophy; it is the world of St. John of the Cross and Meister Eckhard; it is the world of a radically incarnational Christology without dogma; it is a world of Descartes, Kant, Racine, Alain, and René Le Senne; it is the world of the *Bhagavad-Gita*, Taoism, and Zen Buddhism; it is a world of folklore and mythology; it is the world of resistance and rebellion—a search for the Grail through a half century of great human affliction. It is into that chaos that one descends when one reads Simone Weil. As we take up central moral and political issues buried in the primeval chaos, this book will serve as a guide through some of that chaos with the sole aim of making us all feel a bit more at home, or at least in having exposed ourselves to a "standard" to challenge our "average" or "worst" attempts at understanding.

Simone Weil's moral and political philosophy has both *pragmatism* and *idealism* built into it. It is *pragmatic* because she asks us continually to discern the character of and endlessly to struggle against the debilitating nature of our human world—the ways it humiliates, crushes, politicizes, demoralizes, and generally destroys the human spirit. It is *idealistic* in that she proposes our only hope in our discernment and struggle is to insinuate the ideal into our real human practices, or spiritually put, to wholly desire the incarnation of the eternal into time, into the everyday actions of our human life—to "draw God down" into real human affairs. It is this latter capacity that our modern and postmodern worlds have forgotten, and it is just that spiritual dimension that we will show to be essential to understanding her moral and political thought, and perhaps essential to reviving a meaningful moral and political thought for the new millennium.

NOTES

1. Ludwig Wittgenstein, *Philosophical Investigations* (London: The Macmillan Company, 1953), Part II, 222e.

2. Christine Ann Evans, "The Power of Parabolic Reversal: The Example in Simone Weil's Notebooks," *Cahiers Simone Weil* 19, no. 3 (September 1996): 324.

3. Winch, *Simone Weil,* 190.

4. J. P. Little, "Simone Weil's concept of decreation," in *Simone Weil's Philosophy of Culture,* 28.

5. This is one central theme of the book by Mary G. Dietz, *Between the*

Human and the Divine: The Political Thought of Simone Weil (Totowa, N.J.: Rowman & Littlefield, 1988).

6. Dietz's book is, along with Lawrence Blum and Victor Seidler, *A Truer Liberty: Simone Weil and Marxism* (London: Routledge & Kegan Paul, 1989), important in its focus on the central issues of her political thought, but its interpretive framework is very different from our own. Dietz proposes "to offer some psychoanalytic insights with specific attention to identity theory" for her commentary on Weil's political writings. She says, "The interpretive framework takes its impetus from the methodological presumption that deep interrelationships exist between early conflicts in a thinker's life and later themes and ideas in his or her work" (Dietz, *Between the Human and the Divine,* xv).

Dietz believes Simone Weil to be "an especially appropriate candidate for a psychoanalytic study, . . . She was a clear example of what Erik Erikson has termed 'a contradictory bundle of identity fragments': a woman who did her best to obliterate what was feminine about her, yet who found masculinity a suspect category, a Jew who rejected the Hebrew tradition and professed Christianity while refusing to join the church, a defender of the working class who found all political collectivities suspect, a mystic who renounced this world, yet died literally identifying with France, while denouncing French nationalism" (xvi). There are these contradictions in her life and we will have something to say about all these "contradictory fragments" but from a decidedly different point of view and often with very different conclusions.

7. Winch, *Simone Weil,* 58. A similarity exists between Simone Weil's view of language and that of Ludwig Wittgenstein developed in the same period, the 1930s and early 1940s, though independent of one another. Winch makes a great deal of this comparison.

8. The central idea in this paragraph is analogous to one drawn by James Boyd White about how the language of George Herbert's poetry speaks to contemporary readers. See White, *"This Book of Starres": Learning to Read George Herbert* (Ann Arbor: University of Michigan Press, 1994), 129. Herbert's poetry (his language) was among Weil's favorites. His poem "Love" inspired her most compelling mystical experience. (See WG 68–70.)

9. As found in Fiori, *Simone Weil,* 83. From a letter fragment of Simone Weil dated at the end of January 1933.

10. Simone Weil gives her own account of these religious experiences in her "Spiritual Autobiography," found in *Waiting for God,* 66–69. Simone Pétrement has an interesting discussion of these experiences and how she believed Simone Weil received and understood them. See Pétrement, *Simone Weil,* 339–42. Pétrement writes of her third experience linked with her reading of George Herbert's poem "Love": It was not that Simone Weil may have had an experience of Christ present to her that was astonishing, but "that she believed in the reality of this manifestation" (341).

11. McLellan, *Simone Weil,* 237.

12. As found in *Simone Weil: An Anthology,* introduction by Sian Miles (London: Virago Press Limited), 1986, 57.

13. McLellan, *Simone Weil,* 245. Among the particular essays and papers to which McLellan is referring and which are now published in English are: *The Need for Roots,* "Human Personality" (in SE), "Essay on the Notion of Reading," "Are We Struggling for Justice?" "The Legitimacy of Provisional Government," "Draft for a Statement of Human Obligation" (in SE), "Is There a Marxist Doctrine?" (in OL), "The Love of God and Affliction" [second part] (in SNLG), and "Notes on Cleanthes, Pherecydes, Anaximander, and Philolaus" (in SNLG).

14. Pétrement, *Simone Weil,* from an appraisal of Pétrement's book by Adrienne Rich found on the book jacket. The author was unable to track down any other published source of this remark—even with the help of an Adrienne Rich scholar.

15. Andrea Nye, in *Philosophia: The Thought of Rosa Luxemburg, Simone Weil, and Hannah Arendt* (New York: Routledge, 1994), correctly notes that "the tradition of male philosophers has failed to produce an understanding of divinity, self, value, reality, knowledge viable in the late twentieth century" (xx).

16. This point was made clearly by E. J. Doering, in an unpublished paper given at the 1992 American Weil Society meetings, "Simone Weil: A Woman's Voice," 4. I have borrowed Doering's notion of Simone Weil as "an oral historian for her co-workers." Some of Simone Weil's best thoughts on factory work and women workers are found in letters to pupils and friends in SL 10–23.

17. Clare B. Fischer, "Cassandra's Vision: Two Twentieth Century Women Read *The Iliad* for our time," unpublished essay. In this essay interesting parallels are drawn between Simone Weil and the German writer Christa Wolf.

18. Nel Noddings, *Caring: A Feminine Approach to Ethics and Moral Education* (Berkeley, Calif.: University of California Press, 1984). Noddings says that she wants to root ethics in "receptivity, relatedness, and responsiveness" (2ff.).

19. We shall say more about reading as we progress. Perhaps the best single essay to comprehensively discuss Simone Weil's notion of "reading" is Diogenes Allen, "The Concept of Reading and the Book of Nature," in *Simone Weil's Philosophy of Culture,* especially 95–102 and 109–14.

20. Fiori, *Simone Weil,* 309.

21. Ibid.

22. Ludwig Wittgenstein, *Culture and Value* (Chicago: University of Chicago Press, 1980), 65e.

23. Rush Rhees, *Discussions of Simone Weil,* ed. D. Z. Phillips with Mario von der Ruhr (Albany: State University of New York Press, forthcoming 1998). Rhees's reflections are among the earliest of any British or American philosopher

to have examined Weil's writings seriously and critically. He was moved and often confounded by them. Related to the above remarks he says: "I have understood from her writings what is meant by thanks to God for the realization that one's own existence has no worth; and in this connection, what it means to speak of feeling *equal* gratitude for joy and for affliction. I have not found this understanding in any other religious writer—St. Paul, St. Augustine or Kierkegaard, for instance."

2

"THE SECRET OF THE HUMAN CONDITION": POWER, OPPRESSION, WORK, AND LIBERTY—A BRIEF RETROSPECTIVE

> The secret of the human condition is that equilibrium between man
> and the surrounding forces of nature "which infinitely surpass him"
> cannot be achieved by inaction; it is only achieved in the action by
> which man recreates his own life: that is to say by work.
>
> Simone Weil, "Pre-war Notebook"

In this chapter we will show briefly the evolution of Simone Weil's moral and political thought by looking at some key social and political concepts as discussed in *Oppression and Liberty* (1934) and how decisive changes in her life (connected with political changes in France and Western Europe) between 1935 and 1940 led to a new and sharper focus on the concept of justice in her last writings from 1940 to 1943. Through this, we can trace a transformation toward a more spiritual critique of the human condition and perhaps "unlock" its "secrets."

Simone Weil's earlier moral and political views on liberty, oppression, and society were formed in the intellectual and revolutionary debates raging through the first third of the twentieth century, especially as those were shaped by the dominance of Karl Marx's critique of capitalism and work. But even with Marx as one mentor, her view of the individual and society was as clearly rooted in the thought of Rousseau and Proudhon as it was in Marx and Marxism. Her animated debates with Leon Trotksy in 1933 bear witness to this.[1] The target of her harsh critique of the human condition between the wars was abuse of power viewed historically more than it was the proletariat struggle based on division of labor and forces of production. She placed the latter struggle in a larger perspective than did Marx.[2] She says:

> Once society is divided up into men who command and men who execute, the whole of social life is governed by the struggle for power, and the struggle for subsistence only enters in as one factor, indispensable to be sure, of the former.
>
> The Marxist view, according to which social existence is determined by the relations between man and nature established by production, certainly remains the only sound basis for any historical investigation; *only these relations must be considered first of all in terms of the problem of power.* . . . (OL 71, emphasis added)

It was primarily Marx's *method* for analyzing the role of economics in recent social history that she admired. An "idea of genius" Marx had, writes Simone Weil, was "taking society [rather than the individual] as the fundamental human fact and of studying therein, as the physicist does in matter, the relationships of force." But she goes on to say: "Having had this idea, Marx hastened to render it barren . . . by plastering over it the wretched cult of science of his time" (OL 171). In spite of her anarchistic tendencies, this point of Marx about society as the fundamental human fact and his studying the relationships of force within it had a profound and lasting effect on her subsequent social and political thought. She was to understand force, however, differently from Marx.

On another point, Andrea Nye's brief discussion of Simone Weil's critique of Marxism is very illuminating. Nye shows that Simone Weil believed, contrary to Marxist theory, that ownership need not be oppressive. Nye remarks: "Ownership can be based on a duty of stewardship and responsibility to others and not on exploitation." Oppression has its roots in abuse of power, on "force exerted by one person against another, force that takes the form of power over that other. Even where there is no private ownership, even where property is held collectively, force can be exercised."[3]

For Simone Weil, Homer's *The Iliad* was the first and principle critique of power. After that, historical examination of "the Great

Beasts"[4] shows the nature of the relationship of humans to our natural state. In the end "all power is unstable" (OL 67); neither oppressor nor oppressed escape this fact. Both victors and vanquished, she says, are "brothers in the same misfortune" (IC 39):

> The powerful, be they priests, military leaders, kings or capitalists, always believe that they command by divine right; and those who are under them feel themselves crushed by a power which seems to them either divine or diabolical, but in any case super-natural. Every oppressive society is cemented by this religion of power, which falsifies all social relations by enabling the powerful to command over and above what they are able to impose; it is only otherwise in times of popular agitation, times when, on the contrary, all—rebellious slaves and threatened masters alike—forget how heavy and how solid the chains of oppression are. (OL 72f.)

The disequilibrium of oppressed and oppressor, however an unstable fact of nature, must be seen and responded to. She says there are only two ways of breaking this vicious circle of master/slave or oppressor/oppressed and the fear that each instills in the other:

> either by abolishing inequality, or else by setting up a stable power, a power such that there exists a balance between those who command and those who obey. It is this second solution that has been sought by all whom we call upholders of order. (OL 66)

The liberal strategy of thinking one can abolish inequality she believes as unlikely to succeed as the conservative strategy of sustaining order. Stabilizing power is like chasing chimeras. A balance of *power* is not "a just balance." Nor will the attempt made by humans to master nature and thus "control" nature and "engineer" social arrangements produce "a just balance."

It seems clear that the human condition is caught in the grip of power—oppression of the working class is less a result of abusive means of production by industrial barons or faulty bureaucracies than it is due to more general struggles for power, by "force exerted by one person against another." The issue, then, is how to overcome this condition. In *Oppression and Liberty* she saw little hope of resolution. For her, revolution was not the answer. Revolution could not be carried out by workers who were denied a capacity to think. Furthermore, revolution simply changed who held the power and thus changed little. How do we get ourselves out of this hole we have dug for ourselves? "Everything that has happened since August 1914," she says, shows that we are on a path of "destroying all the conditions for the material and moral well-being of the individual, all the conditions for intellectual and cultural developments" (OL 20). Where are we to place our hopes? she asks. Without a clear and compelling sense of a power other than human power, or without appealing to any transcendent power, there seems no way out except to try to "think our way out." That was her philosophical strategy in the early 1930s. It was not until her later, post-1940 writing that she could confidently say that the predicament we are in was a result of having "forgotten the existence of the divine order of the universe" (OL 168, from the 1943 "London Fragments").

Simone Weil's solution in the early to mid-1930s on how to achieve a more just balance to restore greater equilibrium in society is through a kind of "cooperative," but *not* "collective," use of thought and action: "Nothing on earth can stop man from feeling himself born for liberty. Never, whatever may happen, can he accept servitude; for he is a thinking creature" (OL 83). She wants to try to represent "perfect liberty," she says, "not in the hope of attaining it, but in the hope of attaining a less imperfect liberty than is our present condition" (OL 84). Individual action takes center stage here, "an heroic conception" of an individual striving against all odds, but with thought and action seeking this freedom in cooperation with others. We are not made "to be the plaything of the blind collectivities that [we] form with [our] fellows, . . . but in order to cease being delivered over to society as passively as a drop of water to the sea, [we] would have to be able both to understand and to act upon [our society]" (OL 97f.). She continues:

> True liberty is not defined by a relationship between desire and its satisfaction, but by a relationship between thought and action; the absolutely free man would be he whose every action proceeded from a preliminary judgment concerning the end which he set himself and the sequence of means suitable for attaining this end. It matters little whether the actions in themselves are easy or painful, or even whether they are crowned with success; pain and failure can make a man unhappy, but cannot humiliate him as long as it is he himself who disposes of his own capacity for action. (OL 85)

"To sum up," she says, "the least evil society is that in which the general run of men are most often obliged to think while acting, have the most opportunities for exercising control over collective life as a whole, and enjoy the greatest amount of independence" (OL 103). It is this emphasis on "the greatest amount of independence" that Mary Dietz sees as the major flaw in Simone Weil's view of politics, that is, in the relation between individual and society. Dietz argues that Simone Weil fails, in rejecting all "collectives," to seriously consider a notion of the "public sphere" of politics that might lead to a reasonable idea of community. She contrasts Simone Weil's view with that of Hannah Arendt.[5]

The "secret of the human condition," then, involves thoughtful action that restores equilibrium and recreates our individual lives within the "surrounding forces of nature." These forces, she says, "infinitely surpass" us so our task is a daunting one. In *Oppression and Liberty* she speaks of cooperation while emphasizing the importance of freedom of the individual. She says very little about how and with whom one is to cooperate. She says only that we "have to be able both to understand and to act upon our society." Even when she offers a solution in one phrase: "the only possibility of salvation would lie in a methodical coop-eration between all, strong and weak, with a view to accomplishing a progressive decentralization of social life," she takes it back with the next: "but the absurdity of such an idea strikes one immediately. Such a form of cooperation is impossible to imagine, even in dreams, in a civili-zation that is based on competition, on struggle, on war" (OL 120). What "our society" is, other than the place where competition, oppres-sion, and war crush us, is not revealed to us in this critical essay.

There is *this hint* of her ideal cooperative social order which she says might serve "as a standard for the analysis and evaluation of actual social patterns"—though this, too, she sees as "farther removed from the actual conditions of human existence than is the fiction of a Golden Age." This ideal standard would be "a society of men free, equal and brothers. . . . Each would see in every work-fellow another self occupying another post, and would love him in the way that the Gospel maxim enjoins. Thus we should possess, over and above liberty, a still more precious good; for if nothing is more odious than the humiliation and degradation of man by man, nothing is so beautiful or so sweet as friendship" (OL 100). The "Gospel maxim" to love another as you would love yourself and the beauty of "friendship" are of "a scale of values conceived outside time" (OL 100). Here we have a rumor of the transcendent in an ideal of friendship and a partial answer to Dietz's criticism. It points us, however, not toward a public sphere understood by "liberal democratic" standards, but toward a society bound by human obligations and love and friendship—a public sphere where a true "just balance" might be realized among humans. We still have here what would be called a liberal vision of society, but one with more "socialistic" or communitarian ideals.

This ideal, however, is not developed in *Oppression and Liberty* and must await an awakening with a different perspective—a religious or spiritual one, one that has its conception "outside" or "beyond" time. This awakening will, from 1935, take a classical mystical course of self-emptying and being filled for Simone Weil. The course she takes is to sink to a point of total despair—a "dark night of the soul"; to be "visited" or "graced" by a power outside time and space—a supernatural power; and to be given "new eyes to see and ears to hear" aspects of the human condition not fully recognized before. At the time of writing *Oppression and Liberty* such a realization is only a fictional idea. Not until she goes through her own dark night can the fiction become a new and possible ground for "actual social patterns" in her thinking.

Whatever optimism and idealism there is in her idea of liberty as expressed in this important and prophetic essay is crushed in the next year when she undertook to experience firsthand the conditions of factory work with the actual oppression of the workers and tried to reflect on how workers might exercise some control over their lives in such conditions. Nothing, she said, had prepared her for such profound humiliation. In a letter to a friend in January 1935 about her factory work she says: "It has changed my whole view of things, even my very feeling about life. I shall know joy again in the future, but there is a certain lightness of heart which, it seems to me, will never again be possible" (SL 15). Later in some autobiographical remarks she writes:

> After my year in the factory . . . I was, as it were, in pieces, body and soul. That contact with affliction had killed my youth . . . what I went through there marked me in so lasting a manner that still today when any human being, whoever he may be and in whatever circumstances, speaks to me without brutality, I cannot help having the impression

that there must be a mistake and that unfortunately the mistake will in all probability disappear. There I received the mark of a slave. . . . Since then I have always regarded myself as a slave. (WG 66f.)

Finally, this "mark of a slave" is a characteristic expression, although rather opaque, that we must try to shed some light upon before moving to our central analysis of her later moral and political philosophy. In *Oppression and Liberty* enslavement was the destruction of liberty. Those in power would do anything to keep their power: "Every human group that exercises power does so, not in such a way as to bring happiness to those who are subject to it, but in such a way as to increase that power; it is a matter of life and death for any form of domination whatsoever" (OP 16). But beyond oppression and loss of liberty she saw "the mark of a slave" to mean that you are totally at the command of other human beings, that you have no control over your situation. Furthermore, no one pays attention to your condition; no one hears your cries of pain. In this condition it is not that you may experience pain and suffering, but that you are a candidate for what Simone Weil, through her factory work experience, came into contact with: "affliction."

In Weil's later writings the concept of "affliction" replaces the term "oppression." "Affliction is an uprooting of life," she wrote, and involves a combination of physical pain, spiritual distress, and social degradation (see SNLG 171). She sees affliction as symptomatic of our despair and emptiness as human beings. She says:

> Affliction causes God to be absent for a time, more absent than a dead man, more absent than light in the utter darkness of a cell. A kind of horror submerges the whole soul. During this absence there is nothing to love. What is terrible is that if, in this darkness where there is nothing to love, the soul ceases to love, God's absence becomes final. The soul has to go on loving in the void, or at least to go on wanting to love, though it may be only with an infinitesimal part of itself. Then, one day, God will come to show himself to this soul and to reveal the beauty of the world to it, as in the case of Job. But if the soul stops loving it falls, even in this life, into something which is almost equivalent to hell. (SNLG 172f.)

These latter factors she came to experience in her factory year. She sadly and unexpectedly found them in work itself. This unwittingly prepared her for the several mystical-like experiences linked to Christianity she had in the late 1930s, and subsequently for her more spiritual view of morality and politics.

Blum and Seidler see her factory work experience also linked to her subsequent religious experiences. They see the two encounters providing her with what was "a new language to convey what needs to be said" about human suffering and a new political morality. They write: "The experience of factory work seemed to lead Weil to give up thinking in terms of the 'oppression' of working people. For Weil this language was too tied to the discovery of the social sources of oppression . . . [and] seemed to foreclose the possibility of giving full recognition to the moral issues involved—to how people are hurt, the depths to which they are made to suffer within work."[6] Now, more than ever, work must be understood as a fundamentally spiritual category—one that gives humanity dignity and meaning. It was no longer adequate to fight for a "right" to work or even workers' "rights" or higher wages, but work itself must be seen as a moral category that defines our humanness and not simply a means of economic survival. The conception of work that had developed through the industrial revolution had led to enormous social disarray. She could no longer look upon work as a means to some other end. To become acutely aware of the human suffering and degradation—the affliction—that accompanied work must be seen at the heart of re-civilizing society in an industrial and post-industrial age. Work must be understood as "the action by which [one] recreates [one's] own life" (FLN 18). She continues in her "pre-war notebook":

> By work, man creates the universe around him. Remember the way you looked at the fields after a day's harvesting. . . . How differently from a person going for a walk, for whom the fields are only a scenic background! In preceisely *this* consists the power of a true monument of work over the universe that surrounds it. (FLN 18)

In this "recreative" work, we struggle with nature and "free" ourselves from bondage to it. We must change the very nature of our understanding of work. She went so far as to say later in *The Need for Roots*: "Our age has its own particular mission, or vocation—the creation of a civilization founded upon the spiritual nature of work" (NR 96).[7]

Because work itself is understood as a moral category, the devastation Weil felt from the factory work she undertook was a fundamental moral, as well as physical and emotional, uprooting. Her factory work experience met all the criteria of affliction. This, as we said, prepared her for *reading* her subsequent experiences in the Spanish Civil War, in the Portuguese village, and at Assisi and Solesmes as transforming her conception of liberty from freedom *from constraint* to freedom *to obey* (consent). These also unfolded for her the meaning of both the absence and the presence of God that would form the basis of the limits and possibilities of both moral and political action. If affliction is "an uprooting of life," then the end of all moral and political thought and action should be the "re-rooting of life" and a new idea of work and of what constitutes a "worthy" civilization must be re-thought.

One final note on work. When Simone Weil came back to reevaluate Marx and Marxism in her very last London essays, we see again that there was an idea in Marx that she wanted to develop and which Marx had either dropped or "rendered barren." The idea she singles out was one Marx had in the early stages of his career when she believed he was not yet a materialist: it was "to work out a philosophy of labour in the spirit very closely akin, at bottom, to that of Proudhon" (OL 169). In this idea, human action is placed in opposition to matter and not reduced to it. It was her desire to develop this idea that Marx had left fallow. Her idea was to show the creative tension that comes from the relationship of human beings in opposition to and physically struggling with matter. This tension was part of analyzing the dynamics of "forces" in society mentioned above. To show this would require a "philosophy of labour" not yet worked out in the twentieth century.

The "philosophy" would not only be a critique of what was then wrong with the industrial workplace and its oppressive conditions but would address the reconstruction of the workplace and its institutions, turning them into places of human and social rootedness. Beyond that, work would place one in harmony with the wider world—make one feel at home and engaged in work for a good purpose.[8] Work was, in fact, what she finally believed would bring about a spiritual transformation of one's being in the world. The following example captures what she saw as the difference between, on the one hand, unfree oppressive labor in a flawed civilization where constraint, fear, and isolation surrounded work rendering it a meaningless gesture and, on the other, free labor in a "worthy" civilization where consent, control of the work process, and a sense of purpose filled one's working:

> A happy young woman, expecting her first child, and busy sewing a layette, thinks about sewing it properly. But she never forgets for an instant the child she is carrying inside her. At precisely the same moment, somewhere in a prison workshop, a female convict is also sewing, thinking, too, about sewing properly, for she is afraid of being punished. One might imagine both women to be doing the same work at the same time, and having their attention absorbed by the same technical difficulties. And yet a whole gulf of difference lies between one occupation and the other. The whole social problem consists in making the workers pass from one to the other of these two occupational extremes. (NR 95)

This example shows that when work moves from coercion to consent it not only changes the character of what is called work, but it turns physical labor (in this case intricate needlework) from a condition of homelessness to being at home in one's work. She also believes that any transformation that takes place associated with such work has both "this world and the world beyond, in their double beauty . . . present and associated in the act of work" (NR 95). Being at home with one's work in this way transfers to a sense of being at home in one's society and country. "As long as working men are homeless in their own places of work, they will never truly feel at home in their country, never be responsible members of society" (FWK 64). Thus a step is taken in solving "the whole social problem." Realistically and sadly, however, she says "we are not, at present, either intellectually or spiritually capable of such a transformation. We should be doing well if we were able to set about preparing for it" (NR 95). Such preparation, as we shall discuss later, is part of her plan for "educating for civilization."

With her emphasis on human suffering and affliction, on an injustice done to an individual and what one must do to be just, it is easier to see how Simone Weil's thought is "moral" than to see how it is "political." What is the link between these two, and how does her way of thinking allow us to understand the meaning of a moral and political life as closely tied to one another? What we call "political" has simply to do with the most basic questions human beings have about living together—questions about power and justice, about the legitimacy of authority and government, about the limits of individual freedoms in society, and about how humans living together in communities are to organize their lives peacefully and productively.[9] These are precisely the questions on which Simone Weil's last writings focus.

With these last writings before us, we will argue that there is in Simone Weil's thought, first and foremost, an intense preoccupation with the dynamics between power and justice as compassion. Her many discussions of justice bring into focus not just an individual who is harmed, but they *show* us the necessity to lose our self in the other, the one harmed. This takes the spotlight away from the personal and places it on the one outside one's self. This is not yet to make moral action in the form of compassion a public and political matter, but it does release us significantly from the liberal ideal of preoccupation with one's self-concerns. Secondly, as she critiques the human condition, we see clearly how myopic and willful we have become and that we should, rather, step back and give attention to the interactions of humans in their public and social environments—where human beings interact with other human beings for better or worse. This attention, thirdly, brings to prominence several important issues that can only be seen as issues for both individual moral action and as civic obligations. Moral individuals are also citizens who must order their lives by laws, have voluntary associations in communities, and shape their education through sustaining the spiritual treasures of their respective pasts. This is a public, and thus a political, arena for action. It is in this transformation from individual self-concern to seeing one's self in a context of moral and civic responsibilities where justice intersects with politics for Simone Weil.

Finally, these decisive moments from 1935 through 1939 give Weil, as Blum and Seidler said above, "a new language to convey what needs to be said." The rest of this book explores the meaning of this new language for understanding her moral and political thought and also what the implications are for contemporary moral and political action that her ideas create for us. The spiritual transformations that were clearly, but surely incompletely, begun in her moral and political thought from the late 1930s must, finally, be completed in our own appropriation of her thought. In each subsequent chapter we will engage one or more contemporary thinkers whose ideas mirror some of Simone Weil's. Most of these thinkers were unaware of her writings, which, we believe, make her thought all the more compelling for its prophetic qualities. In this way her ideas serve as guides for our thinking.

NOTES

1. Pétrement, *Simone Weil,* 187–91. See also McLellan, *Simone Weil,* 98f.

2. My interpretation here diverges from McLellan's by emphasizing the larger perspective on power. McLellan, however, provides a lengthy and important discussion of Weil's political views and relation to Marxism in the early 1930s leading up to her pivotal work *Oppression and Liberty.* See his chapters 3, 4, and 5. For a detailed study of Weil's relation to Marxism, see Blum and Seidler, *A Truer Liberty.* Their chapters on "Work" and "Morality, Truth and Politics" are useful as background for a few themes developed in this book.

3. Nye, *Philosophia,* 69. See OL 65.

4. The Great Beast comes in a number of forms in Simone Weil's writings. The Roman Empire and the Third Reich are prime examples, but all forms of totalitarian regimes manifest the same evils. She details the nature of this evil in her essay, "The Great Beast: Some Reflections on the Origins of Hitlerism" (1939–40), in SE 89–144.

5. Dietz, *Between the Human and the Divine,* 71–81. We take up Dietz's criticism further in our chapter seven, "Community and Politics."

6. Blum and Seidler, *A Truer Liberty,* 187.

7. See Clare Fischer, "Simone Weil and the Civilization of Work" in *Simone Weil's Philosophy of Culture* (189–213), for a comprehensive look at her notion of "the spiritual nature of work" and its relevance to our present age.

8. See ibid., 200–5.

9. This is a summary of a standard definition of what "political" means and what "political theorists" are preoccupied with. See the widely used political theory reader: *Princeton Readings in Political Thought,* ed. Mitchell Cohen and Nicole Fermon (Princeton, N.J.: Princeton University Press, 1966), 1.

3

RETHINKING JUSTICE AND RIGHTS

> In her political thinking [Simone Weil] appears as a stern critic of
> both Right and Left; at the same time more truly a lover of order
> and hierarchy than most of those who call themselves Conservative,
> and more truly a lover of the people than most of those who call
> themselves Socialist.
>
> T. S. Eliot, introduction to *The Need for Roots*, viii

LIBERALISM, COMMUNITARIANISM, AND SOCIETY

What is a liberal society? Charles Taylor gives us two ways to approach a liberal society. First is in terms of its characteristic forms, such as "representative government, the rule of law, a regime of entrenched rights, the guarantor of certain freedoms"; and second is "as one that is trying to realize in the highest possible degree certain goods or principles of right."[1] The first focuses on law and governance; its approach is more descriptive and neutral, and a greater sense of individual protections prevails. The second approach stresses the normative features of trying to realize certain moral ends or principles of right, and there is also more of a sense of common pursuit. These two different approaches alter the way one conceives of the relationship between an individual and her society. We will see the importance in this difference as we proceed further.

From the perspective of our post–World War II culture, in the second half of the twentieth century, we can read certain developments into what we call "liberal society"—whose roots, of course, go back to eighteenth-century enlightenment principles—which disclose limitations or weaknesses in our moral, political, and economic life. These weaknesses were not only anticipated by Simone Weil in the first half of our century, but she sounded clear alarm bells to their dangers. Her alarms were mostly ignored as being too far out of the mainstream, as utopian, or even as mad. Let us for a moment illustrate where we stand today on some social-political issues in the framework of liberal society to help us understand what Simone Weil's concerns were that were ignored.

The liberal tradition of political philosophy, going back to Thomas Hobbes and John Locke, and articulated today in writers like John Rawls, Robert Nozick, and Richard Rorty, is increasingly under attack for its "possessive individualism"[2] and "a growing ideal of a human agent who is able to remake himself by methodical and disciplined action."[3] These concerns are being more urgently discussed in view of the spread of a global free-market economy, individual greed, and the breakdown of a sense of a "common good" within specific societies. Current views of a liberal society have emphasized the role of a social and political order as one that protects individuals from harm and from others taking something from them (in particular, goods and property), and thus "freeing" persons for unencumbered individual pursuits. On this view it is asked: Just what is an individual's public civil role and what responsibilities go with that role? No single answer is forthcoming, but several things need to be noted more clearly.

One current, and perhaps dominant, liberal theory being espoused in the English-speaking world is what is called "procedural liberalism." Charles Taylor summarizes this view as follows: Society is seen as "an association of individuals, each of whom has a conception of a good or worthwhile life and correspondingly, a life plan," but which excludes "a socially endorsed conception of the good."[4] The liberal society, in our climate of individualism, views society instrumentally, "as the dispenser of security and prosperity" to the end of individual pursuits.[5] Taylor is not pleased with this kind of liberalism and notes that those who support a society because of the prosperity and security it generates are like fair-weather friends: They are bound to let you down when you need them.[6] When it fails to protect them in their personal pursuits or no longer allows them to live out their "life plan" in an unencumbered way, they seek greener pastures. In such an instrumental view there is little, if any, sense of common good or solidarity or civic pride or patriotism.[7] To achieve these latter civic bonds requires a commitment to certain ideals: safeguards for citizen dignity, a sense of shared history, and some sense of obligation to one's fellow human beings. These are communitarian ideals. To redress radical individualism, Taylor wants us to redraw the political map so that it might include a liberalism that is more holistic rather than atomistic—one that might include some communitarian ideals and retard the crass instrumentalism that comes with individualism. He approaches liberal society in his second sense: "as one that is trying to realize in the highest possible degree certain goods or principles of right." This kind of society requires some notion of community with institutions and associations in order for its moral goods to be realized and sustained.

The contemporary communitarian view, espoused by theorists like Taylor, Alasdair MacIntyre, Elizabeth Wolgast, Michael Sandel, and Stanley Hauerwas, sees each human being as "thickly situated," embedded in a social environment, reacting to and shaping his or her life from strands already present. Sandel says: "We cannot regard ourselves as independent [from society] . . . [we must understand] ourselves as the particular persons we are—as members of this family or community or nation or people, as bearers of this history, as sons and daughters of that revolution, as citizens of this republic." Though my life is subject to revision, it does have "contours"—a defining shape arising from my "projects and commitments" as well as from my "wants and desires."[8] This, Sandel and others would argue contrary to Rawls and Nozick (or against procedural liberalism), is as true for understanding my public life as it is my personal identity. Public and private, in fact, are not so easily separable.

Another point of importance for understanding Simone Weil's view on liberal society is that Western liberal democracies have tended to define a civil society in terms of an economy—that is, as Taylor says, "as an entity of interrelated acts of production, exchange, and consumption which has its own internal dynamic, its own autonomous laws. This crystallizes in the eighteenth century with the work of the physiocrats and, more definitively, with Adam Smith. . . . The 'economy' now defines a dimension of social life in which we function as a society potentially outside the gambit of politics" and is given a central place in civil society.[9] This releases society from its historical roots. This point helps explain, in part, the rise of the importance of "rights" as the dominant "civil" concept to preserve security and prosperity, especially when what needs securing is our measure of prosperity, that is, our money, property, and other material goods. This becomes the new focus for "rights" and throws the discussion of justice as equality and fairness toward the sharing or distribution of goods. Justice, going back to Athenian democracy, has always been more closely linked to a conception of a moral or civic good and has had little to do with economic "goods." On the liberal view, as individualism, economic success, and pluralism increase, a shared conception of some moral good recedes and an individual's "rights" and "life-plan" have greater need of particular protection. This is seen in a particularly strong way with the increase in litigation to ensure individual protection of rights—even to the point that the United States is often referred to as a "litigious society."

Simone Weil as an astute observer and one deeply embroiled in the debates swirling around capitalism and Marxist economics saw the dangers in the social order yielding too much to purely economic concerns of either kind. She also saw that individualism would lead us away from any clear notion of a common good. She saw that the word "rights" was taking on its own capital-R life in the context of a society ruled by economic concerns and gaining coinage over a meaningful use of "justice." This is why, as we will see, she thinks of "rights" as linked with "bartering" and "exchange," as having their "own region" in which they operate—a region far from justice.

The current picture of liberal society gives us an autonomous individual and then tries to construct a social order that would best preserve and allow that autonomy to flourish. With this picture before us, we can now return to Simone Weil's perspective on the individual and society and understand it better. Her very idea of philosophy will not let us divide an individual from her society so easily, and it will not let us lose sight of a common good she believed to be at the heart of all human beings which must be reflected in their moral and political life. We will see that justice for Simone Weil is not a product of some purely rational choice even if a person could remove herself from complicating life circumstances. In fact it is precisely because of the complicated circumstances in life that every human being *must struggle from those circumstances to justice*. Although her view of justice shares some things in common with the current communitarian view, it is much more radical and unorthodox.

In her own words, Simone Weil had already articulated much of the current scenario. The liberal—even utopian socialist—conception of justice that we have inherited from enlightenment ideas and Marx is what Simone Weil calls "a noble sentiment," but "very poor in intellectual effort"; it conceives of justice as "desiring liberty, dignity, well-being, happiness and every possible good for all" (OL 172). This avoids evoking any notion that might suggest something beyond the human, though it does embrace a certain human striving. With respect to liberal moral thought, Simone Weil says that one mistake into which we are continually falling "is the belief that moral phenomena are exact copies of material phenomena; for example, that moral well-being results automatically and exclusively from physical well-being" (OL 178). Here we have echoes of a natural moral theory and a Protestant work ethic. Here, too, she believes that civic society is more than organization for production (Marxism). And a second mistake "is the belief that moral phenomena are arbitrary and can be brought about . . . by an act of will" (OL 178). Here we can see a kind of Nietzschean relativism. She is clear that justice is not "of this world," but it may be *in* this world by virtue of the supernatural (OL 177).

Blum and Seidler provide this perspective on why Simone Weil believes we must continue to undo our confusion about "rights" and "justice":

> Within democratic regimes we see politics as a competition among interest groups using whatever power and persuasion they have at their disposal and must assume that the "public interest" will somehow be served through this process. Weil, however, knew that the powerless, weak, and impoverished will continue to suffer, though she was aware of the difficulties of thinking justly in the realm of politics. "Human intelligence—even in the case of the most intelligent—falls miserably short of the great problems of public life" (EL 90). But this difficulty does not abolish the duty to seek solutions or at least to work to establish certain guiding ideas.[10]

The new "guiding ideas" that Simone Weil works to establish are those of justice as love and compassion—a new virtue—which includes a fresh view of law, a new judicial system, and a revision of how we should educate citizens for "civilization." All these she develops within her spiritual perspective.

If, as we saw earlier, Simone Weil's philosophy is found in action and practice, then the individual cannot be separate from her cognitive and social practices, and it is artificial to construct an idea of an individual apart from its linguistic and social contexts. Eric Springsted makes the point in this way: "To know, to be human, is to be engaged in a specifically human activity, which is at least to be related by a whole set of socially instituted actions to other human beings." Simone Weil linked persons and political associations. Her project, Springsted continues, was not "trying to create ideal political situations that are objectively fair and fitted to human 'nature,' but . . . trying to make people fair and just who are already socially related. The point is to get *them* to see that their societies are not artificial constructs, but organically related to the very beings who think them and inhabit them. . . . A good part of the problem is to get them to see their very knowledge of themselves as their own activity."[11] The way of seeing—reacting to—another human being is a moral and political activity. Such seeing and reacting to is not a secondary capacity that humans acquire but is central to their being human. This is shown in an unusual way by the emphasis given to the concept of attention in her discussion of justice and rights in morality and politics.

"The point then of political philosophy for Weil," concludes Springsted, "is to make the relation [mutual attending and care between human beings] apparent and central in any state, and to arrange the relations within any political and social association so that these relations may be advanced to the greatest degree possible."[12] This clearly is an approach to a liberal society in Taylor's second sense—trying to realize certain goods or principles of right [justice] in the highest possible degree. We must now see what our "goods" are and how such mutual attending and care relate to justice.

"RIGHTS" AND "JUSTICE"

A reminder from our first chapter: Simone Weil says, "Our lives are lived, in actual fact, among changing, varying realities, subject to the casual play of eternal necessities, and modifying themselves according to specific conditions within specific limits" (SE 157). Her thought is concrete and connected with time and a culture; it uses both fictional and real life narratives to open our eyes to a subject. With the subject of justice she first suggests that it has lost its meaning and been replaced by a "vacuous" notion of "rights" which "makes us forget the value of life." She also draws our attention to "the circumstances in life which give rise to" a meaningful use of the concept of "justice." She shows us what Elizabeth Wolgast, following Wittgenstein, calls "the grammar of justice." For Simone Weil, the grammar of justice has more to do with injustice—in doing all one can to avoid doing an injustice—than with developing a theory of justice. Here, again, she invokes the behavior of Socrates before the courts: "Socrates' rule in life: not to defend justice, truth; but not to do injustice, not to betray truth" (N 30). Wolgast, in a spirit reminiscent of Weil, says: "To call something unjust is to take it out of the realm of disinterested reportage. . . . saying that something is a wrong or injustice *marks it* for moral indignation and moral concern."[13] Wolgast also says: "Instead of fastening our attention on justice the substantive, let us examine some of the contexts where justice is invoked, that is, complaints against injustice. In the face of wrong, justice is demanded and cried out for, and with passion and intensity. 'We must have justice!' and 'Justice must be done!' are its expressions, and they characteristically have imperative force as well as urgency."[14]

In Simone Weil's terms we must first "read" the circumstances of life that give rise to injustice and feel its "imperative force" and "urgency." "Readings" for her make up the fabric of life. As something appears to us or "enters into us by our senses"—imposes itself upon us —we must "read" it (ER 300f.). This makes it ours and we know it by our reading. We insinuate ourselves into life's situations, react to them, and learn to overcome their obstacles. This is what is meant by our perceptions as a "sort of dance." With respect to justice, we invoke cries for it when we are visibly impacted by forms of injustice all around us. Fear, pain, cruelty, humiliation, and attention to the suffering of a human being are the ordinary encounters that will go to make up our reading of the circumstances that give rise to injustice and evoke a concern for justice. To learn to read such circumstances is one of the "services" we can render to the afflicted. We must, she says, find "the words which can give resonance, through the crust of external circumstances, to the cry which is always inaudible: 'Why am I being hurt?'" (SE 24). Again, evoking a parallel with Socrates, Rush Rhees says that Socrates awakens in his interlocutors and his readers through Plato "the sense of what is degrading: or the sense of good and evil."[15] It is this same sense that Simone Weil awakens in her readers through her discussions of justice. We will turn first to her discussion of "rights," then look at her understanding of the grammar of justice.

Simone Weil calls our attention to the concept of "rights" in a characteristically unexpected way. She forces us to look again at this clash before our eyes. In the midst of World War II, when so many "rights" were being abused, she writes in her essay "Human Personality": "[to say] 'I have the right . . .' or 'you have no right to . . .' evoke[s] a latent war and awaken[s] the spirit of contention. To place the notion of rights at the center of social conflicts is to inhibit any possible impulse of charity on both sides" (SE 21). "Rights" is used "as a banner or a hostile slogan," for example, by both sides in the Right to Life and Women's Rights debate (or should we say in their "latent war" using Capital letters). When one side speaks, we brace ourselves for the next countercharge—any "impulse of charity" left this current discussion over "rights" long ago. Then we read, again in Weil: "Thanks to this word ["rights"], what should have been a cry of protest from the depth of the heart has turned into a shrill nagging of claims and counter-claims, which is both impure and unpractical" (SE 21). Instead of the "shrill nagging of claims and counter-claims," we should be listening to the cries of women manipulated by fear and propaganda; to the circumstances that may agonizingly warrant a woman's choice and those that are self-serving and may lack compassion for new life. Andrea Nye interprets Simone Weil's point in this way:

> Much of feminist political and social activism has remained within the conceptual framework of rights. Women have claimed the right to speak in public, to vote, to run for political office, to go to university, to compete for jobs. In the attempt to keep abortion legal, which takes so much contemporary feminist energy, a fetus's right to life is opposed to a woman's right to choose. Weil suggests another way of thinking about abortion and about social issues of concern to women, as questions not of rights but of obligation. Rejecting both the morality of the institutional Christian churches, which support the pro-life position, and the liberal philosophy of rights which supports the pro-choice position, a Weilian feminist might listen to women themselves as they attempt to make sense of their lives in order to come to a

binding sense of what must be done to restore social balance and create a society in which obligations do not conflict.[16]

In the case of abortion, and in other difficult cases, is "rights" the correct concept to use? Are we listening to one another? Are we missing something deeper? Continuing to help us out of this "nagging" problem we have gotten ourselves into, Simone Weil writes the following:

> Relying almost exclusively on this notion [of rights], it becomes impossible to keep one's eyes on the real problem. If someone tries to browbeat a farmer to sell his eggs at a moderate price, the farmer can say: 'I have the right to keep my eggs if I don't get a good enough price.' But if a young girl is being forced into a brothel she will not talk about her rights. In such a situation the word would sound ludicrously inadequate. (SE 21)

But how do we keep our eyes on the real problem? It is not just a violation of rights this young girl has experienced—she has suffered an *injustice,* and we mean by this that she has had great harm done to her which cannot be understood as a "right" taken. What has been taken and what could be returned in place of the sexual violation? The real problem cannot be resolved by compensation; her cry must be heard.

In answer to the question, "What right has been taken?" one might hear the response from the legal community: "the fourth amendment 'right to privacy.' " But this does not touch the nerve center of this type of violation. An example, used by Simone Weil, similar to the offense of forcing a young girl into a brothel is that of rape. J. P. Little comments on this violation. She says that rape involves "the destruction of the moral being of the individual, the infinitely small but precious capacity for consent."[17] What is legally called a person's "right to privacy" does not adequately cover such a moral destruction. Consent is at the heart of our freedom. "Having the right to . . ." always involves *something a person has*, and what is truly sacred, the seat of justice and one's moral being for Simone Weil, *is wholly impersonal*. What is lost is the sacred core of one's being, not something that can be replaced by a court of law or even some compensatory action by the violator. By using the notion of the "impersonal" in a human being, Simone Weil avoids the suggestion that there is some *property* in us that can be taken or must be protected. Also following Little's discussion of the logic of decreation we see that justice relates to the "uncreated" part of our being, that which does not easily consent to the necessity of events unless it is totally crushed; justice cries out to the extent that it is not being worn away by circumstances of force—"Why am I being hurt?"

To have bought into rights language is to believe that power can be counterbalanced by power. To say "if we could just achieve equal rights . . ." means I must either snatch rights from someone else (one who has a disequal amount) or impose an ideology by force or persuasion to "guarantee" rights in a more or less coercive way (even by civil law). This way of thinking will not easily go away. But in Simone Weil's thinking the only substantial way to counterbalance force is neither through force nor through a more equitable distribution of rights. Rather, it is through attention to injustice and a kind of justice that has as its most active ingredient love.

"Rights," Simone Weil says, "have no direct connection with love" (SE 20), and justice has primarily to do with seeing that no harm is done to another human being. And this, of course, is her point: to contrast our use of "rights" with "justice," and to force us to see that, as she says, "at the very best, a mind enclosed in language is in prison" and that "to be unaware of being in prison" is to be "living in error" (SE 26). Reading the details of situations in our human life helps us to move from "error" to "truth." (We will return to this movement later in considering "justice" as a "supernatural virtue.") Although our readings of all human texts are from a perspective, there are some readings that are more adequate, or truthful, than others. There are no perfect readings.

We must ask: Isn't there something fundamentally askew, in error, about our "rights" talk when it lays so close to matters of life and death—when it no longer is linked to an exchange and a commodity? Simone Weil even suggests that "rights" talk is suited to the marketplace (the farmer and his eggs) and when applied to such issues as human violation it leads to a certain moral mediocrity—but then, the clash of rights over abortion at best shows our mediocrity in thinking and in dealing with human lives. A different language and sensibility are needed to move us from our mediocrity.

This moral mediocrity into which we have fallen runs very deep and we may not be able to extricate ourselves easily. To change the nature of our "rights" talk, as Peter Winch says, "concerns the whole language in which questions about justice are commonly raised, at least in the second half of the twentieth century." Winch, in his discussion of Simone Weil's distinction between "rights" and "justice," reminds us that John Rawls's whole enterprise in *A Theory of Justice* (a theory that has become near canonical) uses "rights" language, "or at least deals in the conceptions that ['rights' language] expresses." Simone Weil's view of justice challenges Rawls's whole way of conceiving "justice."[18] Winch continues as follows:

> The *inspiration* for a demand for rights may well be a concern for justice; it may be that in some circumstances to struggle for rights is the best way of struggling for justice. But that does not mean that the struggle for justice is the same as the struggle for rights; the one struggle may be successful and the other not—maybe that is even more often than not the outcome. And if the distinction is forgotten, there is the danger that a concern for rights will take one farther and farther away from justice; or that the quest for justice will be entirely submerged.[19]

There is a clear and present danger, for example, in the South African situation that "justice will be entirely submerged." It must be clear to all that no final settlement on "rights" should be made without "justice" that includes "charity" and genuine "attention" to the decades of harm done to the non-white majority by the former white rule. This is what that country's "Truth and Reconciliation Commission" has been about. There are, of course, other situations in Africa and elsewhere where "rights" talk is woefully inadequate to the decades of suffering experienced by millions under despotic rule, ethnic hatred, and other injustices.

If we take Simone Weil's point about the "shrill nagging" of "rights" talk, then we have even a harder task to move from error to truth. We have to see how turning over the concept of "justice" in the sense that her philosophical procedure recommends might change our course and make us think differently.

We have before us in the powerful essay "Human Personality" two distinct notions: "rights" and "justice." Weil summarizes the difference between them in these ways:

The notion of rights is linked with the notion of sharing out, of exchange, of measured quantity. It has a commercial flavor, essentially evocative of legal claims and arguments. Rights are always asserted in a tone of contention; and when this tone is adopted, it must rely upon force in the background, or else it will be laughed at. (SE 18)

Justice consists in seeing that no harm is done to men. . . . [it is associated with the cry] "Why am I being hurt?" (SE 30)

The other cry, which we hear so often: "Why has somebody else got more than I have," refers to rights. We must learn to distinguish between the two cries and to do all that is possible, as gently as possible, to hush the second one, with the help of a code of justice, regular tribunals, and the police. Minds capable of solving problems of this kind can be formed in law school.

But the cry "Why am I being hurt?" raises quite different problems, for which the spirit of truth, justice, and love is indispensable. (SE 30)

The spirit of justice and truth is nothing else but a certain kind of attention which is pure love. (SE 28)

Simone Weil says, "If you say to someone who has ears to hear: 'What you are doing to me is not just,' you may touch and awaken at its source the spirit of attention and love" (SE 21). It, therefore, requires a much more detailed analysis of the concepts of "attention" and "love" in Simone Weil to begin to open her reading of the concept of justice. Justice for her is related to the readings we give to the principalities and powers of our world and to individual persons. For Simone Weil a correct reading must focus attention on the "whole human being" and on the faintest cry of those who are hurting all around us (cf. SE 9, 11, and WG 114f.).

Before we go on to her account of her new virtue of justice, let us step back in our analysis for a moment. We have become unaware of the prison that language has placed us in. What is the error here? "Rights" language has imprisoned the concept of "justice." They have been reduced to mean the same thing. Rights and justice have, as Simone Weil observed, been placed "at the centre of social conflicts" and thus "inhibit any possible impulse of charity." In Simone Weil's own earlier conception of justice—before her factory experience in 1935—social conflicts were at the center of justice concerns. Pay disputes and work conditions were to be negotiated with the management to improve rights and offset or balance social inequities. Before her factory experience she was a leading advocate for social rights and was bent on changing things. Within two to three weeks of factory work she succumbed to "the daily experience of brutal constraint" (SL 21). This she could only characterize as the condition of a slave. "Slavery has made me entirely lose the feeling of having any rights," she said (FW 211 and SL 22). Neither negotiation nor revolt seemed possible for the workers.[20] She came to the startling revelation that as a worker under the prevailing conditions she experienced firsthand, she "possessed no right to anything" (SL 22). This, she says, "killed my youth"; it marked her for the rest of her life. After her factory year, it was clear to her that "rights" talk could no longer sustain the moral debate regarding justice.

With the loss of rights so complete and so devastating, what meaning is there left for it? If neither rational negotiation nor revolution can restore one's rights, do we give up on justice as well? A new concept entered her soul as a result of this experience, that of profound humiliation. What she had thought to be a matter of cutting loose the workers from their oppressors' chains was now understood to be a much more complex phenomena—one of restoring human dignity in the context of slavery. As shown earlier, no longer was oppression seen as bound to social conflicts, but it was rooted in the suffering, humiliation and physical constraint placed on the human soul—a mark of what she now called "affliction" (*malheur*). She now had to rethink the concept of justice altogether.

To help us analyze the difference between "rights" and "justice," she turns our attention to classical Greek literature and offers us an alternative reading of the meaning of justice. She turns us to Creon and Antigone, to Hector and Achilles—object lessons in how "justice" language works and how "rights" language in Antigone's voice, for example, is so utterly unthinkable, or as she said earlier "ludicrously inadequate." Antigone feels a deep sense of injustice in not being allowed to bury Polynices and indignantly defies Creon's order. Antigone says, "I was born to share, not hate, but love" (SE 20)—an expression foreign in an age of litigation and moral relativity.[21] Justice is "companion of the gods"; it connects up with "love," she says, and "rights has no direct connection with love" (SE 20).

In 1939–40, she wrote her essay on the *Iliad*, where "force" is shown to be the dominant pressure placed upon human beings—now not just those persons who might find themselves a victim of some form of oppression, but on all human beings. She writes:

> Force is as pitiless to the man who possesses it, or thinks he does, as it is to its victims; the second it crushes, the first it intoxicates. The truth is nobody really possesses it. The human race is not divided up, in the *Iliad*, into conquered persons, slaves, suppliants, on the one hand, and conquerors and chiefs on the other. In this poem there is not a single man who does not at one time or another have to bow his neck to force. (IL 11)

There is no reason to think that the circumstances of human life have changed for us as we continue to imprison our human world with the arms race, the nuclear threat, various forms of economic oppression, and multiple forms of human cruelty. We have, in Weil's terms, overstepped a limit and thus lost "equilibrium which ought to determine the conduct of life" (IL 15).

If we stand in our human world in a state of disequilibrium and have yielded to force as a way of life, is there anything that can restore our equilibrium? For the Greeks, Weil says, "justice and love" are the balancing factor. It is this necessity of human misery under the constraints of force that is a precondition to the recognition of justice and love. She says of the *Iliad*, "Justice and love, which hardly have any place in this study of extremes and of unjust acts of violence, nevertheless bathe the work in their light without ever becoming noticeable themselves, except as a kind of accent" (IL 30). *All* of Simone Weil's post–factory year works are "accented by" and *many* are "bathed in" the light of justice and love. So what is "justice" if it cannot be reduced to "rights"; if it cannot be rationally negotiated?—"eggs for the right price," "no increased productivity without better work conditions and wages?" Rather, as we have noted, justice "awakens at its source the spirit of attention and love" (SE 21). We must now focus on the concepts of "attention" and "love"—two concepts seldom, if ever, heard in the vocabulary of "rights" talk or in the vast majority of twentieth-century philosophical debates (moral or political)[22]—in order to understand her notion of "justice."

"JUSTICE" AND "ATTENTION"

In her essay "Human Personality," "attention" is given a prominent place. This is done in the context of discussing the limitations of a "rights"-based morality or political philosophy and the virtues of a "justice"-based morality or political philosophy. The link between "attention" and a political philosophy clearly comes from her view of philosophy itself as action and practice. "Attending" is an action and practice of human beings to the world and to other humans. Springsted says: "Attention . . . is a first-person activity. . . . Attention is primarily . . . a certain moral stance to others that involves the one who is paying attention." Attention "*is a moral activity that creates* the very human person by actively responding to his or her desire for good."[23] The public social order is a kind of mutual "attending" society and its disorder can be seen as a lack of such attending—"one becomes fully human," says Springsted, "by acting in a fully human way toward others—that is, by paying attention to them."[24]

Attention has to do with discernment—discernment of what someone is saying, discernment of the kind of protest a person makes who is being harmed, discernment of the social conditions that create the climate for injustice or even misunderstanding, and discernment of myself as an equal subject of affliction. Peter Winch writes:

> There are special obstacles *in the soul of the reader* in the way of recognizing protests at real injustice. "Attention" is necessary; and the peculiar difficulty of my attending to someone in such a situation is that it requires me to understand that we are both equal members of a natural order which can at any time bring about such a violation of whoever it may be, including myself. That is, I cannot understand the other's affliction from the point of view of my own privileged position; I have rather to understand *myself* from the standpoint of *the other's* affliction, to understand that my privileged position is not part of my essential nature but an accident of fate.[25]

Acknowledging the reality of affliction means saying to oneself, as Simone Weil says:

> I may lose at any moment, through the play of circumstances over which I have no control, anything whatsoever that I possess, including

things that are so intimately mine that I consider them as myself. There is nothing that I might not lose. It could happen at any moment that what I am might be abolished and replaced by anything whatsoever of the filthiest and most contemptible sort. (SE 27)

When Simone Weil says justice is "seeing that no harm is done to men" (LPG 94), the "seeing" here implies that one read both the nature of the harm being done to another and making certain that the particular harm is stopped. This involves recognition of the other as a human being and being able to put oneself in the other's place. She says clearly:

Love and justice—to be just toward a being different from oneself means putting oneself in his place. For then one recognizes his existence as a person, not as a thing. This means a spiritual quartering, a stripping of the self; conceiving oneself as oneself *and* as other. (N 292)

To do this requires a considerable degree of attention.

The cultivation of attention is a task that requires discipline: a self-emptying, waiting, "a spiritual quartering"—what she calls a "non-active action." As difficult as this seems, it is something that any human being can acquire. At the most basic level attention can be cultivated in school studies, in attention to the natural world, and in a variety of forms of meditation. One of Simone Weil's most original pieces was written in 1942 for a friend, Father Perrin, who would be addressing young students on a mission to Montpellier. It is titled: "Reflections on the Right Use of School Studies with a View to the Love of God." In this essay she argues that school exercises develop "a lower kind of attention," but the pearl in this for adolescents is that such exercises *can* be "extremely effective in increasing the power of attention that will be available at the time of prayer," provided the studies are approached with the "higher" purpose in mind and not carried out for grades or under threat of reprisal. Students should apply themselves equally to all tasks and not show preference to one subject over another, for the importance here is "increasing the power of attention" rather than winning school success. An unnoticed feature in this process is giving close attention to "each school task in which we have failed . . . trying to get down to the origin of each fault" without complaint or excuse. She notes that the temptation is great to overlook the faults. But if the purpose is to prepare ourselves for the love of God, we must not refuse to give attention to our faults (WG 108f.). Attention to faults helps in acquiring the virtue of humility.

She defines attention in this way: "Attention consists of suspending our thought, leaving it detached, empty, and ready to be penetrated by the object. . . . Above all, our thought should be empty, waiting, not seeking anything, but ready to receive in its naked truth the object that is to penetrate it" (WG 111f.). Not to give this kind of attention to school studies has its consequences: "All wrong translations, all absurdities in geometry problems, all clumsiness of style, and all faulty connection of ideas in composition and essays . . . are due to the fact that thought has seized upon some idea too hastily, and being thus prematurely blocked, is not open to the truth" (WG 112). Ultimately being open to the truth is to be open to another human being's affliction, and such openness begins in very rudimentary ways. She concludes:

> So it comes about, paradoxical as it may seem, a Latin prose or a geometry problem, even though they are done wrong, may be a great service one day, provided we devote the right kind of effort to them. Should the occasion arise, they can one day make us better able to give someone in affliction exactly the help required to save him, at the supreme moment of his need. (WG 115)

At the end of this essay, Simone Weil moves us toward the importance of attention for the love of God and the love of our neighbor. Her remarks speak directly to our being social beings and the obstacles we encounter in that process.

> Not only does the love of God have attention for its substance; the love of our neighbor, which we know to be the same love, is made of this same substance. Those who are unhappy have no need for anything in this world but people capable of giving them their attention. The capacity to give one's attention to a sufferer is a very rare and difficult thing; it is almost a miracle; it *is* a miracle. Nearly all those who think they have this capacity do not possess it. Warmth of heart, impulsiveness, pity are not enough.
>
> In the first legend of the Grail, it is said that the Grail belongs to the first comer who asks the guardian of the vessel, a king three-

quarters paralyzed by the most painful wound, "What are you going through?"

The love of our neighbor in all its fullness simply means being able to say to him: "What are you going through?" It is a recognition that the sufferer exists, not only as a unit in a collection, or a specimen from the social category labeled "unfortunate," but as a man, exactly like us, who was one day stamped with a special mark of affliction. For this reason it is enough, but it is indispensable, to know how to look at him in a certain way.

This way of looking is first of all attentive. The soul empties itself of all its own contents in order to receive into itself the being it is looking at, just as he is, in all his truth.

Only he who is capable of attention can do this. (WG 114f.)

Of course, her central point is the attention given to human beings rather than to things or matter or even school studies, but getting somewhere begins with the first step. Winch brings to our awareness a feature of attention that is often overlooked, that is, when we give our attention we may find an obstacle in the way of something else we set out to do. Thus we are urged by Simone Weil to learn to attend "in a certain way" that is oriented to the object of attention and not oneself. Winch says: "To recognize the existence of another human being is to acknowledge a certain sort of obstacle to some projected actions: that is to say, it is to acknowledge that there are some things one *must* do and some things one *cannot* do in dealings with the other which hence constitute a limit to the ways in which we can pursue our projects."[26]

This very recognition and its consequent limiting effect on our projects, Winch argues, are the result of "an initial primitive, unreflective reaction . . . later refined into a mode of behavior."[27] In other words, our human practices are governed by learning a series of moves and reactions to circumstances that range from stepping out of the way of a passerby to avoid being bumped, to involving the passerby in some mutual activity by gaining her consent. To do the latter we must have attended to the behavior of the other sufficiently to have gained her trust. We could, of course, also coerce the other's behavior by some threat or oppressive action. The point is, however, that from such "primitive, unreflective reactions" we learn to stop and reflect, to be attentive to others. Winch sees this as related to Simone Weil's striking phrase from "The *Iliad*," i.e., "that interval of hesitation, wherein lies all our consideration for our brothers in humanity" (IL 14). Winch concludes that it is this "tendency to hesitate in certain circumstances [that] is the seed out of which grow certain kinds of thinking about our fellow human beings,"[28] and ultimately out of which can grow a "geometry" of human relations that embodies justice within the human community.[29] *Such a quality of attention to another human being is the fundamental building block for her moral and political thought.*

A crucial factor in Simone Weil's conception of justice is that of consent, and consent requires a, more or less, condition of equilibrium. But such equilibrium is nearly impossible. The actual human condition is more like our not waiting for others' consent, but in exercising the power we have or can get away with, or consenting out of fear of power or by promise of reward. (Cf. SJ 1f.) "Consent," she says, "is made possible by a life containing motives for consenting. Destitution, privations of soul and body, prevent consent from being able to operate in the depths of the heart" (SJ 5).

This point is illustrated clearly by legal scholar Catherine A. MacKinnon in an essay discussing the difficulties in changing U.S. laws concerning rape. "Consent is supposed to be women's form of control over intercourse," notes MacKinnon. But "the law of rape," she continues, "presents consent as free exercise of sexual choice *under conditions of equality of power* without exposing the underlying structure of constraint and disparity."[30] And the constraints not exposed are the *inequality* of power in a coercive relationship. What motives does a woman have to resist an unwanted sexual assault? Already the social conditions in our culture start with disequilibrium between men and women. "The deeper problem," says MacKinnon, "is that women are socialized to passive receptivity; may have or perceive no alternative to acquiescence; may prefer it to the escalated risk of injury and the humiliation of a lost fight; submit to survive."[31] "The problem," she says, "is that the injury of rape lies in the meaning of the act to its victim, but the standard for its criminality lies in the meaning of the act to the assailant."[32]

Furthermore, the man believes of a woman who has already had "sex" that he is not taking anything away from the woman—because she's already had "that" taken. So no crime, in any proprietary sense, is perceived. Also, little credence is given to the *dignitary harms* in court because, as MacKinnon says, "[They] are nonmaterial [and] ephemeral to the legal mind."[33] Given how the deck is stacked in the social and legal situation, the "possibility of change in the direction of justice" seems virtually impossible. We have not even begun to look at the "injustice" in this case. We have failed in giving it proper attention.

Let us turn to another example. If I have been given reason to distrust my parents, a friend, my school authorities, my government, why should I consent to their wishes or commands? They may coerce me with rewards or threat of punishment, but this further reduces my motivation to consent—or it changes consent to a kind of involuntary submission. Only if I can trust and believe whatever authority to which I willingly submit myself can I willingly consent "in the depths of [my] heart." This is illustrated clearly in Václav Havel's book, *Living in Truth*, and by the whole lack of trust and finally a people's withholding their consent that brought down the Eastern European regimes in 1989. Havel writes that the price of "living a lie," of living in deceit only to maintain some bearable life, is too high; it is a "profane trivialization" of inherent humanity. "To live in truth" requires a new realignment with the "human order." He says,

> [The] task is one of resisting vigilantly, thoughtfully and attentively, but at the same time with total dedication, at every step and everywhere, the irrational momentum of anonymous, impersonal and inhuman power—the power of ideologies, systems, *apparat*, bureaucracy, artificial languages and political slogans.[34]

To be able to "live in truth" is a precondition to consent. Simone Weil says that to preserve consent religiously and "to try to create conditions for it where it is absent, that is to love justice" (SJ 5). And "to the extent to which at any given time there is some madness of love amongst men, to that extent there is some possibility of change in the direction of justice: and no further" (SJ 5). More will be said about the "madness of love" later.

More than anything, Simone Weil wanted "to think with truth *at the same time about the affliction of men, the perfection of God, and the link between the two*." Near the end of her life she despaired that "both in [her] intellect and in the center of [her] heart" she had lost her ability to do that (SL 178, emphasis added).

Today, as clearly as ever, politics is identified with power, and Simone Weil teaches us to "look at" power and learn not to respect it. We have cynically come to expect truth and morality to be compromised if not abandoned by politics. We do not even expect our politicians to tell the truth. Simone Weil was not cynical about this for it was a fact of the gravity of this life; her response is to learn to live morally in the light of God's perfection, even if that seems an impossible task within our human situation. She wanted, say Blum and Seidler, "to transform politics to a concern with morality and the everyday conditions of people's lives."[35] That meant, of course, paying attention to those everyday conditions and also thinking clearly about where we had gone wrong to jettison morality in our political and public life. Blum and Seidler go on to note:

> While we learn within a liberal moral culture to think of equality as a matter of being prepared to put ourselves in the situation of others, we are not helped to recognize the difficulties we face in doing so. We often become surprised at the rage and bitterness that underlay relationships of power and subordination; we cannot face the sufferings of the innocent. We fail to appreciate and even tend to minimize the injuries done to others. . . . At best all we often do is pretend to listen, but really we do not want to know. We want to keep this affliction at a safe distance for we sense that it would cost us a great deal to open up to it.[36]

It is as if in our liberal moral culture we continually deny suffering because we know that we have nothing in us morally that would enable us to face its worst forms, much less make us equal to the task of doing anything about it. The only tool we are willing to wield is talk. It is as if Simone Weil's response is to call us to moral arms—asking us to "fasten our attention" on injustice and its complaints, as Wolgast suggested, then to love unconditionally.

Simone Weil's positive conception of politics was to try and restore human dignity and self-worth through a new focus on the spirituality of work as a way of overcoming the bondage of nature. She also thought attention must be given to a system of law that had truth and a common good as its guide, to our educational system, and to re-rooting ourselves in meaningful human communities. Above all, these may best be achieved by cultivating our capacity for attention and then turning our highest degree of attention on our human condition and its affliction and on God *at the same time*. The link between the two is expressed by her as a new virtue—a supernatural virtue—she calls justice.

If Simone Weil says that all human beings are to be treated with equal respect, she does not say that that means everyone is the same, nor that there should be equal distribution of goods. Justice has to do not with how "things" are distributed—it has nothing to do with "things" (property, rights, etc.) at all. It has to do with preventing harm being done to every and all human beings and with creating a social climate where every human being has the power to consent and to refuse. The strategy for such prevention and consent is knowing by attending to the circumstances that give rise to the harm-doing and slavery. Therefore, proper attention to our human world and the suffering within it and compassion to those who suffer are what serve the ends of truth and justice. They are what unveils what is "supernatural" or sacred in our world; they bring God down through our love. In her search for a more moral political order, Simone Weil was *not*, as Springsted noted earlier, "trying to create ideal political situations that are objectively fair and fitted to human 'nature,' but trying to make people fair and just who are already socially related."[37]

Most of the discussion in this chapter has been the preparation of the soil so we can plant Simone Weil's new seed of justice. In addition to attention, the fundamental aspects of her view of justice are love, friendship, and compassion seen in their supernatural perspectives. To these we now turn.

NOTES

1. Charles Taylor, "Liberal Politics and the Public Sphere," in *Philosophical Arguments* (Cambridge: Harvard University Press, 1995), 257f.
2. C. B. MacPherson, *The Political Theory of Possessive Individualism* (Oxford: Oxford University Press, 1962).
3. Taylor, *The Sources of the Self: The Making of the Modern Identity* (Cambridge: Harvard University Press, 1989), 159.
4. Taylor, "Cross Purposes: The Liberal-Communitarian Debate," in *Philosophical Arguments,* 186f.
5. Ibid., 196.
6. Ibid., 197.
7. Patriotism can, of course, take the form of a virulent nationalism and be

responsible for a lot of evil and harm. Taylor distinguishes between a malign and a benign patriotism and supports some form of the latter (ibid., 196).

8. Michael Sandel, "Liberalism and the Limits of Justice," in *What Is Justice?,* ed. Robert C. Solomon and Mark C. Murphy (Oxford: Oxford University Press, 1990), 354.

9. Taylor, "Invoking Civil Society," in his *Philosophical Arguments,* 215f.

10. Blum and Seidler, *A Truer Liberty,* 260.

11. Eric O. Springsted, "Of Tennis, Persons and Politics," *Philosophical Investigations* 16, no. 3 (July 1993), 207.

12. Ibid., 211.

13. Elizabeth Wolgast, *The Grammar of Justice* (Ithaca: Cornell University Press, 1987), 203.

14. Ibid., 128. Again she says: "Outrage is required of any person of moral dimension, anyone expecting respect as a member of the moral community, or silence and complacency in the face of wrongdoing are themselves a kind of moral offense" (139). A similar theme is struck in Judith N. Shklar's *The Faces of Injustice* (New Haven: Yale University Press, 1990), where she provides a more historical look at how "the sense of injustice as a fundamental experience plays a relatively small part in classical ethics," and argues for greater attention to "the voice of the victims" in its many forms (85ff.).

15. Rhees, *Discussions of Simone Weil.*

16. Nye, *Philosophia,* 111f.

17. Little, "Simone Weil's Concept of Decreation," 40.

18. Winch, *Simone Weil,* 180.

19. Winch, *Simone Weil,* 181.

20. This point is made in a number of places in both Weil's *Oppression and Liberty* and "Factory Journal." McLellan also makes this point in *Simone Weil,* 109f.

21. See Ann Loades's discussion of Simone Weil's "Antigone," in *Simone Weil's Philosophy of Culture.*

22. Iris Murdoch introduces the notion of "attentive love" into ethics, taking a lead directly from Simone Weil, in her *Sovereignty of Good* (New York: Schocken Books, 1970), and in the last decade or so it is beginning to appear among communitarians and some feminists. Lawrence A. Blum traces the history in his *Moral Perception and Particularity* (Cambridge: Cambridge University Press, 1994), focusing on Murdoch, communitarians, and feminists. We will take up the role of love in ethics in the feminist context shortly.

23. Springsted, "Of Tennis," 209.

24. Ibid., 210.

25. Winch, *Simone Weil,* 182.

26. Ibid., 107.

27. Ibid., 107.

28. Ibid., 108.

29. Ibid., 115–19. Springsted's essay, "Of Tennis," also speaks to these issues.

30. Catherine A. MacKinnon, "Rape: On Coercion and Consent," in *Women and Values: Readings in Recent Feminist Philosophy,* ed. Marilyn Pearsall, second edition (Belmont, Calif.: Wadsworth Publishing Co., 1993), 216, emphasis added.

31. MacKinnon, "Rape," 217.

32. Ibid., 219.

33. Ibid., 215.

34. Václav Havel, *Living in Truth,* ed. Jan Vladislaw (London: Faber and Faber, 1989), 153. See especially Havel's long essay "The Power of the Powerless."

35. Blum and Seidler, *A Truer Liberty,* 302.

36. Ibid., 283.

37. Springsted, "Of Tennis."

4

A NEW VIRTUE OF JUSTICE: LOVE, FRIENDSHIP, AND "MADNESS"

"SUPERNATURAL JUSTICE" AND LOVE

It is in the connection of love to justice that we see most clearly why Simone Weil's return to the concept of justice enables us to call it a *new* virtue. In the classical Aristotelian sense, a virtue is acquired through practice. For Simone Weil, justice strictly speaking is *not* an acquired virtue; it is given by God in the form of divine love. We will see, however, that it is *related* to human practices like attention and undivided love of the other, even though not acquired by them. To have this new virtue—"the supernatural virtue of justice"—one must consent to this love given by God; and this level of consent comes from the most sacred part of our being—the "uncreated" part in us that desires God's love. Simone Weil says, "Human consent is a sacred thing. It is what man grants to God. It is what God comes in search of when like a beggar he approaches men" (SJ 2). To grant this most sacred thing to God, however, requires that I renounce all those "created" parts of myself that yield to power; that create motivations in me for *not* consenting.

A picture emerges in this rather uncommon "language game" of Simone Weil's concerning this new "supernatural virtue." The picture is that God holds all the cards but needs our human consent to play out the divine hand. The short of it is that the supernatural virtue of justice is the product of the gratuitous intervention of divine love and that this love is asymmetrical. The central qualification of this intervention is that it happens when, and only when, our human practices are *of the form that is love.* Any human practice that is of the form of love must presuppose mutual human consent and thus what we, as human beings, call up by consent is that part of us that is one with God and is thus God. Justice, therefore, is consenting to God to have God made present in our human practices which are, themselves, of a form that is God's love, i.e., of a form of unconditional love—a love that we rarely, if ever, recognize clearly.

To try to understand this rather abstract notion in another way, let us illustrate by using two examples from Simone Weil. She used these examples to make a different point, but they translate her uncommon thought to a common idiom. The point they will illustrate is that, while "rights" always operate within a *horizontal symmetry* on a social scale, "justice" operates within a *vertical asymmetry* on a cosmic scale.

The first illustration comes from "Human Personality." She says that the gram is inferior to the kilogram on the scales, then goes on to say:

> But there can be a scale on which the gram outweighs the kilogram. It is only necessary for one arm to be more than a thousand times as long as the other. The law of equilibrium easily overcomes an inequality of weight. But the lesser will never outweigh the greater unless the relation between them is regulated by the law of equilibrium. (SE 33f.)

In relation to the cosmic scale, where human actions are related to divine love, the kilogram is in the arena of human practice and could only normally be balanced by a counterweight on the social scale equal to it or overcome by a heavier weight. The gram, on the cosmic scale, however, is a non-material counterweight—it is like the mustard seed or the pomegranate seed—and when placed on the scales with the disequal arm of supernatural justice, balance or equilibrium can be achieved. On this cosmic scale the asymmetry of God's love to our human action is evident. God, though unseen and not to be spoken of, can implicitly balance the scales on this earth through our attention to injustice and the genuine human practice of unconditional love to our fellow human beings.

Consider a second example. This comes from Simone Weil's essay "On Bankruptcy," written in 1937:

The payment of debts is necessary for social order. The non-payment of debts is quite equally necessary for social order. For centuries humanity has oscillated, serenely unaware, between these two contradictory necessities. Unfortunately, the second of them violates a great many seemingly legitimate interests and it has difficulty in securing recognition without disturbance and a measure of violence. (SE 149)

The first (payment of debts), however, survives, and it is considered scandalous to default on debts. She gives this example: "Even in the fifth century B.C. the aged Cephalus, to convince Socrates that he had always lived according to justice, made the claim: 'I have told the truth and paid my debts.' Socrates doubted if this was a satisfactory definition of justice. But Socrates was a troublesome person" (SE 148). Rights, it could be argued, rest on such balance of debts within society. To have a right to something means that it cannot be taken away without equal compensation. Our courts of law are set up to oversee the enforcement of fair if not equal compensation. And it is necessary to social order that such balance is maintained.

But "Socrates doubted if this was a satisfactory definition of justice." Both Socrates and Simone Weil were, of course, "troublesome." Social order, however, is not only based on this symmetry of debt payment; it is also based on the asymmetry of non-debt payment. One implication here is that sometimes debts must be cancelled or forgiven to maintain social order. If unfairness has resulted in gross imbalance, e.g., between rich and poor, and the one who suffers from the unfairness cannot compensate loss, then to avoid revolt or risk further unfairness, a debt may be cancelled. (This has got the world economic community all knotted up at present, due to the enormous debts of poor nations to first world banks and the inability, almost unthinkability, of the Western banks to write off the debts. There is the growing awareness that such may be a necessity to survive globally. This, of course, is not an unconditioned forgiveness of debt, for the act of forgiveness is to preserve a possibly worse financial loss. It is, however, a kind of gratuitous act.) Simone Weil notes:

> The revolt by which the Roman plebeians won the institution of the tribuneship had its origin in a widespread insolvency which was reducing more and more debtors to the condition of slavery; and even

if there had been no revolt a partial cancellation of debts had become imperative, because with every plebeian reduced to a slave Rome lost a soldier. (SE 149)

There is a deeper sense to her notion of nonpayment of debts regarding justice, however. This relates to the human scale of affliction where any notion of "repayment" or "compensation" seems totally meaningless (as in the case of the sexual violation of a woman, or of cruelty imposed by armed force to perpetuate fear). As was noted earlier with the case of the violated woman, what "right" has been taken away and how could it be replaced? Or, in the second case, is repayment of cruelty to be some return of cruelty in kind? This second kind of payment is, however, part of judicial systems based on retribution and is embedded in those social scales based on balance of power.

The asymmetrical aspect of justice is created by the weight of necessity and how, given our equal vulnerability to misfortune, we all at some time bow our necks to force. This also means that we must all become acquainted with affliction, even to the point, as Weil suggests, of becoming slaves with no sense of rights whatsoever. Acquaintance here begins with attention—attention to things in the natural world, to school studies, and then to human beings through a succession of "intervals of hesitation." But it continues with love, that is, an unconditional, noncompensatory act of compassion toward one who is afflicted. The human world, however, knows little of such unconditional love, and thus the love has its source from outside the human world—it appears to be "love from nowhere," a form of "madness." We can flatter ourselves that we will read a situation in the right way, says Weil, and thus act justly; but invariably we give a "wrong reading of justice" leading to another exercise of our power (GG, 122). "Readings," she says, "—except where there is a certain quality of attention—obeys the law of gravity. We read the opinions suggested by gravity (the preponderant part played by the passions and by social conformity in the judgments we form of men and events). With a higher quality of attention our reading discovers gravity itself, and various systems of possible balance" (GG 122). And the "system of possible balance" that we must look for in the case of bringing justice about lays outside the natural world. Simone Weil says:

> Only by the supernatural working of grace can a soul pass through its own annihilation to the place where alone it can get the sort of attention which can attend to truth, and to affliction. It is the same attention which listens to both of them. *The name of this intense, pure, disinterested, gratuitous, generous attention is love.* (SE 28, emphasis added)

Balance or equilibrium here can neither be found in nor function within a social order. Rather it has its meaning in a larger cosmic order—what may be called a divine *milieu*. The counterbalance to the weight of natural necessity is God's grace. For Simone Weil one clear model of such counterbalancing grace is the crucifixion. The cross represents the divine intersection with the world—our only pure example of an unconditional love. The cross, in fact, is a sign of an incarnation where God, having taken leave of the world to allow humans to act, reenters by our consent. Here, again, we have links with the concepts of "decreation" and "grace."

The harmony and equilibrium that operate on the cosmic scale—a justice that embraces divine love—must recognize the asymmetry

> that nothing in the world is the center of the world, that the center of the world is outside the world, that nothing here below has the right to say *I. One must renounce in favor of God*, through love for Him and for the truth, this illusory power which He has accorded us, to think in the first person. He has accorded it to us that it may be possible for us to renounce it by love. (IC 174, emphasis added)

Ultimately, then, justice is beyond human control, but it is also manifest within and through human action by attention, renunciation, and fellow-love. In this sense justice is possible within the world, but it is the supernatural virtue of justice that is manifest here. "The criterion for those things which come from God," she says, "is that they show all the characteristics of madness except for the loss of capacity to discern truth and love justice" (FLN 351). Our "madness" from the perspective of the cosmic scale is *not* to recognize our limits and our abuse of power, and *not* to read our actions as "just" *by our own measures.* "Madness" understood on the social scale is not to bow to power and risk becoming a slave. Simone Weil found few examples of how a human might understand justice as possible through human behavior within the world. One that she did find compelling is in the Egyptian *Book of the Dead*, spoken by a soul on the way to salvation.

The model here for "uncontaminated" justice—justice as far as is humanly possible—should show all the marks registered in *The Book of the Dead*:

- To show no scorn for God and to show reverence for the truth
- To listen for and be attentive to words of right and truth
- Not to strike fear in any person
- To make no person weep and let no one suffer hunger
- To act without arrogance or expectation of favor (LTP 13f.; cf. also SE 131 and 45f., N 369, and WG 144)

If we do these things, God's grace takes care of the rest and balances the scales; in our just love God's love is present.

This *new* virtue of justice, this supernatural virtue, understands the word "justice" in the same way it understands "God," "truth," "beauty," and "love." These are words, says Simone Weil, which "illumine and lift up toward the good"; they refer to "an absolute perfection which we cannot conceive"; they are "the image in our world of this impersonal and divine order of the universe" (SE 33f.). In another context she makes this very telling remark about these words of this "impersonal and divine order": "Humanism was not wrong in thinking that [these words] are of infinite value, but in thinking that man can get them for himself without grace" (SE 53). To think we can get justice without grace is to remove the term from its divine order.

This is clearly *a very radical formulation of what justice is* considering the nearly three hundred years that have been spent on the "modern," secular formulations within which we operate in Western democracies. If, however, we go back to Socrates, Lao Tzu, and Confucius, and even earlier to *The Iliad* and Egyptian concerns with harm and hunger, their desire for homecomings and hot baths, where balance, harmony, and peaceableness (*ataraxia*) are our chief aim both personally and publicly, then Simone Weil's struggle to give us a *spiritual* reading of justice does not appear quite so radical or novel. Add to this the crucifixion where God descends to suffer humiliation and affliction, and the Gospel message of unconditional love of neighbor Simone Weil wants to bring forward—what was only a "hint" in her writing at the time of *Oppression and Liberty*—and her radical spiritual vision begins to come into focus.

In her later reflections, Simone Weil goes so far as to say that there is "no distinction between love of our neighbor and justice" (WG 139). In fact she says: "Only the absolute identification of justice and love makes the coexistence possible of compassion and gratitude on the one hand, and on the other, of respect for the dignity of affliction in the afflicted—a respect felt by the sufferer himself and the others" (WG 140). The important feature in what we are calling the asymmetrical aspect of justice is that "the supernatural virtue of justice consists of *behaving exactly as though there were equality* when one is the stronger in an unequal relationship" (WG 143, emphasis added). Thus, if you are in a position of power or control or wealth relative to another human being, there must be mutual consent between the parties, and the weaker party should in no way feel humiliated, or the stronger superior. The fact will remain, however, that the condition of inequality will persist by necessity. That is why a "supernatural" virtue is required to bring about justice. "In true love," says Weil:

> it is not we who love the afflicted in God; it is God in us who loves them. When we are in affliction, it is God in us who loves those who wish us well. *Compassion and gratitude come down from God, and when they are exchanged in a glance, God is present at the point where the eyes of those who give and those who receive meet.* The sufferer and the other love each other, starting from God through God, but not for the love of God; they love each other for the love of the one for the other. This is an impossibility. That is why it comes about only through the agency of God. (WG 151, emphasis added)[1]

To understand this remark with all its radical implications is a key to understanding the grammar of Simone Weil's new virtue of justice.

The whole grammar of justice is transformed into a new virtue when viewed on this cosmic, supernatural scale. Our human nature balances power only and will tend to preserve in unequal amounts the power one has (whether an individual or a government). We will not, according to Simone Weil, "naturally" move in a benevolent or sacrificial manner to preserve the good against what she calls "necessity" or "gravity." The sooner we recognize our human limitations, the greater becomes the prospect of being open to grace or "the agency of God."

She sees this factor as implicit in every culture around the globe—historically and contemporaneously. "Grace," she says, "is the law of descending movement. An ascending movement is natural, a descending one supernatural" (N 308). This formulation of justice in terms of grace is hardly bizarre—it appears so only against the enlightenment background of modern political thought where all is conceived solely in terms of "human rational agency."

To complete our picture of the new virtue of justice we need now to speak of friendship and the "madness of love" before turning toward Simone Weil's conception of a moral and civic order anchored in her *compassion-based morality* as opposed to the *rights-based moralities* dominant in Western political theory.

THE IDEAL OF FRIENDSHIP

In the social order of the world, love of neighbor is best exemplified by compassion; but, says Simone Weil, a purer relationship between human beings than love of neighbor is friendship. In addition to the commandments that we love God and love our neighbor, Jesus said, "love one another" (John 13:34; Jesus called this "a new commandment"). Simone Weil calls this "a third commandment" (FLN 128). In love of neighbor there may be inequality. Although just love "consists of behaving exactly as though there were equality," it is likely, given the natural order, that "one is the stronger in an unequal relationship" (WG 204). She says:

> Friendship has something universal about it. It consists of loving a human being as we should like to be able to love each soul in particular of all those who go to make up the human race. . . . The consent to preserve an autonomy within ourselves and in others is essentially of a universal order.
>
> There is not friendship where distance is not kept and respected. . . .
>
> Pure friendship is rare. (WG 206f.)

Friendship allows each person in the relationship his or her complete autonomy. You cannot either "wish to please or . . . desire to dominate" a friend: "In a perfect friendship these two desires are completely absent.

The two friends have fully consented to be two and not one, they respect the distance which the fact of being two distinct creatures places between them" (WG 205). In love of neighbor no such relation of "equality" is necessary; we do not require absolute autonomy of knowledge of the other's needs or desires. In the second commandment we act *as we* would want to be loved. To some degree we measure the kind of love given, and it is not dependent on a particular association with the one loved. Although the difference between love of neighbor and friendship is subtle at times, it is reflected in the difference between what Simone Weil sees as the "second" and the "third" commandments and in the knowledge and association one necessarily develops with a particular friend which is not a necessary part of love of neighbor.[2] The goal of friendship is to establish a bond of affection and respect with another human being without any degree of necessity—you love one another without needing one another or expecting anything from the other, or not desiring the other. A friendship is sustained because "each wished to preserve the faculty of free consent both in himself and in the other" (WG 204).

Simone Weil gives us two historical examples when such pure friendship may have been an accepted part of life. The first was during the Golden Age of Athenian democracy and is expressed perfectly in Plato's *Symposium,* when in a speech by Socrates he reveals what he says he "learned [about love] from a woman of exalted wisdom, named Diotima" (SNLG 128). The second was in the culture of Languedoc in southern France during the eleventh and twelfth centuries. In both these examples there was an aspiration to "impossible love"—a love that saw few barriers between human beings, which abhorred vice, understood consent as central, and embraced chastity as a virtue. She even discusses how such love tolerated love between men (in the *Symposium*) and between women (in the chivalrous love of Languedoc) (SE 49). There is a tacit approval of homosexual love as equal to all perfect love with the limiting features that it never be covetous, has mutual respect and consent at its heart, and be chaste, that is, show no desire in the relationship. Chivalrous love does not covet the other person: "It is simply a patient attention toward the loved person and an appeal for that person's consent" (SE 50). This impossible love appears to be the same kind of rare love of another she calls pure friendship.

Andrea Nye has identified in an early writing of Simone Weil, "On Freud," this view of sexual love:

> Weil, although she adopted chastity for herself, did not see sexual union as necessarily impure. Sexual union is analogous to fusion with the mother or with God, and so is divine. *"La reaction, le respect de ce qu'on aime constitue l'essential de la pudeur. Ce qu'on aime est sacre"* (O I:278). Sexual love is pure when there is respect for the other person, when she is loved as a whole person, and when there is mutual pleasure. "All perversion consists in ceasing to consider the loved being as a person, in considering him as an object, and notably an object divisible into parts." (O I:279)[3]

This view is refreshingly sensitive amidst all the noise of contentious moralisms about sexual love heard today. It is consistent with her later views of the perfect love of friendship and the wholeness of every human being. To contemplate such examples as these, she says, "should stimulate us to seek for our own particular source of spirituality" which gives us clues to one of "many bridges between God and man" (SE 45f.).

Simone Weil insists that Plato's philosophy is not "a search for God by means of human reason," but a wisdom that oriented "the soul towards grace" (SNLG 99). At the heart of this wisdom is love. Love always directs itself to God. This is why when true love in the form of friendship or compassion to another human being is shown, it is nothing other than God's love being enacted to the other.

This idea of a relationship between two people where one considers the loved being "as a whole [autonomous] person" and where "mutual respect is shown" takes an interesting turn in the writing of contemporary French thinker Luce Irigaray (born 1930). Although Irigaray does not seem to have been aware of Simone Weil's views on friendship and perfect love of another, her view of love and sexual difference has some striking resemblance to Weil's views on friendship.

Irigaray, not surprisingly, finds Diotima's speech on love in the *Symposium* a fertile starting point. Irigaray believes there cannot be any liberation of women short of freeing women from the masculine images that define them in our culture. Women must define themselves in their own terms and not in the terms of the other (men). The relationship between men and women, for Irigaray, must emphasize sexual difference and generate mutual respect from a sense of awe and wonder about each other's otherness. There can be no covetousness or desire that controls the relationship. Even sexual love must be a consequence of mutual wonder and awe at the other's difference. Irigaray writes: "Wonder keeps the two sexes non-interchangeable regarding the status of their difference. It maintains between them a free and attracting space, a possibility of separation and union. . . . There would never be an overstepping of the interval."⁴ The relationship of men and women must go beyond equality. "The liberation of women," Irigaray writes, "goes well beyond the frame of feminist struggles which nowadays too often go no further than critique of patriarchy, separatism, or the claim to equality with men, without putting forward new values to live sexual difference with justice, civility and spiritual fertility."⁵ Here we have something very close to Simone Weil's notion of "consent to preserve an autonomy within ourselves," where two persons in friendship "respect the distance which the fact of being two distinct creatures places between them" (WG 205f.), and where each is allowed "to seek [his or her] own particular source of spirituality" (SE 45). Direct union can only be with God, says Simone Weil. Irigaray, too, says that the relationship between men and women must reserve room "for God." Simone Weil's ideal of friendship, it could be said, also has at its heart the values of "justice, civility and spiritual fertility."

In the second historical example, besides showing us friendship in chivalrous love, Simone Weil also provides a genealogy of the decline of the spiritual in Western culture. First she differentiates between what she calls the "true Renaissance" from the "false Renaissance." In the "false Renaissance," the one we know best of the fifteenth and sixteenth centuries, she says, "people thought that they could turn away from Christianity towards the Greek spirit. . . . From then onwards, the spiritual element in the life of Europe has diminished until it has almost shrunk to nothing" (SE 47). It was from here that she says humanism developed and was reinforced by the eighteenth-century enlightenment and the Revolution. By the Revolution she is no doubt referring to the French Revolution of 1789, but could also add the Revolution linked to the historical materialism of Marx, that is, the 1917 Russian Revolution. "What had happened," she asks, between the true Renaissance of the eleventh and twelfth centuries found in *langue d'oc*, and the false one? The true Renaissance perished with "the murder . . . of *langue d'oc*" and with it "Romanesque civilization came to an end." She believed that the civilization of Languedoc was the purest in all Medieval Europe because it embraced a spirituality with "a living link" to the "traditions of India, Persia, Egypt, Greece, and perhaps others as well." These were "traditions which offer us inexhaustible spiritual treasures." The link was cut in the thirteenth century (SE 47f.).[6] The inspiration of Languedoc was that they recognized and understood force and yet rejected it "with loathing and contempt. This contempt," she says, "is the other face of the compassion which goes out to everything that is exposed to the ravages of force." Love in friendship is the total rejection of force or coercion of any kind (SE 48f.). The compassion and "chivalrous love" of Languedoc had as its object "a human being; but it is not covetousness. It is simply," as noted earlier, "a patient attention towards the loved person and an appeal for that person's consent. . . . In this land, as in Greece, human love was one that bridges between man and God" (SE 50).

So what can we learn from this civilization? Simone Weil tells us to contemplate the beauty of that remote age, and as we do that "with attention and love, in that same measure its inspiration will come to us and will gradually make impossible the ignominies which constitute the air we breathe today" (SE 54). This particular advice will be taken to heart in our concluding chapter as we contemplate what Simone Weil's entire moral and political philosophy, with all of her concrete examples, may have to say to the ignominies of today (that is, the waning years of the twentieth century) and our moral and political practices in the air we will breathe tomorrow—in the century that lies ahead.

Simone Weil also gives us a brief glimpse of her idea of friendship in *Oppression and Liberty* when she tries to picture, as we noted before, "a society of free men, equal and brothers. . . . Each would see in every work-fellow another self occupying another post [imagine here shop floorman and machine operator seeing the self in one another with equal respect and autonomy], and would love him in the way that the Gospel maxim enjoins. Thus we should possess, over and above liberty, a still more precious good; for if nothing is more odious than the humiliation and degradation of man by man [there is no friendship on the shop floor], nothing is so beautiful or so sweet as friendship" (OL 100).

The purity and rarity of friendship are what make it "a miracle" for Simone Weil. In a perfect world where we would "love one another," where friendship was the norm, there would be no need of justice. But in the world we have, it is a Herculean task just to try and love your neighbor as you love yourself. Neighbors are those nearest to you, wherever you are—that is, those nearest you whether they be spouse, child, parent, coworker, fellow citizens, strangers, or enemies. These are our neighbors in the world we inhabit. The world we have is a world of necessity where we both "wish to please" *and* "desire to dominate": it is a world where power and force are the daily reminders of inequality and uprootedness, where jealousy and envy, greed and covetousness, pride and hatred keep the hope of justice just that—a hope for which we must struggle and without which our world would be worse than hell.

So a peaceful social order requires a continual struggle for justice, and the hope stays alive with signs of compassion for those who hurt and by the inspiration of those moments of rare and pure friendships that come to our attention and which show us some of the "bridges between God and man."

THE "MADNESS" OF JUSTICE AND LOVE

In a number of places, but most forcefully in her late London writings, Simone Weil says that this higher justice—this new virtue—requires a certain kind of "madness": it requires thought and action that go against the stream of the situation of power and oppression on the human level. When, within the social order, we take such contrary actions, we are called "mad."

To help clarify Simone Weil's unusual use of the term "madness" by juxtaposing it with "love"—"the madness of love," "mad love," and justice implying a kind of "madness"—we will note here the way in which "madness" is used by Michel Foucault in his well-known and influential *Madness and Civilization* (1961). Foucault differentiates (a) "madness" as seen before "the Renaissance," "linked to the presence of imaginary transcendences" and ascribed to those who bore the "stigmata" of coming "from the world of the irrational," from (b) "madness" in "the classical age"—after his landmark year of 1656—when madness was perceived in a person because the person crossed "the frontier of bourgeois order of his own accord, and alienate[d] himself outside the sacred limits of its ethic."[7] It is clear that Simone Weil believed we must cross the frontiers of the current social order and ethics "of our own accord" and also that we must alienate ourselves outside the bourgeois ethic. To defy a "rights based" morality is enough to be branded "mad." "Madness" for her bore not the "stigmata" of "imaginary transcendences"; rather the "stigmata" that her "madness" bore was witness to God incarnate and crucified as love, the stigmata of the cross as well as all "ways" that intimate an incarnation of divine love in human practice. Whereas Foucault's second madness, post-1656, is defined within a post-Renaissance secular context, Simone Weil's use combines and modifies Foucault's two notions to construe "madness" as a concept that is out of sync with our modern secular culture. Maybe hers is a postmodern idea of madness, just as her idea of justice goes beyond our modern conceptions of justice.

No more perfect expression of Simone Weil's understanding of the "madness of love" can be found than in this remark of Søren Kierkegaard:

> Divine compassion, however, the unlimited *recklessness* in concerning oneself only with the suffering, not in the least with oneself, and of unconditionally recklessly concerning oneself with *each* sufferer—people can interpret this only as a kind of madness over which we are not sure whether we should laugh or cry.[8]

If we laugh, of course we are like Lao Tzu's "worst student who hears about the way"—we are repulsed by its ridiculous demands and alien ethic. Lao Tzu concludes, however, that "If he did not laugh it would be unworthy of being the way." The way of compassion is hard. It is this kind of love as compassion that is offensive to most contemporary sensibilities, but it is precisely that new virtue Simone Weil calls us to practice if we are to be just.

Even though we may be deprived of consent "in the depth of the heart" by all manner of "privations of soul and body" (SJ 5), such privations must be challenged. Hope against hope, "justice," she says, "has as its object the exercise of the faculty of consent on earth. To preserve it religiously wherever it exists, to try to create conditions for it where it is absent, that is to love justice" (SJ 5). And she concludes, as was quoted earlier, "To the extent to which at any given time there is some madness of love amongst men, to that extent there is some possibility of change in the direction of justice: and no further" (SJ 5).

Thus, when Simone Weil asks, "Are we struggling for justice?" she is in essence asking us how "mad" are we among our fellow human beings? *And she answers*: to the degree that we refuse harm-doing and prevent harm being done to other human beings (SE 31); to the degree that we resist all forms of evil and encourage conditions for the flourishing of the good; to the degree that we are willing to "hurl" ourselves "into risks"; and to the degree that we are grateful to God and love unconditionally, we *are* mad and *are* engaged in the struggle for justice.

This madness of love derives its meaning, in part, in the midst of moral ambiguity, when there is no clarity for us to set our moral compass. Which way shall we turn to do good and avoid harm? How are we to sustain our health, wealth, and wisdom without harming others? Because most ethical waters are deep and wide, the possibility of a steady, right course is not always straightforward. The way of justice is never easy. Simone Weil was always struggling to see her way through a sea of moral ambiguity.

Andrea Nye refers to Simone Weil's way as a kind of "goodness in human affairs," and that "the remedy for social injustice cannot be more power; it can only be goodness."[9] Nye continues:

> Goodness is not an idea, but a way of acting in that world: attentive, listening, capable of response to claims for justice. If, as feminist critics have pointed out, it is men who have exercised most of the destructive power that Weil describes and men who continue to seek that power in elections and commerce, it is women, for whatever the reason, who are more likely to have the communicative goodness Weil describes. If this is true, the recruitment of women for public office is not only redress of past discrimination, but a positive means to a more just society. For Weil, more important than the structure of institutions is the character of the persons who administer them. It is through good individuals that Weil's divine goodness, those infinitely small grains of the divine, permeate and leaven human affairs.[10]

There are few relatively unambiguous examples of such good people who have navigated the seas of moral ambiguity with courage and clarity, who show goodness in human affairs. When an example does come to light, it shows all the marks of Simone Weil's madness of love.

One thinks of Gandhi or Dorothy Day or Mother Theresa of Calcutta, but one of the most moving examples shown through the lives of ordinary people is found in the story of the people of the village of Le Chambon-sur-Lignon who, during World War II, placed themselves at risk out of gratitude to God and in unconditional love to save the lives of Jewish children.[11] They did so on their own accord, guided by their traditional religious aspirations and what Hallie called the "mysterious virtues" of compassion and generosity. Their actions were motivated by others' needs and a witness to what Simone Weil called "the supreme and perfect flower of the madness of love"; they rekindled "the smallest traces of . . . the fragile earthly possibilities of beauty, of happiness and of fulfillment . . . all with an equally religious care" (SJ 9). It is ironic that while Simone Weil was talking about mad love and desperately trying to find a way to practice it in her war-torn homeland, the people of Le Chambon were "madly" at work loving those most afflicted—Jewish children fleeing from certain death. One wonders if Simone Weil would have had the patience to love as did the Chambonnais—or whether by this time her death wish was too strong. The example set at this time in Le Chambon was precisely the kind of pure expression of justice as compassion Simone Weil advocated.

In his story about Le Chambon, Hallie tries to get to the root of "how goodness happened there." He is particularly drawn to Magda Trocmé, wife of the community's pastor and leader, André Trocmé, whose goodness seems unusually pure and unencumbered by ethical theory. In *Lest Innocent Blood Be Shed*, the story of the whole village is told and a number of good people are discussed, while in his followup book, *Tales of Good and Evil, Help and Harm*, Hallie focuses on Magda's goodness.

In *Tales*, Hallie draws a comparison of the ambiguities found in twentieth-century morality to Goethe's Faust. Faust had two souls in one body, each wanting to tear itself away from the other. Hallie sees in himself a human torn between these two souls, living two distinct kind of virtues. The first kind of virtue grows from acting in terms of one's own self-interest and preservation; it "rests on the sound biological and psychological bedrock of self-preservation."[12] Of this kind there are what he calls "little virtues" like thrift and caution; "they protect our hides" and are commonsensical—reasonable ways of behaving in order to preserve our lives and comforts. The second kind of virtue includes "mysterious" actions, ones "motivated by another person's needs"—"you are not the center; the helped person is." This virtue is expressed in compassion and generosity. This seemed both impractical and "unnatural," but to the Chambonnais, especially to Magda, exercising a "mysterious" virtue became an ordinary, natural practice as they went about welcoming strangers and saving lives.

Simone Weil, too, has a sense of the two souls of Faust: Force or power is a rule in the natural, social order and we work to avoid harm and maintain some reasonable balance of power; we work to exercise the "little virtues" and stay out of harm's way. Compassion and generosity, however, enter from "outside" and require us to do some good. Both souls and the virtues that spring from them commingle in the human being; they both find expression in and through our lived-body as we read the world we encounter. It is a continual struggle to see which will win out. The mysterious virtues require grace. To position the self to receive such outside help, one must annihilate the "I" and "wait" in attention to the cries of those in need of help. Then one is prepared to exercise those "mysterious virtues" and be an instrument of the madness that is God's love.

Singlemindedness in the service of others, or "recklessness" concerned only with the sufferer, is another way of understanding this goodness in human affairs that Simone Weil calls "mad"—where compassion and generosity appear completely selfless. Hallie provides another tale of such goodness. The "plot" of the story of Joshua James, the nineteenth-century patron saint of the U.S. Life Saving Service (later to become the Search and Rescue arm of the U.S. Coast Guard), and his "surfmen" and fellow villagers of Hull, Massachusetts, is embodied in "benevolence, hospitality and helpfulness." What Hallie discovered in this "immovably centered" man was a goodness that was visible in the form of his being—in what he did to save lives for almost sixty years.[13] "His power to spread life," says Hallie, "did not lie in one of his deeds, like what he did in the storm of '88. It was his whole persistent, centered, life-giving life that was the very *form* and essence of [his] decency."[14] "Moral beauty happens," concludes Hallie, "when someone carves out a place for compassion in a largely ruthless universe. It happened in the French village of Le Chambon during the war, and it happened in and near the American village of Hull during the long lifetime of Joshua James."[15]

When this kind of "moral beauty" or goodness happens in the

midst of power struggles and suffering in our world, Simone Weil's new virtue of justice seems alive and well. In such justice God is the balancing principle for the moral good being done and God is present in the help given to others.

For Simone Weil, madness is a passion for love and justice and a belief that without love and justice we banish God from our world. God is present in the person within whom God's love is alive; she says, "compassion is the visible presence of God here below" (FLN 103). Madness for her has God, in Wittgenstein's words, "moving around in the grammatical background" and "embodied in [the] grammar" of one's very life. God must be, as Kierkegaard said, "the middle term" in whose company one discovers one's neighbor. It is this Kierkegaard calls "divine compassion." What we need, says Simone Weil,

> is for the spirit of justice to dwell within us. The spirit of justice is nothing other than the supreme and perfect flower of the madness of love. . . . The madness of love draws one to discern and cherish equally, in all human milieu without exception, in all parts of the globe, the fragile earthly possibilities of beauty, of happiness and of fulfillment; to want to preserve them all with an equally religious care; and where they are absent to want to rekindle tenderly the smallest traces of those which have existed, the smallest seeds of those which can be born. . . . *The madness of love . . . radiates irresistibly through accent, tone and manner, through all thoughts, all words and all actions, in all circumstances and without any exception.* It makes impossible those thoughts, words and actions through which it cannot radiate. (SJ 9, emphasis added)

The madness of love is the purest possible expression of this new virtue of justice; it draws us to see another's hurt and want to help—to stop it "in all circumstances and without any exception." This madness calls for the impossible; it is perceived by our "modern" world to de-mand the "irrational"; it demands a kind of "recklessness." It clearly demands we step outside the frontiers of our current social order, as Foucault noted, and adopt both a radical ethic of love—a "mad love" in Simone Weil's words—and what appears to many to be a "mad" mode of speaking and acting. The madness of love draws us to cherish all human beings equally but also to discern and cherish "the fragile earthly possibilities of beauty . . . to want to preserve them with an equally religious care." This madness linked with the "super-natural" extends to how our bodies flow into the natural order of our world. To morally live in a way of compassion and gratitude within this social order is like a dance filled with a total madness—a madness "radiat[ing] irresistibly through accent, tone and manner, through all thoughts, all words and all actions, in all circumstances and without any exception" (SJ 9).

NOTES

1. Here is a perfect example of "essential contradiction" being resolved in correlation as discussed by André Devaux, "On the Right Use of Contradiction According to Simone Weil," in *Simone Weil's Philosophy of Culture.*

2. See Diogenes Allen and Eric Springsted's discussion of friendship and love of neighbor in chapter seven, "The Love of Particulars," in their *Spirit, Nature and Community: Issues in the Thought of Simone Weil* (Albany: State University of New York Press, 1994), 113–31. Their interpretation is set in an interesting discussion of the differences they have with Peter Winch and Rowan Williams on the nature of love in Weil.

3. Nye, *Philosophia*, 248f. Nye's reference to "O I:278" is to Weil's *Oeuvres Complète*, Tome I, volumes 1–2 (Paris: Gallimard, 1988).

4. Luce Irigaray, *An Ethics of Sexual Difference*, trans. Carolyn Burke and Gillian C. Gill (Ithaca: Cornell University Press, 1993), 13. My comparison of Irigaray's relationship rooted in sexual difference with Weil's ideal of friendship was triggered by a interesting discussion of Irigaray found in Fergus Kerr, *Immortal Longings: Versions of Transcending Humanity* (London: SPCK, 1997), 89–112.

5. Irigaray, *je, tu, nous: Toward a Culture of Difference*, trans. Alison Martin (London: Routledge, 1993), 12. Irigaray queries: "To demand equality as women is, it seems to me, a mistaken expression of a real objective. The demand to be equal presupposes a point of comparison. To whom or to what do women want to be equalized? To men? To a salary? To a public office? To what standard? Why not to themselves?" (Irigaray, *je, tu, nous*, 12). Kerr goes on to discuss an explicit theology in Irigaray's position that requires an idea of God that serves as a horizon for women's identity, as the free and autonomous subject of whom they are the images. Women have no such divine mirror and thus are alienated. Irigaray writes: "Women are deprived of God, they are forced to comply with models that do not match them, that exile, double, mask them, cut them off from themselves and from one another, stripping away their ability to move forward into love, art, thought, toward their ideal and divine fulfilment." Iri-

garay, *Sexes and Genealogies,* trans. Gillian C. Gill (New York: Columbia University Press, 1993), 64. See also Kerr, *Immortal Longings,* 101–12).

6. There are, of course, a multiplicity of ways to explain the decline of Romanesque culture in the twelfth and thirteenth centuries, leading us through the later middle ages to the rise of humanism in the Renaissance. Not the least of these is the reintroduction of Aristotle's physical and metaphysical writings from the Arab world into Western medieval culture and its subsequent absorption into Christian theology through Thomas Aquinas's works, and Aristotle's empirical methods which open a path toward the scientific revolutions of the fourteenth through seventeenth centuries.

7. Michel Foucault, *The Foucault Reader,* ed. Paul Rabinow (London: Penguin Books, 1984), 136. To my knowledge Foucault was unaware of Simone Weil's usage of the term "madness."

8. From *Practice in Christianity: Anti-Climacus,* S. Kierkegaard, ed., 27 September 1850. See the broader discussion of this remark related to Kierkegaard's notions of "pathos" and "offense" in the appropriation of love in Harvie Ferguson, *Melancholy and the Critique of Modernity: Søren Kierkegaard's Religious Psychology* (London and New York: Routledge, 1995), 170 (Ferguson's larger discussion of this in his chapter six is very illuminating).

9. Nye, *Philosophia,* 121f.

10. Nye, *Philosophia,* 122.

11. See the account of this village's actions in Philip P. Hallie, *Lest Innocent Blood Be Shed: The Story of the Village of Le Chambon and How Goodness Happened There* (San Francisco: Harper & Row, 1979). In Hallie's followup study (published posthumously), *Tales of Good and Evil, Help and Harm,* introd. John J. Compton and afterword by Doris A. Hallie (New York: HarperCollins Publishers, 1997), he focuses on just a few central characters in the drama of Le Chambon, including a German commander, Julius Schmäling, in the Haute-Loire during the height of the community's rescue activities, and other persons who understand the virtue of helping others in need. See pages 60–83 for his discussion of Schmäling.

12. Hallie, *Tales,* 41ff. and larger discussion through page 54.

13. See especially Hallie, *Tales,* Chapter 10, "The Hands of Joshua James."

14. Hallie, *Tales,* 172.

15. Ibid., 173.

5

THE WAY OF JUSTICE AS COMPASSION

> Compassionate love . . . is the only just love.
>
> Simone Weil, "New York Notebook"

ENDOWING JUSTICE

Let us discuss how a society might *endow a struggle for justice*. Such an endowment could not be established simply by having a few people, or even a majority, who might choose to love their neighbor or consent to authority and show compassion when they see harm done in their midst. The liberal ideal that thought a majority goodwill would fix all has been unmasked; it is *un*willing to face up to life's necessities, for it is simply too hard and its vision of humanity too limited. We have settled for "little virtues," seeking self-protection and comfort backed by our rights-based morality.

A real endowment for justice, in Simone Weil's view, requires more than a little goodwill; it requires "great virtues"—nothing less than "the perfect flower" which is "the madness of love." Such an endowment requires *a new way of thinking about the moral order of human beings and human beings thinking and acting in that new moral way*. The new moral way for Simone Weil has as its most fundamental principle that we live in a world where we cannot escape our divine origins and remain alive; a world that is itself sacred, but that sacredness is shrouded by our forgetfulness and lack of attention to what lies before our eyes. To breathe as a human being is to breathe with a divine breath; to act morally is to act with love, which is to act with the compassion of the love of God, to all human beings—especially those who are afflicted.

This new moral way for Simone Weil has its primary focus on how each individual should act toward every other individual. We have seen that for her this involves awareness of the human condition surrounding us and re-rooting ourselves with others in ways that require building human connections—associations with others and community environments to ensure trust and consent. Thus her moral philosophy leads us into a subtle web of social and political connections. It is in relation to time and through our moral action that good citizens are formed. Human community for Simone Weil is built from the bottom up; from the way one person treats another and the reactions one receives from the treatment. This is what we referred to earlier as the "sort of dance" through which just relations and just societies are formed. We will see as we move on through chapters 6, 7, and 8 that formal institutions like laws and government, communities and countries, and education depend in large part on a people's past and how they are creatively carried forward. But, foundational to all orders, personal or public, is our being "bodily in" relation to others and our surroundings—"reading" what is before our eyes and reacting in ways that move the struggle for justice forward. The main dynamic of this movement is attention, desire for the good, and compassion.

Although there is no systematic formulation for the endowment of a moral order that Simone Weil describes, we can give it some structure in order to see it in contrast to the "rights-based" moral order that we have inherited. There are four primary components to Simone Weil's "compassion-based" moral order:

1. That all human beings desire good and seek to avoid being harmed
2. That all human beings should be given equal respect and that consent is always theirs to give
3. That "obligations come before that of rights"
4. That compassion is the way of God's love in the world

These reveal her point of view on what it means to be human and embody the new virtue of justice as both an individual matter and one to be lived within the public sphere. We will discuss these four components briefly, then devote considerable time to the centrality of compassion, comparing it with current views in the ethics of love, care, and compassion.

The Human Desire for Good

In "Human Personality" Simone Weil writes:

> At the bottom of the heart of every human being, from earliest infancy until the tomb, there is something that goes on indomitably expecting, in the teeth of all experience of crimes committed, suffered, and witnessed, that good and not evil will be done to him. It is this above all that is sacred in every human being. (SE 10)

And in her "Draft for a Statement of Human Obligations" she says:

> There is a reality outside the world . . . outside space and time. . . .
> Corresponding to this reality, at the center of the human heart, is the longing for an absolute good, a longing which is always there and is never appeased by any object in this world. (SE 219)

Furthermore, she says that humans "whose attention and love are turned towards that reality are the sole intermediary through which good can descend from there and come among men" (SE 219). "The combination of these two facts—the longing in the depth of the heart for absolute good, and the power, though only latent, of directing attention and love to a reality beyond the world and of receiving good from it—constitutes a link," she says, "which attaches every man without exception to that other reality" (SE 220). These words are about as foreign to modern political theory as one could find. So we need to press further to understand them.

It is in this "indomitable expecting" and in our "longing" for the good that our humanity resides. However cruel, uprooted, afflicted, oppressed, or oppressive we may be, Simone Weil sees this seed of the sacred in every human being. It is the "impersonal" center of our human being—and by each human being she means not a part of them, their soul, or personality, or gender, or race, but "the whole of him [or her]. The arms, the eyes, the thoughts, everything" (SE 9). As I can extend my body to the world, to others in the social order of the world, by touch, sight, and thought, as I can give attention and react to nature and to other human beings, I am in touch with and expressing what is sacred in me. This feature of me as a human being is what I carry into the world as a social being—as one who responds to others, sees them and attends to and cares for them.

This is clearly a point of view that is not in vogue, if even intelligible, in our time among political theorists and philosophers. There is a deep reluctance to talk about the sacred or the "supernatural"—skepticism is the favored form of "critical" approach to our knowledge of the self and the natural order. But the idea that a society could be built upon a notion of a common good, inherent in the world or human nature, or that virtues might be as much a part of civic life as personal behavior, is not new with Simone Weil. The very idea is one she derives from ancient Greek philosophy, and she sees it as having been a part of Egyptian, Chinese, and Indian civic cultures as well. It was even a clearly debated subtext standing behind the framers of the U.S. Constitution.

Her understanding of human nature is the primary motivation for why humans live for others and become involved in civic concerns. That we depend on "a reality outside the world" is not an alien idea even though it stands in stark contrast with the new "rational" philosophical ideas leading to enlightenment views of the individual and society. In her view, the very notion that "I" might be independent from and prior to "a society of others" is impossible.

Let me briefly point to some salient features of John Rawls's view in his seminal work, *A Theory of Justice*, to mark this contrast. To set up his picture of what must go into a theory of justice, Rawls begins with his well-known thought experiment. We must remove ourselves from all social relationships and proceed from "a veil of ignorance"—an individual must assume a rational, objective point of view where he or she can set aside whether they are rich or poor, black or white, male or female and thus create (imagine) a social order that would be fair and equal regardless of their "personal" position and attachments. All specific interest must be suspended. Rawls says that to establish a theory of justice "should not require a knowledge of contingent particulars, and surely not a reference to individuals and associations."[1] To ensure an impartial theory, "no one knows his place in society, his class position or social status; nor does he know his fortune in the distribution of natural assets and abilities, his intelligence and strength, and the like. Nor, again, does anyone know his conception of the good, the particulars of his rational plan of life."[2]

Rawls admits that such a perspective as he is providing with his "veil of ignorance" notion "is not a gathering of all actual or possible persons."[3] Of course, Simone Weil would say that it is not a gathering of *any* possible persons, that there is nothing actual about it. It does reflect a logical point of departure for one who has traced so carefully, as Rawls has, the modern liberal enlightenment tradition. It is just that tradition, however, that Simone Weil wants to set aside. She wants to start anew *with* a conception of the good she believes to be a part of what being human means, and she gets that meaning by *looking at* real individuals with their myriad of associations, that is, ethnic associations, gender, class, culture, etc., and the way that their interaction with other human beings has shaped their present reality. Human interactions, she believes, are also constrained by "gravity"—the necessity that we are caught in a mesh of oppressive forces in a world of matter—and we must struggle with those forces. Work, with its physical labor, is an essential part of that struggle as well as recognizing what is good in us and longing for it—all these can trigger spiritual transformations in our world.

To confirm that all humans have some conception of the good, she might suggest a thought experiment of her own and have us ask ourselves: Why have we not given up? Why has the human world remained so resilient given its history of cruelty? Were we solely secular beings with no "indomitable expecting" and "longing" in our hearts for the good, we would have self-destructed long ago. But there is the sacred, a spiritual quality that sustains hope and desires that good and not harm be done to each human who has breath. There are two radically different starting assumptions here. One presupposes a notion of the eternal in time and accounts for individuals and society with all their human liabilities within a spiritual perspective (Simone Weil's view); and one makes no such assumptions and starts with an abstracted conception of an individual as a rational being, then begins to conceive of a social environment suited to hypothetical needs (a Kantian/Rawlsian liberal view).

The Necessity of Equal Respect

Both the liberal "rights-based" view and Simone Weil's view put great value on equality of persons, on treating people as equals. For

Rawls that is an *a priori* given, while for Simone Weil, although at the heart of being human there is equality of persons—as the point of their sacred being—as a matter of social fact we are far from equal. The human world in her view is in great imbalance, and those who have power will deny equality in others and do all they can to preserve their power. This is, she says, "the whole of Realpolitik" (SJ 1). For this reason, "divine intervention" is the only countervailing power that can tip the scales and balance things out. Without such a divine link our world would sink to utter despair and death. To consent to this reality "outside" us and recognize our humanness is a first step in invoking such aid. Invoking such aid means that we practice both "attention and love" and that we do all we can to ensure another's ability, in the circumstances they are in, to exercise the power to refuse and have the liberty to consent. Even rulers should be made to see that the consent of subjects is more in their interest of maintaining authority than is tyranny. Without consent there can be no justice: Consent gives us the capacity to draw God down through attention and love. Consent is the only thing that can disarm power—the power of one person over another or the power of the principalities of this world.

The Priority of Obligations

As we have seen, liberal moral political views come at the price of accepting "individualism." Protection of individual liberties is given the highest priority. This requires a long list of "rights" that are not to be interfered with. "Rights" talk is gradually taken out of its moral context and drifts toward a legalistic context—or at least what we call "rights" becomes a morally neutral notion. As a morally neutral notion, rights carry no positive obligations.

For example, if a friend is being mugged, I may believe it is the right course of action, morally, to intervene and prevent or stop the mugging. But on a "rights-based" liberal view moral ambiguity creeps in. There is no intrinsic "right" that a person be helped, and there is no positive "right" that obligates me to help.[4] Or if I see poverty, I am under no obligation to be generous. And because my notion of a good and any life-plan I may have to realize it may be different from yours and everyone else's goods and plans, I am in no way compelled to agree with your course of action. I may criticize your good and your plan, but

I will be inclined to choose not to interfere so that I do not invite your interference with my good and plan. You can see the easy slide into moral relativism or moral neutrality. The possibility of moral concensus or a common good diminishes as individualism increases, and the stake I may have in protecting my good from another's goes up as my moral concern decreases.

Simone Weil has a clear way of shifting this slide to moral neutrality. The opening sentence of *The Need for Roots* reads: "The notion of obligation takes precedence over that of rights, which is subordinate and relative to it" (NR 3). J. P. Little, in *Simone Weil: Waiting on Truth*, says that in this one sentence Simone Weil "dispenses with several centuries of thinking on the fundamental principles of social organization, including, of course, all the national and international charters for the protection of human freedoms from the American Declaration of Independence and the French Revolutionary Declaration of Human Rights onwards." Little goes on to show how in *The Need for Roots* Simone Weil criticizes "rights" on two grounds:

> firstly, a right is worthless except in conjunction with its corresponding obligation; it is of no use to me to have rights if no one else recognizes them. Secondly, and more importantly in Simone Weil's eyes, rights belong to an inferior order, and are always conditioned by particular circumstances. The notion of rights is a legal one (in French *le droit* means both "right" and "the law"), and is linked to that of quantity, exchange, property.

On the other hand, moving from rights, which Simone Weil believed to be primarily a Roman idea, she says the Greeks gave us a notion of justice. Little concludes, reiterating our discussion in chapter 2:

> Justice is based on mutual consent, and the cry of someone suffering injustice is "Why am I being hurt?" The notion of rights, being based on property, produces a different cry: "Why has he got more than I have?" (EL 38). The notion of obligation is unconditional, since it is situated on a higher plane than that of rights; the only difficulty lies in grasping the theoretical basis for the obligation towards ones' fellow-beings, and then finding practical expression for it.[5]

The theoretical basis for obligation Little finds in the "Draft for a Statement of Human Obligations," written at the same time as *The Need for Roots*. In the "Draft," Simone Weil writes:

> Whoever has his attention and love turned in fact towards that reality outside the world recognizes at the same time that he is bound, in both public and private life, by the unique and perpetual obligation, according to his responsibilities and to the extent of his power, to alleviate all those privations of the soul and the body capable of destroying or mutilating the earthly life of a human being whoever he may be. (SE 222, Little's translation)

The "practical expression" for this obligation—the exercise of our responsibilities in public and private life—is found in our fourth point, in compassion as the way of the human expression of God's love.

Compassion as the Way

Finally, to endow justice in human social relations we must understand the full implication of compassion; we must see the very way of justice as compassion-based.

The public moral order, which is inseparable from our private morality, is the place where God must dwell. Both what is called the private and the public spheres have their meaning in the larger *milieu*—a cosmic or divine *milieu*. Always examining the place of the free individual caught in relation to time, Simone Weil wants to know the limits of human power and action—how, and with what limitations, we can exercise our moral and political being in this world. She comes to only one conclusion: "Liberty without supernatural love—that of 1789—is something absolutely empty, a mere abstraction, without the slightest possibility of ever becoming real" (N 466). What is meant, then, by "supernatural love" in terms of our liberty and moral action as a citizen of this world and how can it become *real*? How can the new virtue of justice prevail?

If we are truly living our humanness, attending to another human being as a citizen of this world, then "God is present at the point where the eyes of those who give and those who receive meet." "Compassion and gratitude," she says, "come down from God." When our heart moves toward God [the Good] in expectation and hope, in praise and gratitude, *and* toward other human beings in love and compassion, our heart is making the same movement: "Praise to God and compassion for creatures. It is the same movement of the heart" (FLN 102). "Compassion," she says, "keeps both eyes open on both the good and the bad and finds in each sufficient reasons for loving. It is the only love on this earth which is true and righteous" (NR 173).

A presupposition to a moral social order for Simone Weil is consent to the reality outside us, an aspiration toward and an openness to this larger divine *milieu*. This consent must then be united with compassion. In her notebooks she gives her most compelling remarks on compassion. There she writes:

> God is absent from the world, except in the existence in this world of those in whom His love is alive. Therefore they ought to be present in the world through compassion. Their compassion is the visible presence of God here below.
>
> When we are lacking in compassion we make a violent separation between a creature and God.
>
> Through compassion we can put the created, temporal part of a creature in communication with God. . . .
>
> Compassion is what spans this abyss which creation has opened between God and the creature.
>
> Compassion is the rainbow. (FLN 103)

Compassion "keeps both eyes open on both the good and the bad . . . on this earth." And through compassion we put "the created, temporal" part of us "in communication with God." God is present as love and compassion move toward the other, and this movement is in the direction of justice. In another of her unequivocally clear remarks she says simply: "Compassionate love . . . is the only just love" (FLN 95).

In her image of compassion as a rainbow—an image in which light is tied to physical phenomena and tails into the sky or which originates from above and arcs to the earth, a natural image of unsurpassed aesthetic beauty—we are given a moral perspective on our world unlike any in the mainstream literature of Western moral philosophy (at least not up to the 1940s). In her time, and even now, this is a moral image "in a different voice," expressed through a woman's eyes, enabling us to hear and see something differently. With this image we are given a way of responding and giving voice to "the heart which cries out against evil" (SE 11) which, as we will see later, requires a new infrastructure including a radically revised judicial system, the development of human community, and a conception of education that can endow a sense of justice to our larger public and political life.

AN ETHIC OF LOVE, CARE, AND COMPASSION

An important difference between a compassion-based and a rights-based morality is found, in part, in the perspective of the person doing the moral thinking. We do not wish to "genderize" Simone Weil's moral philosophy here; that would go against much of what she so desperately thought crucial in all human thought and public practice, that is, striving for "truth" not for just a point of view. It is instructive, however, given the lay of the current landscape in moral philosophy, to look at important differences in how one approaches the truth just as we did with the rights-based moral views. Simone Weil's concerns in her moral philosophy have to do with the language used and the practices that follow from them. Because rights-based moral philosophies have been tied so closely to the language of economics and fairness, practices based on them tend to reflect concerns for property, security, distribution of goods, and compensation. How can we say this language and these concerns get us closer to the truth about how we ought to live? *There is in her recasting of ethical concerns a clear language shift intended to evoke a behavior shift.* Her choice of moral concepts like attention and love, friendship, consent, care for the afflicted—those who hunger and are in need of assistance—and, above all, compassion and her clear priority of obligations over rights has no small effect on how we construct our moral and public lives.

Her selection of these concepts is not accidental, nor is it a conscious choice based on gender considerations. It is rather, first, *a natural convergence* of her own experience on the one hand—much of which is crucially related to her being a woman (as in the case of the kind of factory work she could get) and its effect on her and other women (as she records in her "Factory Journal" and elsewhere) and in the kinds of teaching placements the ministry of education gave to her. Second, it emerges her particular reading of the Gospel with its incarnational ethic of suffering, love of one another, and compassion for the marginalized in society. She also found her own experience and her reading of the Gospel to converge with Antigone and Electra; with the Egyptian Book of the Dead's concern with attention to words of truth and to people who weep and are hungry; with the "chivalrous love" of the people of Languedoc which showed "a patient attention towards the loved person" (SE 50); and with compassion-oriented views found in some post-exilic Old Testament writings and especially in ancient Hindu, Buddhist, and Chinese texts.

This natural convergence of hers toward a moral and political thought that is compassion-based has since been taken up by both feminist philosophers and some who advocate "virtue ethics"—though for different reasons and from different experiences. Some feminist philosophers suggest that their ethics have an intrinsic connection with being female, while most simply refer to their ethics as placing concepts such as care, love, and trust at the center of its concerns. Both generally place their views over the ethical views of Kant and Nietzsche and utilitarian ethics.[6] There is also a long tradition in moral psychology following Freud, Erik Erikson, and Lawrence Kohlberg which has argued that males and females have different ethical concepts connected with their respective moral and cognitive development, and that male moral and cognitive development is superior to that of the female. These are highly disputed claims within both moral psychology and philosophy. Carol Gilligan's work, and others', have caused us to take greater notice of the fact that in Western philosophy, concepts of care and love have been rarely, if ever, incorporated into the standard moral theories (all male) over the past three hundred years.[7] Both the psychological and moral development theories and the rights-based moral views embedded in Western moral theory have been substantially muted in the recent literature. We may have reached a point in the literature where gender considerations can no longer be separated—where both points of view must be inclusively embraced in our moral thinking and discourse. Any meaningful moral theory must take into account compassion-based views which do, in fact, connect more centrally with women's concerns—especially those related to maternal obligations in raising a child, in moral education, and in other virtues of being a loving parent. To forget these aspects of morality undercuts the importance of maintaining stability of morality over several generations.[8]

Simone Weil's moral thinking and discourse are more narrative and contextual and thus have a more inclusive character. They are linked clearly to the social and political debates, to conditions in the workplace, to human suffering in time of war, and to injustices due to various forms of everyday economic and political oppression. Hers is a view, as we noted earlier, that is more "thickly situated," thus turning attention to injustices that occur to every human being.

If we assess Simone Weil's ethics by current mainstream views, it would appear less Kantian/Rawlsian and more connected in some ways with "virtue ethics" or communitarian views as discussed in chapter two. It would also converge with certain feminists' views. There is little doubt that the focus among contemporary women writers in ethics on care and love, trust, reciprocity, and compassion reflects concerns that were central to Simone Weil's moral and political thought. There are even a few direct lines of influence from Simone Weil to be found in Iris Murdoch, Mary McCarthy, Flannery O'Connor, and Sara Ruddick. The point here is not to suggest that Simone Weil's thought has something feminist about it, nor that she was the forerunner of feminism—both suggestions would be a violation of the way she thinks. There is, however, a different cast to her language and her examples and to how human moral practice gets played out. This difference in cast is not unrelated to the fact of Simone Weil's particular voice—how she perceives or "reads" the world she sees and the manner of her engagement with it. One only has to read the short, but philosophically pivotal piece, "Essay on the Notion of Reading" (*"Essay sur la notion de lecture"*) and her essay on *"The Iliad"* to see this.

To illustrate, let us look at some features of an ethic of care that directly reflect the concerns put forward by Simone Weil. One feature given focus by Sara Ruddick is what she calls "maternal thinking." This is a kind of thinking that develops a capacity to sustain life and love in a child. Such thinking contributes to moral stability across generations. Ruddick writes:

> To a mother, "life" may well seem "terrible, hostile, and quick to pounce on you if you give it a chance." In response, she develops a metaphysical attitude toward "Being as such," an attitude I call "holding," an attitude governed by the priority of keeping over acquiring, of conserving the fragile, of maintaining whatever is at hand

and necessary to the child's life. It is an attitude elicited by the work of world-*protection,* world-*preservation,* world-*repair* . . . the invisible weaving of a frayed and threadbare family life. . . .

Holding, preserving mothers have distinctive ways of seeing and being in the world that are worth considering. For example, faced with the fragility of the lives it seeks to preserve, maternal thinking recognizes humility and resilient cheerfulness as virtues of its practice. In so doing it takes issue with popular moralities of assertiveness and much contemporary moral theory.[9]

Though Simone Weil's views about chastity and her own body would have limited the range of her "maternal" thinking, she was a daughter, and her moral instincts as we have seen have the quality Ruddick calls "holding." Recall Simone Weil's example of the two women sewing a layette where the expectant mother sews for love of the child and her labor is focused and joyful (NR 95). In another example she describes a mother who senses a child's need when the child "leans toward [a shiny object] and quite forgets it is beyond his reach. Then his mother picks it up and puts it near him" (FLN 325). In this way the mother attends to a child's need and maintains what is "necessary to the child's life." The mother becomes herself "a conserver" of the child's fragility and desires. Ruddick supports her notion of this "holding, preserving" attitude by discussing Iris Murdoch and Simone Weil's focus on "the capacity for attentive love."[10] Although she is not a mother, echoes of this attitude and of humility and resilient cheerfulness are to be found in Simone Weil in her reading of *The Iliad,* her essay on "School Studies," and throughout the *Notebooks* as in the second example given above. "Compassion," she says, "consists in paying attention to an afflicted man [or crying child] and identifying oneself with him in thought. It then follows that one feeds him automatically if he is hungry, just as one feeds oneself. Bread given in this way is the effect and the sign of compassion" (FLN 327).[11] This remark of Simone Weil's is precisely the kind that would not be found in the literature of modern moral philosophy.

Nel Noddings, who has provided us with the most sustained philosophical discussion of an ethic of care, emphasizes the relationship between the "one-caring" and the "cared-for." She starts, like Simone Weil and Wolgast, with our human condition and its injustices and takes the concept of "*relation* as ontologically basic" and recognizes "human encounter and affective response as a basic fact of human existence."[12] Caring, she says, is completed in the other, thus the cared-for "reciprocally" contributes to the caring relationship. Noddings' focus is on "how to meet the other morally . . . without recourse to notions of God or some other external source of 'sanctity' in human life."[13] Hers is an ontology of natural caring—we are motivated to care because we want to be in a caring relationship and we perceive this to be "good." "Our earliest memories of being cared for and our growing store of memories of both caring and being cared for" develop in us a "caring attitude" and sustain a kind of ethical consciousness for us. Nurturance of this attitude should be a primary aim of all education.[14]

Already we see a Weilian emphasis here on completing oneself morally in the other, though the motivation is different. For Noddings there is an internal, natural motivation arising from "memories of being cared for," while for Simone Weil it is God's love stirred in one's soul that motivates care for or loving another. Furthermore, Noddings sees the importance of obligation as part of a caring relation. From the natural caring attitude, as we enter a caring relation, follows commitment on behalf of the cared-for (I pick up my crying infant; I bind the wounds of one injured in a fire; I at least think about diving into the lake to save a drowning person). These all evidence some level of commitment arising from my impulse to care. If I am to behave *as* one-caring, then "I ought" to commit to a person in need—to make that person one cared-for. "The source of my obligation," says Noddings, "is the value I place on the relatedness of caring."[15] Whereas Noddings' "ethical must" arises from a natural sentiment, Simone Weil's arises from "supernatural love." Both, however, see the ethical relationship realized or completed only *in the act of caring or loving*. For Simone Weil justice requires the "must" love of risk with no self-regard, which pushes Noddings' caring relation one step further to the ideal of compassion.

There are many suggestive parallels (as there are also some clear differences) in the way the contemporary ethic of care develops some earlier moral themes struck in the literature and life of Simone Weil. I have drawn attention to only a few of these parallels. All these points are not unrelated to the fact of the point of view of the writers and the way in which they write themselves into their ethical texts. Simone Weil's view would differ, however, from these current ethic of care discussions in three important ways: 1) there would be less concern for "caring for the self" in relation to the other, with a clearly different concept of self operating as well; 2) Simone Weil has a clearer, or at least more distinctive, sense of "responsibility" focused around her notions of "obligations" and "consent"; and 3) her view presupposes the "supernatural virtue" of justice, or a clearer spiritual horizon which serves as a balancing card in the practices of a moral life. It is this latter view that may be most important, for it gives her moral thought a universal applicability. Some Kantian influence lurks in the background for Simone Weil where the dignity and equal moral worth of all human beings are concerned, but not by some principle of Reason—rather by a sense of the sacred in life.

The thing to remember here is that Simone Weil's moral and political philosophy is not, and could not be in her way of thinking, intended as an ethic for a particular group, be they women or "proletariat." It is not even an ethic for the poor, even though it may resonate with that aspect of "liberation theology." It is not an ethic to simply provide us with a point of view on a particular kind of person. It is a moral and political philosophy that she believes applies to all human beings, equally, and without exception. It is rooted in our human aspiration for the good, moving through human experience with all its obstacles to bring about "a just balance" through compassion. In this last point it has the distinct advantage of bringing the "supernatural" into the arena of human action to help balance the scales. Having said this, it is nevertheless worth our noticing from whose voice this moral philosophy came, and the fact that the voice is a woman's is significant. *This may in fact be one of the important reasons that her thought is so disarming within the present moral landscape that we have inherited.*

THE "TAO" OF COMPASSION

The real force of Simone Weil's "compassion-based" morality as opposed to a "rights-based" morality is that it carries *the obligation* to love one's neighbor—even ideally "to love one another" in perfect friendship—and to engage in such loves "madly." This carries the full force of a divine moral authority. Eric Springsted makes this point as follows: For Simone Weil "the recognition of this supernatural good carries an obligation to act on it, to bring its light into play in the natural world. . . . She also says that, to be just, a state must ensure that 'all forms of power are entrusted, as far as possible, to men who effectively consent to be bound by the obligation to all human beings . . . and who understand the obligation' " (SE 223).[16] The origin of the good we seek comes from God and is seated in the impersonal part of every human being who goes on indomitably expecting that good will be done to her or him. In all our relations with others, in all voluntary associations and in all states that rule by consent of the governed, there is justice if, and only if, and where, and only where, there is compassion—when and where human beings are engaged in the action and practice of being moral in this unconditionally loving way: "Compassionate love . . . is the only just love" (FLN 95). Having an obligation gives our moral action, as was noted earlier, an "imperative force as well as urgency."

We have mentioned a number of times Simone Weil's admiration for Buddhist and Chinese texts largely because she found in them a morality rooted in compassion. She frequently referred to one Chinese tradition, Taoism, in her last writings, and she specifically remarked on the sayings of Lao Tzu and the *Tao Te Ching* over half a dozen times.[17] She wrote while in Marseilles: "Every Taoist saying awakens a resonance in us, and the Taoist texts evoke by turns Heraclitus, Protagoras, the Cynics, the Stoics, Christianity, and Jean-Jacques Rousseau. Not that Taoist thought is not original, profound, and new for a European, but like everything truly great it is both new and familiar; we remember, as Plato used to say, having known it on the other side of the sky" (FW 284). As she "meditated on Taoist sayings," Simone Weil resonated with the Tao, the Way. It was "both new and familiar"; it reminded her once again of the importance of justice as compassion, which she had been passionately thinking about and trying to find ways to practice all her life. Let us look at a few of her own meditations on Taoists' sayings.

Simone Weil admired two things in Taoism. The first is the notion of "non-active action" and the second is the importance of compassion. The first she sees as the same as her attention and waiting. In the notebooks she writes, "The Tao acts without effort" (N 213), and "Attention: non-active action of the divine part of the soul upon the other part [that part caught in the vise of power and self-interest]" (N 262). She then makes note to the archer of the Taoist, a parable attributed to Lao Tzu which she had earlier recounted as follows:

Ref. to Taoist technique of attention. "To destroy locusts in full flight, it is enough simply to see in the whole universe the particular locust aimed at and nothing more: you cannot then fail to hit it. To become an archer, you should lie for two years under a loom and not blink your eyes when the shuttle shoots back and forth; then for three years, with your face turned to the light, make a louse climb up a silk thread. When the louse appears to be larger than a wheel, then a mountain; when it hides the sun; when you see its heart, you may then shoot: you will hit it right in the middle of the heart." (Lao Tse) (N 30)

This note recounting the parable followed a remark urging us to keep all aspects of a situation before our attention: "Let the attention be directed above all towards the chosen aspect, so that the action may be carried out" (N 30). In a third reference to the parable of the archer and the louse, she writes: "The attention should be directed towards the object . . . never towards the self (archer of the Taoist); it comes from the self—the only real thing one can do after committing a fault is to contemplate it" (N 128).

In the three times she calls up this parable, the message is the same as developed in the first legend of the Grail in *Waiting for God* where the seeker of the Grail must turn all attention to the guardian—to the afflicted in this world—in an effortless attentive witness of the seeker's compassion.[18] This waiting and attention, this active inaction, give assent to divine agency but do not excuse the way one must love and care for another in particular situations.

Later in the notebooks comes a remark that is perhaps her most profound in linking her own thought with Taoism. She writes: "Non-active action . . . Love is on the side of non-active action, of powerlessness: Love which consists of loving simply that a thing should *be*, of not wanting to tamper with it" (N 541). In the larger context of this remark, in a most difficult passage to unpack—full of allusions to the Trinity, Krishna, and Taoists' non-active action—she discusses the opposition between power and powerlessness in God and its relationship to human beings in the world. The object of attention must not be manipulated as a thing—power must not be directed toward it. God operates in this world only as love, powerlessness. She says, "Obviously, we can only see with our eyes and can only imitate God-in-his-powerlessness, and not God-in-his-power" (N 542). Our non-active action is of the form of justice as compassion that is a true expression of God's powerlessness in love being enacted through us. The implications of this passage for analyzing our public, political reality of human relations with "principalities and powers" are far-reaching and radical, just as were the personal and political implications of the *Tao Te Ching*.[19] This opposition, contradiction even, comes very close to the spirit of Lao Tzu and the Tao itself and points a way to peace in the sense of quiet and being in a state of equilibrium. Real peace can only occur between enemies, according to Lao Tzu, when a victor returns what the victim has lost or "exacts no payment from the people."[20] The way takes its lead from a condition of powerlessness: "It is the way of heaven to take from what has in excess in order to make good what is deficient."[21] And Lao Tzu concludes: "So the wise do without claiming, achieve without asserting, wishing not to show their worth."[22]

This "non-active action" of the Tao is an essential ingredient in compassion, just as compassion is central to justice. If one is truly attentive when it comes time to act, one will not act according to a self-conscious mode, but according to the divine and spontaneous mode of *wu wei* (non-active action), which is the mode of action of Tao itself. One will be acting in the way of justice as compassion.

The second part of Taoist thought that attracted Weil was its focus on compassion. In *Notebooks* 284–5, she discusses compassion following this remark: "I am the Way. The Tao, non-active action, is an equivalent form." Here, what resonates for her in the Way is sacrifice—it reminds her of the life of Jesus and the Cross—but more particularly she is reminded of compassion in terms of accepting the suffering of others and undergoing suffering oneself. Christ as the Way calls up parables of self-sacrifice and a life lived toward the marginalized in society: "The capacity for pure compassion is exactly proportional to the acceptance of one's own suffering" (N 284). To refuse to accept one's own suffering "places an obstacle in the way of compassion. It is the refusal to recognize oneself in the misery of others—which necessarily wears an ugly appearance. (Lack of humility; compassion is never pure without humility.)" (N 284–5).

In Book Two, LXVII, of the *Tao Te Ching*, compassion and humility are seen as cherished treasures—we read the following:

163   The whole world says that my way is vast and resembles nothing. It is because it is vast that it resembles nothing. If it resembled anything, it would, long before now, have become small.

164   I have three treasures
Which I hold and cherish.
The first is known as compassion,
The second is known as frugality,
The third is known as not daring to take the lead in the empire;
Being compassionate one could afford to be courageous,
Being frugal one could afford to extend one's territory,
Not daring to take the lead in the empire one could afford to be lord over the vessels [officials].

164a   Now, to forsake compassion for courage, to forsake frugality for expansion, to forsake the rear for the lead, is sure to end in death.

165   Through compassion, one will triumph in attack and be impregnable in defence. What heaven succours it protects with the gift of compassion.[23]

Here, the *Tao* of justice—within the empire and its proper mode of leadership—rests primarily in compassion, but also in prudence and humility. Compassion and renunciation precede courage and taking the lead in matters of community or state. The latter follow only from the former. If compassion, prudence, and humility are forsaken, it is fatal. These are the treasures of the *Tao*. In this same spirit, and once again linking her thought with the Taoist, Simone Weil says: "Love which never compels, which is never compelled, is supernatural love, charity." And she continues:

> To call by the same name *Tao*, way, on the one hand the way leading toward God, and on the other hand God himself—doesn't this imply an idea of mediation? "I am the way" [John xiv, 6]. And in these passages concerning the Tao and the man of perfect wisdom, isn't there a foreshadowing of the incarnation—or more than that even? (N 457, see also LTP 27f.).

A love that is uncompelled is a love that has removed the "I" from the loving and rules out false idolatry. Humility. By referring to the "incarnation," the important thing to remember is God *descending* so that the love shown to one another is God's love as powerlessness in particular acts of compassion and not my love. Compassion is here shown in three ways: love that never compels or is compelled, attention to suffering, and humility in care toward another. The particular link of God with the human condition—the manner of mediation—is spelled out by Weil in very explicit ways, which we will now examine.

Simone Weil enriched her philosophical and spiritual understanding and its modes of expression by embracing other non-Western and non-Christian religious traditions. By embracing their respective concepts embedded in a way that may seem unorthodox in Western culture, she brought them into her own moral and spiritual way of thinking. Thus, her use of concepts like "incarnation," "attention," "non-active action," "self-renunciation," "humility," "powerlessness," "sacrifice," "God," "love," "compassion," and "justice" carry with them a culturally plural sense; they embrace many cultures and show the meaning of such concepts, or the *Tao*, to be universally embedded in human life and practice. One common feature in this *Tao* is the way in which the divine and the human are related to one another.

Returning to her notion cited earlier that we must find a link between God and the human condition, we can see that linkage in her compassion-based morality. Even with all Weil's talk of a "supernatural realm" and her frequent metaphors of "above" or "outside" this world, Blum and Seidler underscore that "she never saw the spiritual as an independent and autonomous realm but as something whose reality has to be expressed in the relations between people." They even say that "in this way her spirituality was essentially material."[24] Their second remark, however, is misleading in light of the development of her thought. It is not simply a matter of emphasis as to how we understand the connection between the "supernatural" and the "natural"; we cannot reduce her spirituality to the material. Simone Weil believed there was another realm *but we could say or know nothing of it outside its being present in this world*. Its being present in the world does not make it material. We must remind ourselves that it was fundamental to her philosophical procedure, as Peter Winch reminded us, "to root the concepts which are most important to her in actual, very concrete features of human life." God, the good, justice, and beauty are all shown to be either present or absent relative to our human practices in this world. Winch asks the question: "Does Simone Weil have a theory about the nature of the universe, as divided into two realms, the natural and the supernatural?" He answers with "a qualified no." The question, he says, is not an easy one to answer.[25]

We have referred to the spiritual as a prism through which thought and actions are understood by Simone Weil. A prism refracts light from another source, and the refracted light may take several paths as it comes out, affecting what we say and do in its current refracted paths. To act *in this light* is more than just having a different perspective or point of view; it enjoins the light, and the light has a direct effect on the path taken. Simone Weil uses a slightly different light metaphor but I believe to a similar end. She says:

> The Gospel contains a conception of human life, not a theology.
>
> If I light an electric torch at night out of doors I don't judge its power by looking at the bulb, but by seeing how many objects it lights up.
>
> The brightness of a source of light is appreciated by the illumination it projects upon non-luminous objects.
>
> The value of a religious or, more generally, a spiritual way of life is appreciated by the amount of illumination thrown upon the things of this world.
>
> Earthly things are the criterion of spiritual things.
>
> This is what we generally don't want to recognize, because we are frightened of a criterion.
>
> The virtue of anything is manifested outside the thing.
>
> If, on the pretext that only spiritual things are of value, we refuse to take the light thrown on earthly things as a criterion, we are in danger of having a non-existent treasure.
>
> Only spiritual things are of value, but only physical things have a verifiable existence. Therefore the value of the former can only be verified as an illumination projected on to the latter. (FLN 147)

Even though there is a source of light on one side of the prism and a bulb makes illumination of objects possible, it is clear that the emphasis here is to be on "the amount of illumination thrown upon the things of this world." "The value of [spiritual things] can only be verified as an illumination projected on a [physical thing]," and such a projection is a direct consequence of our attention and love, of our compassion-based morality. Winch says that "her insistence that 'earthly things are *the crite-*

rion of spiritual things' shows that we are not being offered a 'metaphysics of the spiritual,' but a certain way of thinking about the earthly."[26] In no uncertain terms, she says that "we are in danger of having a nonexistent treasure" [that is God or the spiritual would be nonexistent] if we "refuse to take the light thrown on earthly things as a criterion!" Winch believes that the seeds for this idea were present in her thinking well before her religious experience and before, as she said, "Christ came down and took possession of me" (WG 69), but I think it also clear that not until that experience could she have had the clarity she does about the "incarnational" nature of the spiritual in the form of a "supernatural virtue." This provides the new language needed to articulate her new virtue to replace morally bankrupt practices.

A morality based on reason—as "rights-based" moralities are—could not grasp the crucial notion of "affliction" and does not, in and of itself, require a notion of the "supernatural." Talk of "spirituality," and much less an incarnational spirituality connected with morality and justice, was simply not and still is not a part of discussions in Western political and moral philosophy. Blum and Seidler argue that the only place where such spiritual ideas are present in political discussions are in the liberation theologies of Central and South America. There a voice is given to the poor and oppressed even if they too often go unheard.[27] Simone Weil's new virtue of justice rooted in her compassion-based morality provides all human beings with a means of restoring their voice—a voice that has a capacity within the human realm of drawing God "into the fray."

The very notion of morality as "compassion-based," which is at the heart of her political philosophy, emerges when she clearly identifies with the compassion of Christ both *in his life* lived for the other—for those who were thirsty and hungry, outcast, and in need of assistance—and *in his death* on the cross when Christ himself cried out "Why am I being hurt?" She did not, however, see this as an original idea. It had its precursors in her reading of pre-Socratic Greek literature such as the *Iliad* and *Antigone*, and she found similar themes in *The Egyptian Book of the Dead*, the *Bhagavad-Gita*, and Taoist literature.

One last note on Simone Weil's notion of compassion, which has another interesting parallel in "Oriental wisdom," is her understanding of it as embedded in the human community. This time the parallel is found in Confucius's notion of the secular public world as "sacred" when morality is practiced through holy rite and ceremony. Although Simone Weil did not "resonate" to Confucian sayings as she did to Taoist's, Oriental wisdom and specifically ideas from China are seen as important in re-civilizing our Western culture, and we have noted how Lao Tzu understood non-active action in running the affairs of "empire"—the way must embrace above all, prudence, humility, and compassion. Confucius believed that "when we see [another person] as participant in communal rite rather than as individualistic ego, [that person] takes on to our eyes a new and holy beauty. . . "; the person is seen as a "holy vessel."[28] A difference is that for Confucius there is no realm outside this world. We will explore again just what Simone Weil may mean by such a realm. In our chapter on community and politics we will also say more about this Confucian "secular as sacred" moral perspective. Not only does it have some parallels with Simone Weil's view of justice found in community and traditions, but it will help us focus on another link or bridge between the spiritual and the moral in public life, that of public and religious ceremony.

NOTES

1. John Rawls, *A Theory of Justice* (Cambridge: Harvard University Press, 1971), 132. This important work, of course, has been critiqued many times, and my use of it does not depart from a number of standard criticisms. However, I know of no direct comparisons between his view and Simone Weil's that emphasizes what I do.

2. Rawls, *A Theory of Justice*, 137.

3. Ibid., 139.

4. There are some exceptions to this. Curiously in French law, unlike U.S. and British law, this is qualified by what is sometimes called a "good samaritan" law which says that if you come upon a person in danger, and you have the skills to help (you are a doctor, strong swimmer, etc.), you are obliged to help. If you can help and do not, you risk both social opprobrium and legal sanctions. Simone Weil would understand this as a point in law and social order that moves in the direction of justice. We will see in the next chapter her view on this. I do not know the historical origin of this law. This point was brought to my attention by Christine Ann Evans.

5. Little, *Simone Weil: Waiting on Truth*, Berg Women's Series (Oxford: St. Martin's Press, 1988), 85.

6. Among a number of essays in feminist ethics, those of Nel Noddings' "ethics of care" avoid some of the worst difficulties of "ghettoizing" ethics by gender and may come closer to the spirit of Simone Weil's compassion-based moral philosophy. Noddings says: "The ethics of caring is not intended as an ethic only for women. An ethical orientation that arises in female experience need not be confined to women. . . . This is exactly why an ethic of caring puts great emphasis on human interdependence and on moral education." Noddings discusses some of the difficulties in "genderized" ethics in her "Ethics from the Standpoint of Women," in Pearsall, *Women and Values,* 383–88. See also in the same volume: Carol Gilligan, "In a Different Voice: Women's Conceptions of Self and of Morality," 342–68, and Sara Ruddick, "Maternal Thinking," 368–79. Also see Joan Tronto, "Beyond Gender Difference to a Theory of Care," *Signs* 12 (1987), and Annette Baier, "What Do Women Want In A Moral Theory?" in *Virtue Ethics,* ed., Roger Crisp and Michael Slote, Oxford Readings in Philosophy (Oxford: Oxford University Press, 1997). Finally, for a more systematic treatment of love's role between humans and God from a radically feminist perspective, see Irigaray, *An Ethics of Sexual Difference.*

7. Søren Kierkegaard and Max Scheler may be exceptions, though their ethical views are not usually included in "standard moral theories." In the dispute among moral psychologists, Carol Gilligan's *In a Different Voice* (Cambridge: Harvard University Press, 1982) has been an important study in broadening the vocabulary of mainstream ethics. See also Lawrence A. Blum's "Gilligan and Kohlberg: Implications for Moral Theory" and "Gilligan's Two Voices," in *Moral Perception,* 215–67.

8. See Annette Baier, "What Do Women Want?" 266ff.

9. Ruddick, "Maternal Thinking," 371.

10. Ibid., 375–76.

11. There are those who argue that Weil is obsessed with denial of her gender: that her silence on women and their oppression and that she did not champion women's "rights" show her derogatory view toward women. On this point see Rachel Feldhay Brenner, *Writing as Resistance: Four Women Confronting the Holocaust* (University Park: Pennsylvania State University Press, 1997), 156–67. Brenner tries to show that Simone Weil thought that females were "uncreative" (113) and that they wanted to possess only male virtues (156 and 160f.). Brenner says that overall Weil had an "uncritical position on female victimization" (159). On all these points Brenner is extremely short-sighted and fails to understand Weil's concept of the "impersonal" in us—not to mention Weil's whole compassion-based ethics. Furthermore she overlooks the many narrative examples that are being cited and discussed throughout this chapter and others and which were introduced in chapter one. There is certainly no justification for writing Simone Weil off as either demeaning to women (however demeaning she might

have been to her own self) or saying that her ethic of love and compassion is contrary to much feminist ethics.

12. Noddings, *Caring*, 4.

13. Ibid.

14. Ibid., 5f.

15. Ibid., 84.

16. Springsted, "Rootedness: Culture and Value," in *Simone Weil's Philosophy of Culture*, 176. Springsted's essay is a compact and highly original reading of Weil's last London writings, namely: "Human Personality," *The Need for Roots*, and "Draft for a Statement on Human Obligation." This essay, too, is helpful in making sense of how Weil's spiritual view connects to social and political life.

17. The *Tao Te Ching* was attributed to Lao Tzu, who was an older sixth- to fifth-century B.C.E. contemporary of Confucius. Lao Tzu cultivated what was called *Tao*, or way of virtue, aimed at self-effacement and compassion. This is the most frequently translated of all Chinese classical texts and was widely known in the West. Simone Weil could also have been familiar with the popular Taoist sayings of Chuang Tzu (third century B.C.E.). It was after hearing a lecture by M. Marcel Brion at the Society for Philosophical Studies in Marseilles in the spring of 1941 that she turned more intently to reading and reflecting on these Buddhist and Chinese texts. In her essay, "Philosophy," she remarks: "The marvelous passages [Brion] cited were all taken from Taoist writings or Buddhist writings closely related to Taoism. . . . He left his hearers with the desire to spend a few hours in contemplation of Chinese painting; if that is not possible, they may meditate on Taoist sayings" (FW 283).

18. The first legend of the Grail was discussed in chapter three.

19. Among recent thinkers whose position resonates with Simone Weil and the *Tao Te Ching*, I am reminded of William Stringfellow's *The Politics of Spirituality* (Philadelphia: The Westminster Press, 1984), where he attacks modern-day principalities and powers and challenges them with a powerlessness he calls "a monastic witness." There is much that could be said about Stringfellow and Taoism.

20. Lao Tzu, *Tao Te Ching*, trans. with an introduction by D. C. Lau (London: Penguin Books, 1963), 141. Lao Tzu and Lao Tse are different English forms of the same name.

21. Ibid., 139.

22. This is from a new English version of the *Tao Te Ching* by Ursula Le Guin (Boston and London: Shambhala Publications, Inc., 1997), 97.

23. Lao Tzu, *Tao Te Ching* (D. C. Lau translation), 129.

24. Blum and Seidler, *A Truer Liberty*, 181.

25. Winch, *Simone Weil*, 191. Winch's answer is extremely nuanced and has been very helpful in understanding Simone Weil's thought. Allen and Springsted

in *Spirit, Nature and Community*, take up this question and Winch's answer in a sympathetic reading of Winch and conclude with these comments: "Winch claims that the 'supernatural cannot be understood apart from our natural history,' " and Allen and Springsted add a converse to Winch's claim: "That converse is that our natural history cannot be understood apart from our *supernatural history*. This is not to say for Weil that there are two things—nature and supernature—to be played off against each other, or which explain or are explained by each other. Rather, to understand anything well involves seeing its natural and supernatural histories. *And to see that one has a supernatural history and that one's life is not adequately described apart from it, is precisely to see one's natural history in a certain light as well*" (89).

26. Winch, *Simone Weil*, 199.

27. Blum and Seidler, *A Truer Liberty*, 192 and an extended discussion on pages 283–309.

28. Herbert Fingarette, *Confucius: The Secular as Sacred* (New York: Harper and Row, 1972), 77. Fingarette's reading of Confucius is extremely helpful in thinking about differences in moral outlooks.

6

CIVIL SOCIETY AND THE LAW

Every human being needs to have multiple roots. He needs to receive practically the whole of his moral, intellectual and spiritual life through the intermediary of those milieux in which he naturally participates.

Simone Weil, *The Need for Roots*, 43

MORALITY AND SOCIETY

To be rooted in one's life personally and publicly within a spiritual framework is the goal of Simone Weil's just society. It is in this specific framework that compassion is the moral vehicle for justice. Eric Springsted says: "For Weil, it is the idea of roots that finally bridges the cleavage between the limited values of social necessity and the undefinable values of supernatural justice."[1] What are the kinds of things in the natural and social order in which we live that provide us with a sense of rootedness? This chapter and the next two chapters provide some of Simone Weil's answers to this question. They also will explore some broader moral and political implications of her views. We could say that the kinds of things we are looking for are "in" but not altogether "of" the natural or social order. It is in this human world that we are either rooted or uprooted through our actions and practices, but rootedness also has a spiritual aspect. To be rooted, Simone Weil says, we must organize "our moral, intellectual and spiritual life through . . . those milieux in which [we] naturally participate" (NR 43), and those milieux in which we naturally participate are families, professional associations, education and civic life, communities, and nations—everywhere we do commerce and interact with other human beings.

Simone Weil's ideas on justice, rootedness, and society were not taken very seriously in her native France after World War II, but insofar as there was any truth in her ideas, they were sustained in the world and were bound to find expression again wherever cries of injustice and oppression might be heard. Since the war there have been many areas in our world where such cries of injustice have been voiced. Among the clearest voices were dissidents in Eastern Europe and the Soviet Union and liberation movements in Latin America and Africa. In Europe, beginning symbolically with the descent of the Iron Curtain and ending with the razing of the Berlin Wall (1945–89), the citizens of the post-totalitarian systems of Eastern Europe struggled with the same issues of power and oppression that Simone Weil had earlier identified. A dissident in postwar Poland, Hungary, or Czechoslovakia, for example, was very much like one of Camus' "rebels." One had to speak the truth to the great inequalities and indignities concealed by the ruling regimes. Rebellion indefatigably confronts evil, said Camus, from a point outside the regime's rules. This was precisely how Václav Havel understood dissidence. Havel called dissidence "politics outside the sphere of power." "The dissident," he said, "does not operate in the realm of genuine power at all. He is not seeking power"; he offers his own skin "because he has no other way of affirming the truth he stands for. His actions simply articulate his dignity as a citizen regardless of the cost."[2] During the liberation struggles in Africa and Latin America, beginning with Ghana in the 1950s through the coming of majority rule in South Africa in 1994, "rebellion" was not limited to a few dissidents but included majority populations of dispossessed—millions sought independence, dignity, and national and ethnic identity as they struggled with colonial dominance, despotic rule, extreme poverty, and massive economic oppression.

The Cold War was a wonderfully ironic response to the "hot" war just completed. The Cold War was a new struggle to preserve power interests, creating a continuing state of uprootedness beneath a veneer of balance of power. All parties continued to do all they could to preserve what power they had and maneuvered to enhance their power. The Cold War was a fiercely fought competition between modern states to preserve power. Masked in capital-N abstractions like "National prestige" and "National security," the so-called "cold" war had everything to do with "economics" and "rights" (property, boundaries, trade, ideological rights over human beings) and a state's ability to make war—and, of course, multiple wars were waged on every continent in the name of peace. The prestige involved on the part of Western free market democracies and Soviet-Sino socialists' republics consisted "in behaving always in such a way as to demoralize other nations by giving them the impression that, if it comes to war, one would certainly defeat them. What is called national security is an imaginary state of affairs in which one would retain the capacity to make war while depriving all other countries of it" (SE 158f.). This, of course, is Simone Weil's account of 1930s European and American culture. Nothing seems to have changed much since then, confirming the acuity of her analysis of the human condition in our century.

The decade of 1990 has been a time of momentous political and cultural realignment and of economic restructuring on a global scale; it is thus a time that is requiring all of our best reflective energies to think about economic, social, and political justice. Above all, however, we are morally adrift and seek some redefinition of who we are as a human community and what forms public life may take to ensure a safe, civil, just, and peaceful future. Simone Weil's ideas offer some insight into this task.

To better understand the application of Weil's ideas in the public political sphere in the specific context of the second half of the twentieth century and into the twenty-first century, it is instructive to look at other philosophers and political thinkers who are trying to give some shape to our current moral and political landscape and who discerned some of the same truths articulated by her. One such thinker is Václav Havel whose unique positions as rebel, poet, liberation leader, and current head of state have enabled him to put his ideas into practice literally before the eyes of all the world. The issues that Havel faced prior to 1989 in his native Czechoslovakia were direct extensions of some of the same political and social issues with which Simone Weil had been preoccupied.[3]

The very fabric of virtually all societies in Europe was in ruin after World War II, and oppression in the form of new totalitarian and post-totalitarian regimes had been passed from fascism to Stalin's Soviet-style communism. (This in itself is an affirmation of her correct analysis in

"The Power of Words" that there was no difference between the meanings of fascism and communism.) The human condition in Soviet-controlled Eastern Europe had become one reflecting what Simone Weil would call "affliction." Havel articulates that condition of affliction in ways that echo her. In an open letter to his country's president, Dr. Gustav Husak, in 1975, Havel speaks of the utter "humiliation" suffered every day by the Czech and Slovak people by virtue of their being forced "to live a lie." He says, "People have a very acute appreciation of the price they have paid for outward peace and quiet: the permanent *humiliation of their human dignity.*"[4] He describes this humiliation of human dignity in great detail with concrete examples in this letter and in his better-known essay "The Power of the Powerless" (1978). What prevails, he says, is *"order without life"*: "Order has been established. At the price of a paralysis of the spirit, a deadening of the heart, and devastation of life. Surface 'consolidation' has been achieved. At the price of a *spiritual and moral crisis in society.*"[5] What does a human being need to overcome such a crisis? Clearly a way of life that is both spiritual and moral and which restores a meaningful sense of life! Havel has his own way of marking out his idea of a spiritual life with an accompanying morality and how we may begin to engage in practices to restore a more just society. What is perhaps surprising about parallels between Havel and Simone Weil is that while both are students of the modern enlightenment, they nevertheless understood the need for a spiritual framework for both morality and politics.

Havel's "Politics and Conscience"—written in 1984 and intended for the University of Toulouse, but for which he was not allowed to leave his country to deliver—begins with an autobiographical story. He tells of his boyhood in rural Czechoslovakia where each day he walked to school "along a cart track through the fields." In the horizon was a huge smokestack which "spewed dense brown smoke." He says that without knowing anything about noxious emissions and the risk to the health of people and the surrounding forests, he did have "an intense sense of something profoundly wrong, of humans soiling the heavens." What did he learn from this ordinary, everyday experience? He was aware that he had not yet grown alienated from nature and that the smokestack upset some natural rhythm of the world. There was a certain primordial sense of good and evil, of concepts like "soiling" and being "at home." He was, he says, still rooted in a world which knows the dividing line between all that is intimately familiar and appropriately a subject of our concern, and that which lies beyond its horizon, that before which we should bow down humbly because of the mystery about it. . . . In this world, categories like justice, honour, treason, friendship, infidelity, courage or empathy have a wholly tangible content, relating to actual persons and important for actual life. At the basis of this world are values which are simply there. . . . The natural world, in virtue of its very being, bears within it the presupposition of the absolute which grounds, delimits, animates and directs it, without which it would be unthinkable, absurd and superfluous, and which we can only quietly respect.[6]

This account could almost be taken as a narrative summary of several important features of Simone Weil's moral philosophy. Its language is more familiar than hers, but conceptually it has many of the basic ingredients of her spiritual worldview. It has the components of nature as sacred, a world that still embraces mystery and depends on a quality of the spiritual; it is a world of "lived experience," of personal responsibility, where categories like justice, honor, treason, and friendship still have meaning and importance.

It is important to detail Havel's view to show that such a spiritual reading of morality and politics is not an anomaly even at the end of our century; it is an illustration that enlightenment morality and politics can be effectively challenged by rebellious, yet practical, civic leaders at the present hour. When truth is the object of one's search for meaning in life, it should not be surprising that ideas converge even when they arise a half a century apart and in different historical and social contexts. Simone Weil would have thought very differently about Czechoslovakia after the war under Soviet control than she had before the war when Germany moved to annex it.[7]

Havel had reflectively developed this vision of the spiritual and moral life through his long and active struggle against his government. During one of his stays in prison, between June 1979 and September 1982, he articulated his maturing moral and political views in letters to his wife, Olga. Let us look at how these views developed. In these letters he is in search of what he calls "the absolute horizon of all life's relativities"—of what, he says, "many experience as God" (November 1980).[8] This idea of an "absolute horizon" is rather imprecise in his early letters but becomes increasingly clear as he tries to relate it to human action, to moral responsibility, and to politics. This horizon is what Havel discovers to be, as he said of his boyhood experience, "that before which we should bow down humbly because of the mystery about it"—the horizon in which "justice, honour, treason, friendship, infidelity, courage or empathy have a wholly tangible content." This horizon "grounds, delimits, animates and directs" our natural world. To Olga he says "there can be no transitory human existence without the horizon of permanence against which it develops and to which . . . it constantly relates" (January 1981).[9]

By September 1981, he speaks of this "absolute horizon" with greater certainty with respect to the role it plays in human life: "The assumption of an 'absolute horizon,' naturally, 'explains' nothing. It is, however, the only source of our hope, the only 'reason' for faith as a (consciously reflected) state of mind, the only existential meta-experience (i.e., an experience concealed within all other experiences) which—without explaining the meaning of life—evokes the hope that it actually does have meaning, encourages one to live, helps one resist the feeling that all is vanity and futility, the pressure of nothingness."[10] And a month later he says: "The meaning of any phenomenon lies in its being anchored in something outside itself, and thus in its belonging to some higher or wider context, in its illumination by a more universal perspective; in its being 'hung,' like a picture, within a higher order, placed against the background of a horizon."[11] The search for the meaning of life is a constant "striving for something beyond us and above us," something to hold onto, but in the striving we discover that it is also "holding on to us."[12]

By spring of 1982, a friend had hand-copied several essays of Emmanuel Levinas in a letter and smuggled them into prison. Havel's letters from that point reflect a focused concern with a sense of moral responsibility and an ethic of love of neighbor (ideas central to Levinas's thought) as this links to the "absolute horizon." He learns from Levinas that we establish our identity when we become responsible; thus our human social and political lives are constituted in our moral practices. He asks himself the question: "What does 'responsibility' mean . . . responsibility not only to the world, but also 'for the world' . . . Whence comes this strange and clearly impractical . . . essence of the moral law, that which is called 'good'?" He thinks the answer is clear:

That curious feeling of "responsibility for the world" can probably only be felt by someone who is really (consciously or unconsciously) in touch, within himself, with "the absolute horizon of Being," who communicates or struggles with it in some way, who draws from it meaning, hope and faith, who has genuinely (through inner experience) grasped it. . . . In other words: by perceiving ourselves as part of the river, we accept our responsibility for the river as a whole (which is folly in the eyes of all proprietors of dams and particular horizons). (March 1982)[13]

Havel's last reflections move closer to how a person is to act in the concrete world—in accepting "responsibility for the river as a whole." He is worried about the "I" as ego getting in the way and says that a true "I" can only be constituted "through a 'you,' [it is] only through a 'we,' that the 'I' can genuinely become itself."

In the nearness of love of another it [the 'I' which becomes a genuine self] comes to know its home; . . . In short, in the experience of the other it experiences everything that it means to be human: the world, Being, its own separateness, its thrownness, its horizons. . . . Face-to-face with the existence of his neighbor, he first experiences the primordial "responsibility for everything" and thus becomes a special creature capable of fellow feeling with a complete stranger, of loving even that which he does not erotically desire or on whom he is not dependent for his existence-in-the-world.

He concludes that "a better outlook for human communality" lies in "love, charity, sympathy, tolerance, understanding, self-control, solidarity, friendship, feelings of belonging, the acceptance of concrete responsibility for those close to one." These are expressions he calls a new "'interexistentiality' that alone can breathe new meaning into the social formations and collectivities that, together, shape the fate of the world" (August 28 1982).[14]

This "interexistentiality" within the "absolute horizon" of relating moves toward Simone Weil's notion of justice as compassion, where attention and love become the very means—a mediator, *metaxu*—between divine and human by which justice as love is present to "shape the fate of the world." For Simone Weil and Havel, "a renaissance of elementary human relationships" and "a better outlook for human com-

munality" happen only in those relationships that take the "other" seriously—which "face-to-face" see another's affliction, "their disturbing
existence," and act responsibly toward it. Havel says, and Simone Weil
could have as easily used these words: "Another person . . . is the only
entity capable of opening the human heart." Havel's "absolute horizon
of our relating" is what gives human beings hope in the face of affliction,
and motivates love, charity, and all "fellow feeling with a complete
stranger." Havel's morality, like Simone Weil's, is clearly a compassion-
based morality—one that should be taken with great seriousness in rethinking human communality in our present world culture.

In "The Power of the Powerless," Havel describes life in the post-
totalitarian systems governing the Soviet bloc countries in the 1960s
right up to the "velvet revolution" he led in 1989, as "coming closer to
some dreadful Orwellian vision of the world of absolute manipulation,
while all the more articulate expressions of living within the truth are
definitively snuffed out."[15] They have become societies where "technology . . . is out of humanity's control [smokestacks which 'soil the heavens,' 'devastate our forests,' and 'endanger the health of people'] . . . has
enslaved us and compelled us to participate in the preparation of our
own destruction." He says "humanity can find no way out."[16] Echoing
the image of the human condition given us by Simone Weil, Havel talks
about how we are "caught up in the 'self-perpetuating' structures of
society" and says to Olga: "The world modern man creates is an image
of his own condition, and in turn, it deepens that condition." He asks:
"Is there really nothing to be done?" Havel's answer is to struggle to
become more autonomous and responsible in small, human ways.[17] He
gives numerous local examples of what these ways could be in "The
Power of the Powerless," and it was because hundreds of shopkeepers,
farmers and workers refused "to live a lie" and were willing to stand in
truth—as an expression of "absolute" powerlessness—that the revolution succeeded.

Also like Simone Weil, Havel notes how our language has lost its
meaning, and its "vacuous abstractions" serve only the ends of propaganda and self-interest, not the end of truth. As Simone Weil says, words
"stupify our minds" and serve only to "make us forget the value of life."
Havel writes to Olga:

> One consequence of this alienating process [linked to the meaning-
> lessness of our words] is the enormous conflict between words and

deeds so prevalent today: everyone talks about freedom, democracy, humanity, justice, human rights, universal equality and happiness, about peace and saving the world from nuclear apocalypse, and protecting the environment and life in general—and at the same time, everyone—more or less, consciously or unconsciously, in one way or another—serves those values and ideals only to the extent necessary to serve himself, i.e., his "worldly" interest—personal interests, group interests, power interests, property interests, state or great-power interests.[18]

He further says in another context that our language only touches people with "ideological gloves":

Life in the system is . . . thoroughly permeated with hypocrisy and lies: government by bureaucracy is called popular government; . . . the complete degradation of the individual is presented as his or her ultimate liberation; depriving people of information is called making it available; the use of power to manipulate is called the public control of power, and the arbitrary abuse of power is called observing the legal code; the repression of culture is called its development; the expansion of imperial influence is presented as support for the oppressed; . . . military occupation becomes fraternal assistance.[19]

Our question following both Simone Weil and Havel is: Are there any practices that could serve the end of a more just and civil social order? Both affirm that whatever practices there are they must be understood within some spiritual frame, "placed against the background of an horizon," which give them their meaning and authority and keep them from becoming, in the words of Jean Bethke Elshtain, "latter-day Protagorean efforts to make man the measure of all things."[20]

For Havel, a number of suggestions serve as *guides for our practices*— "whether economic, political, diplomatic or military"—and he is not ashamed to assert them in a clear and straightforward way as related to his "absolute horizon," to a reality and memory outside us and above us, and to concrete moral responsibility.

Throughout his numerous essays and as pervading themes in his plays—he is first and foremost a playwright—Havel gives shape to a civic life within his moral and spiritual framework. He says that we must place "morality above politics and responsibility above our desires, in making human community meaningful, in returning content to human speaking, in reconstituting, as the focus of all social action, the autonomous, integral and dignified human I."[21] But that autonomous I must not be isolated, nor pursue selfish interests. He says: "We must not be ashamed that we are capable of love, friendship, solidarity, sympathy and tolerance, but just the opposite: we must set these fundamental dimensions of our humanity free from their private exile and accept them as the only genuine starting point of meaningful human community."[22] Havel sees the moral life and social rootedness as possible only in the context of human community.

Finally, Havel says the task for a meaningful moral and political life, both East and West, should be

> one of resisting vigilantly, thoughtfully and attentively, but at the same time with total dedication, at every step and everywhere, the irrational momentum of anonymous, impersonal and inhuman power. . . . We must resist their complex and wholly alienating pressure . . . [and] honor with the humility of the wise the bounds of that natural world and the mystery which lies beyond them.[23]

Havel's words and deeds are a testament to our time in the clear, unequivocal way Simone Weil's were to hers. Human decency and communality, civic responsibility and order, humility, hope, and human compassion are all understood by Simone Weil and Havel in a framework or horizon of the spirit. Both thinkers also understood that these features of a civil society required a legal system that would ennoble the human spirit. We now turn to how Simone Weil conceived the relationship between the moral self, civil society, and the law.

CIVIL SOCIETY AND LAW

Laws help root us. Public institutions and the law are there to assist individuals in ordering their lives: "Whoever is uprooted himself uproots others. Whoever is rooted in himself doesn't uproot others" (NR 48). Not everyone can "root herself." The soul needs some kind of communal order. A legal system operates in a human *milieux* in which we participate and through which we receive part of our moral, intellectual and spiritual life. For Simone Weil it is a bridge between the human and the divine. The law that serves as a guide for a just and equitable social order, just like any moral practices, must be understood from a spiritual perspective according to her. Both laws and judicial exercises of the law are governed, above all, by the truth. The law gains its legitimacy from an "eternal source" (NR 181) and judges "must be accustomed to love truth" (NR 40).

Simone Weil believed that the French Republic's law and its judicial system had long ago lost all legitimacy—"it was completely dead" (NR 180). Furthermore, the war and foreign occupation had provided a break in historical continuity. She writes: The legal system "can no longer be regarded as having an historical basis; [therefore] it must be made to derive from the eternal source of all legality" (NR 181). Such a demand is not an easy one in the legal and political environment of our century, but perhaps after such a war, following on the heels of a previous world conflict and an "economic depression" that shook material confidence, she was not totally mad in thinking that there might be a possibility for some fresh thought. During her final months in London, much of her remaining energy went into sketching an outline of her own legal thought—one that could be "made to derive from an eternal source."[24]

As Simone Weil wrote:

> It is the aim of public life to arrange that all forms of power are entrusted, so far as possible, to men who effectively consent to be bound by the obligation towards all human beings which lies upon everyone, and who understand the obligation.
> Law is the totality of the permanent provisions for making this aim effective. (SE 223)

What is the obligation to all human beings that she says "lies upon everyone," and how should "law" make this obligation work within our public life? We will answer these questions under three headings:

1. Obligation to all human beings
2. Law as a guide to our obligations
3. "Judging" and "attention"

Under each heading our discussion will be brief, highlighting aspects of Weil's view of the law that are relevant to her political thought. These are, in most instances, developed further in the appendix, "The Spirit of Simone Weil's Law" by Collins and Nielsen. We will also comment on and extend some of the "preliminary conclusions" found in their essay.

Obligation to All Human Beings

With Patrice Rolland, Collins and Nielsen say Simone Weil is continually trying to discover "how 'the eternal and unconditional obligation "descends" or incarnates in this world.'" That, of course, matches all that we have been saying about her with respect to supernatural justice and its "incarnation" in human life. Now, how may obligation and the law show the presence of God *in* the world? Obligation can neither be based on social custom, convention or social contract nor rooted in nature because, as she says, it is unconditional. Obligations "belong to a realm situated above all conditions . . . it is situated above this world" (NR 3f.). Her view of the law presupposes what all along we have seen as an essential presupposition to her thought, a spiritual presupposition that enlightenment thinking and liberal political and social theory have continually refused to recognize or intentionally set aside. Liberal social theory wanted to postulate absolute principles—"inalienable rights" and Kantian-like "duties." These were thought of as inherent "natural rights" or rights derived from reason and operated within "the human plane." For Simone Weil the *origin* of obligations is from the eternal realm, while

> the *object* of any obligation, in the realm of human affairs, is always the human being as such. There exists an obligation toward every human being for the sole reason that he or she *is* a human being, without any other condition requiring to be fulfilled, and even without any recognition of such obligation on the part of the individual concerned. (NR 4f.)

Because each human being possesses an aspiration toward the good (an expectation that good and not harm will come to him or her), each commands respect; and because of mutual respect, Simone Weil believes humans have an unconditional obligation not to let a single human "suffer from hunger when one has the chance of coming to his assistance"

(NR 6). Here, again, a good Samaritan law as mentioned above would be a step in the right direction, where one is under legal as well as moral obligation to help if one has the skills to do so. Having this chance is at the root of all compassion-based morality. Mutual respect and moving toward "a state in human society in which people will not suffer from hunger" or harm are the basic premises and the model upon which all other obligations should correspond and upon which all human needs are based (NR 6). It is, precisely, the way of justice as compassion. The object of our obligations, however, take shape *in*, not prior to, our social, public life. Thus it is in that arena of life that we must continually struggle for justice by attending to one another. Mutual attending, as we saw earlier, has to do with how we deal with one another within a variety of human associations—family, community, friendships, voluntary societies, country—in which our obligations are acted upon and human needs are to be met. It is in this public sphere that laws should guide our practices based on our eternal obligations.

Law as a Guide to Our Obligations

It is important to Simone Weil that laws do not get in the way of our thought and actions—they should in no way thwart liberty and people practicing her new virtue of justice. Law should only "counsel," say Collins and Nielsen. Weil says: Law should be easily understood by anyone "with average powers of application" (NR 12), and they "should be sufficiently stable, general and limited in number for the mind to be able to grasp them once and for all, and not find itself brought up against them every time a decision has to be made" (NR 13). She also believes the number of laws should be confined and that no laws should be made to serve special interests. Finally, say Collins and Nielsen, "lawmakers must resist the process of micro-contextualized legislation that attempts to suit law to a myriad of events . . . citizens must play an active role in the legal process, rather than abandoning the process to professional rulers."

All these features of the law are to make it serve as a *guide* to our public life and not a stumbling block on our way to a just society. Laws should enable maximum freedom with the two notions of mutual respect and of preventing any human from hunger and harm, which are always before us as we engage in public life. With eternal obligation comes consent to obey the law. This consent to obey the law can itself be freeing; that is, it assures us of a certain order in which we can pursue projects and come to people's assistance when they have needs.

Laws ought to provide a framework of order, what she calls "a texture of social relationships" (NR 10), that are not repressive and constraining but sufficient as *guides* for all those needs of the soul, such as freedom, obedience, responsibility, equality, freedom of thought, security and truth, which Simone Weil believes essential for any just human society.

For Weil an important role of law in public life is to enable "truth-seeking discourse." "There has been a lot of freedom of thought over the past few years, but no thought," she remarked (NR 33). This loaded remark quickly brings to mind the familiar refrain, "I have the right to say whatever I want!" Thus we say anything and too often *without thinking*. Such unthoughtful speech and action, as she has said so often, leads to empty or meaningless talk, even to murderous propaganda. Today, unthoughtful speech and vicious speech under protection of First Amendment rights lead to hate speech and the pervasive racial and ethnic tensions felt world-wide. And our contemporary instinct to deal with this problem has been to move toward "micro-contextualized legislation" rather than fundamentally rethinking what we mean by human obligation and mutual respect.

To check such unthinking speech and action, Simone Weil has very strong views on punishment. She believes that the more responsible position one has in public life, the more responsibility one must show. Breaches of responsibility bring the harshest punishment to those with power.[25] She provides us with a good example of how power and responsibility should be tied to degrees of punishment. She writes:

> Anyone with power over the fate of other human beings has the ability to commit continual crimes; if he falls into this, criminal punishments are appropriate.
>
> A poor hungry wretch who takes a carrot from a field is punished in his flesh. If this happens often he is sent for his whole life to a place in Guiana much worse than that kept for convicts. A head of government who, from cruelty, insensitivity, hate, inattention, or prejudice, unjustly causes a human being's death or seriously injures him, or does this to hundreds, thousands or millions of human beings,

will perhaps damage his career. He won't have to suffer anything in his flesh.

This is a monstrous inversion of justice. The injustice is not merely monstrous in relation to the afflicted. It is worse in relation to the ruler. With so many opportunities for evil it is cruel to leave him to cope alone with the conflict of good and evil inclinations. A just compassion requires that the part of his soul which wills the good should be helped by subjecting the evil part to fear or punishment.

The people, for its part, would live in a stable feeling of trust in justice and legitimacy if there were an increasing scale of punishments corresponding, level by level, to the scale of social power. Someone who can do almost nothing either for good or evil should have almost nothing to suffer, no matter what he does, as long as he keeps from doing violence to anyone's person. Anyone who consents to occupy a position where he can do much, for good and ill, must suffer if he does ill—in his honour, in his flesh and in his whole destiny.

This is true social equilibrium. It rests entirely on judicial institutions. (LPG 94–95)

Thoughtful action with truth always before us requires, finally, that *we increase our capacity for attention*. This brings us back to one of the basic pillars in becoming just; in recognizing hunger and harm, in stopping harm doing, in securing liberty and peace.

"Judging" and "Attention"

"What is culture?" Simone Weil asks. "[It is] the development of attention."[26] Judges are to play a central role in the shaping of culture. At the heart of her legal system are judges who have a great capacity for attention and who become custodians of culture.

Simone Weil has a very high view of the role of judges in society. She says they must be

> drawn from very different social circles; be naturally gifted with a wide, clear, and exact intelligence; and be trained in a school where they receive *not just a legal education but above all a spiritual one*; and only secondarily an intellectual one. They must be accustomed to love truth. (NR 40, emphasis added)

This "spiritual education" is for the purpose of both recognizing and understanding human obligation as eternal and for discerning when people's actions do not serve the end of truth. This is no less than schooling in attention. At its most practical level, law schools, as was noted earlier, must help students "learn to distinguish between the two cries": [Why am I being hurt? and Why has somebody else got more than I have?] and "as gently as possible, to hush the second one" with the help of a code of justice, tribunals, and police (SE 30). And as Collins and Nielsen note, "Her best single statement . . . on the judiciary and its role in society is set out in her London report 'Essential Ideas for a New Constitution,'" and reads as follows:

> Judges must have much more of a spiritual, intellectual, historical education than a juridical one (the strictly legal domain should only be retained in relation to unimportant things); they [judges] should be much, much more numerous; they must always judge with equity. For them the law should only serve as a guide. This should also apply to previous judgments [judicial precedents].
>
> But there should be a special court to judge the judges, and it should dispense extremely severe punishments.
>
> The legislators should also be able to summon before a court chosen from among their fellow members any judge guilty, in their eyes, of having violated the spirit of the laws. (EL 95)

These judges are subject to intense oversight by other judges and legislators; they are, in Collins and Nielsen's words, very important "public figures who serve as one of the key moral voices of the community." Collins and Nielsen detail many of their moral responsibilities; they are very much like Plato's "custodians of the law." All in all, law is a means, along with education, whereby the "reality *outside* of this world" might be implanted, incarnated, within the reality of *this* world. Simone Weil had great trust that a properly trained judicial presence would be able to right wrongs and keep us from excesses of our rights-based morality. A strong judicial system could provide a language to shape moral right through compassion to avoid contention of rights based on economic and security interests. We have "eternal obligations," but not "eternal rights." We can only wonder at such judges. This may be among her most utopian ideas, but it sets before us, in sharp relief, the failures of most of our known judicial systems and reminds us of the importance of rethinking how justice may be served in public life.

Because of the centrality of attention for both a reflective, thoughtful public and the judiciary, the law should never be static. As a guide it should serve as a map for the terrain of our action and practice. As Collins and Nielsen conclude: "Living *in* the law means living *out* [its high purpose of justice], always attentively applying [its principles] to a myriad of situations. Always thinking; always reading [the human condition]. In living out the law, what is most important is the process of continually orienting oneself towards the good."

In a concluding observation on civil society, let us move forward in time again (from the 1940s to the 1990s) to Havel's reflections. Václav Havel had a dream about his new republic of the future—even if it were to be the realized hope of two peoples: Czech and Slovak.[27] He projected some ends to be realized in a decade, for example, a rebirth in private agriculture. Other dreams like the humanization of work and urban life, educational and judicial reform, the cultivation of democratic institutions, and environmental transformation may take longer than a decade. Simone Weil, too, believed the full transformation to a just and civil society would take time, possibly several generations. Laws and responsibilities would not only have to be absorbed by ordinary citizens, leaders, and judges, but a new system of education would have to be put in place and a sense of civilization restored. She realized, as Collins and Nielsen note, that her "pretty fanciful" ideas would require many "transitional stages." Simone Weil's legal system, like most of the visionary ideas in *The Need for Roots*, was stillborn. But since 1989, Havel's Czechoslovakia, now the Czech Republic, has been going through a number of transitional stages, and should its evolution to a new civic, moral order follow Havel's vision (which it may not) it could become a society that Simone Weil might recognize as partially reflecting the truth that she sought and which contains seeds of her own reflections.

Throughout the struggle for freedom from the repressive regime, Havel was calling for a "moral reconstitution of society"—a spiritual transformation of civic life that would enable his people to overcome "the permanent *humiliation of their human dignity*."[28] He has continued this call after the communist regime fell in his country in 1989. For Havel, as for Simone Weil, the moral reconstitution of society depends upon seeing our civilization bound by common hopes; motivated by the belief that all humans share an "archetypal experience" based on "a higher authority than human authority"; and distinguished by a notion "of a justice higher than earthly justice." In a speech given in 1995 in

Hiroshima, Japan, marking the fiftieth anniversary of the nuclear night-mare, Havel stated: "True goodness, true responsibility, true justice, a true sense of things—all these grow from roots that go much deeper than the world of our transitory earthly schemes. This is a message that speaks to us from the very heart of human [spirituality]."[29]

NOTES

1. Springsted, "Rootedness," 182.

2. Havel, *Living in Truth*, 193f.

3. I am not arguing that Havel was directly influenced by Simone Weil, but that the truth of her thought about our human condition and how we might see our way through it was also independently grasped by Havel and others. One might make a similar case by looking at the example of Nelson Mandela and the liberation struggle in South Africa during the second half of our century, al-though the political and social situation of apartheid South Africa would call for a different kind of reading of the human condition than does postwar Europe.

4. Havel, *Living in Truth,* 31.

5. Ibid., 15. Among other "dissident" activities, Havel was a signator to "The Charter of '77," addressed to the government asking it to join together with its people to throw off its repressive chains and lead its country toward greater human rights and democratic reforms. For this, he and many others served several prison terms.

6. Ibid., 136f.

7. In an essay published in *Feuilles Libres de la quinzaine*, no. 58, 15 May 1938, Simone Weil favored ceding over portions of Czechoslovakia to Germany rather than defending it against German interests. She wrongly believed that if this were done Germany would be satisfied and might not invade Central Eu-rope. In retrospect her argument appears naive, and if a similar argument were to be made about Soviet control (annexation) of Eastern and Central Europe after the war, she would have lost her moral credibility. See "A European War over Czechoslovakia," FW 264–68.

8. Havel, *Letters to Olga* (New York: Henry Holt and Company [An Owl Book]), 1989), 123.

9. Ibid., 147.

10. Ibid., 231.

11. Ibid., 242.

12. Ibid., 243.

13. Ibid., 301.

14. Ibid., 370f.

15. Havel, *Living in Truth*, 112.

16. Ibid., 114.

17. Havel, *Letters to Olga*, 295f.

18. Ibid., 367. One wonders if Havel had not read Simone Weil's "The Power of Words" in *Les Nouveaux Cahiers*, published in 1937 (SE) under the title *"Ne recomençons pas la guerre de Troie."* It appeared again in 1960 in a collection of her essays entitled *Ecrits historiques et politiques.*

19. Havel, *Living in Truth*, 44f.

20. Jean Bethke Elshtain, "A Man for This Season: Václav Havel on Freedom and Responsibility," unpublished manuscript. The same sentiment is noted about Havel in an earlier published essay of Elshtain where she says that his notion of an absolute or " 'higher horizon' opens up rather than forecloses genuine political responsibility." Havel's kind of morality in politics moves toward civic responsibility, not away from it. Jean Bethke Elshtain, "Politics Without Cliché," *Social Thought* 60, no. 3 (Fall 1993), 436.

21. Havel, *Living in Truth*, 149f.

22. Ibid., 153f.

23. Ibid., 153.

24. Ronald K. L. Collins and Finn E. Nielsen's "The Spirit of Simone Weil's Law," first published in *Simone Weil's Philosophy of Culture*, incorporating insight from Patrice Rolland's "Simone Weil et le Droit" (1990), provides us with a comprehensive critique of Simone Weil's legal thought. Since their essay analyzes all of her known central remarks on the law, I have chosen to reprint it with permission from its authors in its entirety in the appendix. Therefore, I urge readers who want a fuller understanding of her view of the law to pause and turn to the appendix before reading further.

25. Collins and Nielsen have said a great deal more about Simone Weil's view of punishment as a kind of moral training and a penal system oriented toward "therapy" in turning criminals back toward the good, rather than "retribution" for crimes. "Crime is a turning away from the good (why would anyone commit a crime if not for some spiritual malfunction?) and a corresponding renunciation of one's fundamental obligations towards others," note Collins and Nielsen. I will not review all the interesting ground they cover in the Appendix.

26. From Weil's London notes and fragments, unpublished translation by Martin Andic.

27. Havel, "A Dream for Czechoslovakia," *The New York Review of Books*, 25 June 1992: 8–13.

28. This Havel did with both his pen and his body. See Havel, *Living in Truth*, 117f. and 31.

29. From Havel's 1995 speech in Hiroshima, "The Future of Hope: Observations on the Subject of Hope from Hiroshima, 'a city where we cannot help thinking of death,' " *Religion and Values in Public Life*, Harvard Divinity School 5, no. 2/3 (Winter/Spring 1997): 2f.

7

COMMUNITY AND POLITICS: HUMAN NEEDS AND SOCIAL OBLIGATIONS

To be rooted is perhaps the most important and least recognized need of the human soul. It is one of the hardest to define. A human being has roots by virtue of his real, active, and natural participation in the life of a community, which preserves in living shape certain particular treasures of the past and certain particular expectations for the future. This participation is a natural one, in the sense that it is automatically brought about by place, conditions of birth, profession, and social surroundings.

Simone Weil, *The Need for Roots*, 43

UPROOTEDNESS AND POLITICS

In an atmosphere of war, Simone Weil believes those caught in its vise lose all perspective on the value of human life. In a letter to George Bernanos following her short foray into the fray of the Spanish Civil War (about two months in 1936, part of which was at the Aragon front on the banks of the Ebro River near Saragossa), she observed that the purpose of any war should "only be defined in terms of the public good, of the welfare of men," and that she had seen firsthand how that purpose had been totally submerged by "useless bloodshed" and cavalier attitudes towards killing. "One sets out," she says, "as a volunteer, with the idea of sacrifice, and finds oneself in a war which resembles a war of mercenaries, only with much more cruelty and with less human respect for the enemy" (SE 175).

In atmospheres of conflict and war which, shortly after the Spanish Civil War, engulfed Europe and Asia and embroiled North Americans on both fronts, Simone Weil's vision of law becomes blurred and her view of justice is temporarily suspended. What obligations humans may have and whatever consent they may will to an ordered or civil public life become subjected to force. As France fell to Hitler, she writes of war itself: "War effaces all conceptions of purpose or goal, including even its own 'war aims.' It effaces the very notion of war's being brought to an end. To be outside a situation so violent as this is to find it inconceivable; to be inside it is to be unable to conceive its end" (IL 22). She also says that the intoxication of force in war "intervenes" and "drowns" the "terror, grief, exhaustion, slaughter of comrades" which "tear at the soul" (IL 23). It took six years to break the cycle of terror and violence and bring an end to the war that was raging at the time she wrote this. Part of what ended the war was a threat of total annihilation of the enemy with a force so powerful that its inventors were morally ambiguous about its development and use. The impact of the use of atomic bombs on two Japanese cities subsequently changed the very meaning of the term "war," and it changed the nature of all moral debates about war. It became (and continues to be) difficult to discuss a public good or human welfare in the frame of possible nuclear holocaust.[1]

War is the most devastating cause of uprootedness for humanity. War, of course, may also result from many kinds of uprootedness. "Whoever is uprooted himself uproots others," says Simone Weil. "Whoever is rooted in himself doesn't uproot others" (NR 48). Arguably, this century surpasses all others in human history for cruelty and sheer loss of life in wars. Human migration due to war and war-caused famine in Africa alone in the past twenty-five years has displaced tens of millions of human beings from their homelands. Although the continental United States has been among a few nations spared physical invasion in the century, its industry has exported its war-making powers in every decade of the century. Arms manufacturing and global distribution of arms from European states, the United States, Canada, Brazil, former Soviet Union, South Africa, Israel, China, and more have placed an automatic weapon in the hands of virtually every able-bodied man in sub-Saharan Africa and Asia and supplied more than two hundred million anti-personnel landmines worldwide. This has resulted in massive social uprootedness and unconscionable human suffering.[2] With all of this it is not difficult to see why we may want to listen more carefully to the "madness" found in Simone Weil's new virtue of justice. It could help us "discern and cherish equally, in all human milieux without exception, in all parts of the globe, the fragile earthly possibilities of beauty, of happiness and of fulfillment" (SJ 9).

Simone Weil died in the middle of World War II and knew nothing of future nuclear holocausts. That development and another half century of regional genocides and massive migrations due to wars would not, however, have surprised her, given her view of how we use power (scientific and political) and how she viewed the state of human uprootedness which she had already brought to our attention. Her spiritual view of justice in a civil society gains even more urgency and credibility in light of the nuclear peril and subsequent continuing armed conflicts.

In her last months she gave us an extraordinary array of thoughts about life in the public sphere. They are sometimes sketchy and stand more as a criticism of the modern state than as a blueprint for a future state. We heard the criticism earlier that Simone Weil's political thought operated primarily in "the private sphere" and that she had little to say about human action in "the public sphere." We have already disputed this criticism, but will now be more explicit in suggesting ways in which her last thoughts might help us give a different shape to public life.

Simone Weil said clearly in her "Draft for a Statement of Human Obligations" that a human soul needs a "disciplined participation in a common task of public value," and it also needs "personal initiative within this participation." She continued:

> The human soul needs above all to be rooted in several natural environments and to make contact with the universe through them.
> Examples of natural human environments are: a man's country, and places where his language is spoken, and places with a culture or a historical past which he shares, and his professional milieu, and his neighborhood. (SE 226)

These "natural human environments" are no less than what we call examples of human community—specific contexts where humans can experience mutual respect, friendship, warmth, shared tasks of value (responsibilities), and some cultural linkage (such as common language, arts, history, and physical work). These all create environments in which the human expectation and aspiration that good and not evil come to human beings can be realized and flourish in a creative and peaceful way.

Before examining some of the natural environments for her notion of community, let us look at some things besides war that she says uproot us. Most of the following things that uproot us—all mentioned in *The Need for Roots.*—will be discussed in greater detail throughout the rest of this book:

- Money, power, and economic domination by one nation over another as found in many forms of colonialism.
- Money wherever it is turned into the sole motive for gain and the primary measure of success.
- Unemployment or loss of meaningful work, that is, work in which one is deprived of any feeling of usefulness, responsibility, or a sense of participation in a common task of public value. Mindless work. The complete divorce between working life and family life. Work that subjects the worker to a machine.
- Education, which has developed a "stovepipe atmosphere" (NR 45), cut off from one's history and culture; education that is too technical or narrowly specialized. Weil does not believe technology is bad in itself, but its use may be and human beings should be educated within a broader humane context to understand technology's applications and meaning. Her vision of education will be discussed in our next chapter.
- The watering down of culture so that the smallest things are elevated. (The rise of "pop" and commercial culture she would view as uprooting—all those things that Søren Kierkegaard says are a matter of "fashion.")
- The depopulation of the countryside and the migration to urban centers she says lead to social death. This is particularly apparent today in Africa and South America, and increasingly so in China, where a massive population shift to cities has uprooted family ties, agricultural production, and a sense of relatedness to local traditions.
- The loss of the past is for her a "supreme human tragedy"; it is "like a child picking off the petals of a rose" (NR 119). This is particularly acute in countries that had been colonized, where

"assimilation" to the colonial power disrupted local cultural patterns.

- The development of a "State" and its bureaucratization "exhausts a country" (a country being a more natural collection of people with some shared past, traditions and language to bind it together). A State eats away a country's moral substance; it "lives on it, fattens on it, until the day comes when no more nourishment can be drawn from it, and famine reduces it to a condition of lethargy" (NR 120). "The State," she says, "is a cold concern, which cannot inspire love, but itself kills, suppresses everything that might be loved; so one is forced to love it, because there is nothing else. That is the moral torment to which all of us today are exposed" (NR 114). No place is this form of uprootedness more apparent than in many current African nation states.
- Finally, we become no better than our age, she says. We must become aware that our age is "poisoned by lies" and that our age "converts everything it touches into a lie" (NR 97). This awareness was so commonplace in Eastern Europe in the 1970s and 1980s that despair finally led those living in lies to dare to speak the truth. The revolutionary effect of truth-telling became plain to all—a far more potent force for change than previous "armed" rebellions or ideological revolutions. The cynicism for politics in the United States is also related to lies. We no longer think of politics as a valued measure for much of anything, except perhaps for the exploitation of desire.

The surprising thing about this list is *how unsurprising it is* to us at the end of the twentieth century. It reads like a litany of the commonplace in our lives, so commonplace that Simone Weil's very idea of rootedness itself seems foreign, even tyrannical.

It is curious that Simone Weil does not say that politics itself is a cause of uprootedness. Individual politicians may sully their art with lies, and they may use their power for money and personal gain. States may do the same and in doing so are a great part of our uprootedness. Politicians are as capable of the same evils as any human beings, but their particular positions of public trust with power make their evils seem worse. It is clear in her view of law and punishment that the greater public responsibilities of politicians should make them subject to harsher punishment for crimes. We know, however, that is not a familiar practice. She does have another slightly more positive view of politics and politicians, in which both can work for the common good and serve to improve our public well-being. How is this so?

It is clear that, generally speaking, she has a rather low view of politics. Politics is, as it has been for centuries, "a technique for acquiring and holding onto power" (NR 218). Insofar as politics and its practitioners are associated with power, they are part of our created, fallen nature, but even such fallen creatures have an "uncreated" part that can aspire to the good, and Simone Weil believes that politicians too are capable of such aspiration. A particularly appropriate time for such aspiration is when an individual or a community or a country has suffered great loss and humiliation as did France with its capitulation to Hitler in 1940. Out of the depths of distress one is more likely to show whatever genius or greatness or good it may have. "The war," she says, "must be made the teacher to develop and nourish" an inspiration in political leaders after the war (NR 215). Re-rooting France, or any community for that matter, requires first and foremost an inspiration that is grounded in the sacred. It also calls for those who will exercise power on the human level to transform the very art of governing. The art of governing must, like poetry, music, and architecture,[3] be composed on several planes simultaneously to achieve the transformed end of justice, since power cannot be an end of governance. She writes:

> Politics, in their turn, form an art governed by composition on a multiple plane. Whoever finds himself with political responsibilities, if in his heart he hungers and thirsts after justice, must desire to possess this faculty of composition on a multiple plane, and consequently is bound, in the end, to receive it. (NR 217)

Politics, properly composed, can be an instrument to receive justice; that is, like attention and love, and like the new virtue found in a compassion-based morality, justice as an absolute value comes down and completes the composition. The human inspiration, if it is in the heart of a politician even, for some local justice—attention to human needs— has the capacity to bring forth the creative intervention of divine justice. Politics and politicians must operate within their human limits, but with the right aspiration to the good they can be an expression of our humanity as sacred. Once again she creates idealized conditions to raise the level of discussion about politics. She also reminds us that "politics are practically never looked upon as an art of so high a category" (NR 218). The fact, however, that politics for so long has been held in such low regard does not mean that our accustomed view could not be changed!

It is not simply politics and politicians that bore the burden of governance; it was the responsibility of everyone knowing that even "the most intelligent . . . is wretchedly below the problems of public life" (EL 90). How do we rise above the problems of public life or even to its level? We do so by struggling for justice and endowing that struggle in a variety of natural human environments, or communities, that would enable people to carry out their obligations to one another. Remember, her thoughts were formulated in the belief that with the end of the war a new opportunity for a new social order presented itself—that with the slate clean a new beginning was possible. She says of this opportunity, "A terrible responsibility rests with us. For it is nothing less than a question of refashioning the soul of a country" (NR 149) and "it must be made to derive from the eternal source of all legality" (NR 181).

So, in starting over, France should take into account what had uprooted it since the 1875 constitution and what had kept it from realizing its pledge to "equality, liberty, and fraternity" in 1789. To avoid these failures she conceived not a new powerful state, but a restructuring around regional and local communities. This would be the new backbone for a just society and the only hope of restoring a civilization. She cautions that all those

> who offer their services to the country to govern it will have to publicly recognize certain obligations corresponding to essential aspirations of the people eternally inscribed in the depth of popular feeling; the people must have confidence in the word and in the capacity of these men, and be provided with means of expressing the fact;[4] they must also be made to feel that, in accepting these men, they give an undertaking to obey them.
>
> Since the people's obedience toward the public authorities is a necessity for the country, this obedience becomes a sacred obligation, and one that confers on the public authorities themselves, seeing that they form the object of it, the same sacred character. (NR 181f.)

To govern properly, nothing less than this sacred trust between governed and public authorities is required. Nothing less will restore integrity to politics.

Thus we see her insistence on "real, active, and natural participation in the life of a community" (NR 43), and "a disciplined participation in a common task of public value" (SE 226). Never, in her last writing, did she waver from seeing the importance of an individual's life in the public sphere. At its best this is what politics should be; it requires "personal initiative" in one's participation in public life as well as cooperation with and consent to legitimate authority. Rootedness was for Simone Weil a complex, multifaceted activity; it involved face-to-face contact among those who share some common environments—work, family, language and culture, and country—and who see justice as the object of their living with one another.

TRADITION AND CREATING "NATURAL ENVIRONMENTS" FOR COMMUNITY

How, then, are we to re-root ourselves? How might politics itself assist individuals in building community in the interest of some public good? How are we to actively participate in the life of a community in a highly pluralistic and democratized society? What becomes clear in Simone Weil's writings concerning public life is that her compassion-based morality applies equally to individual relating *and* to one's natural social communities (professional, neighborhood, and culture-based associations) and country; the way of justice as compassion must contribute not only to local civil peace but to world peace. For example she says that "compassion for [one's] country, the watchful and tender concern to keep it out of harm's way . . . can give to peace, and especially to civil peace . . . something stirring, touching, poetic and sacred. This compassion alone can give us back that feeling we have lacked for so long, and so rarely experienced throughout the course of history, and which Théophile de Viau expressed in the beautiful line, '*La sainte majesté des lois*' " (NR 179f.).[5] And with specific reference to the sufferings her own country was undergoing she writes: "Compassion for France is not a compensation for, but a spiritualization of, the sufferings being undergone," and when such compassion is present toward one's country it "is able, without hindrance, to cross frontiers, extend itself over all countries in misfortune, over all countries without exception; for all peoples are subjected to the wretchedness of our human condition. Whereas pride in national glory is by its nature exclusive, nontransferable, compassion is by its nature universal" (NR 174).

That compassion may instill in a people "something stirring, touching, poetic and sacred" is no small feature of its power, nor is the fact that compassion is universal. She says that a central issue for creating legitimate human community is that one must "breathe an inspiration into a people" (NR 187)—stir their sacred center. Then, personal initiative can enter public life and be focused toward common tasks: "It is . . . necessary that the love of the citizen for his city . . . should be a supernatural love" (N 466).

Usually when Simone Weil talks about mutual relationships or participation in the public sphere, she has in mind an individual's moral relationships where compassion is at its center, i.e., caring for the poor, being a friend, hearing the cry of the afflicted, loving your neighbor, obeying authority, fulfilling one's obligations. These individual acts are not particularly political, nor do they presuppose any specific community structures, though they may contribute to both the welfare of a polis and the building of community. There is, however, another important component to human relating that is more of a social and communal form of action and that depends, as she says, on "a past," on "tradition," and on "place, conditions of birth, profession, and social surroundings." In these, the directions of one's acts are partially shaped by one's place and past. In such "environments" one finds roots and is given a language to participate in the "common tasks of public value." It is here that customs and ritual practice are part of one's language and crucial to the shape of public values and to sustaining a meaningful sense of community and country.

There is an early example from "Oriental wisdom"—particularly in the writings of Confucius—of how a sacred center for public life was stirred in people to form community. Simone Weil's concern with tradition and not losing one's past, and with how to configure a community in such a way as to make its participants feel meaningfully involved and mutually obligated, may be understood more clearly with Confucius' example before us.

It was noted in chapter 5 that Simone Weil did not regard Confucius and Confucianism as highly as she did Lao Tzu and Taoism. But, however distinct and often antagonistic toward the other's "way" these two schools of Chinese thought may seem, the wisdom we may extract from them has Confucianism and Taoism as two sides of a single coin.[6] The Tao was addressed to rulers as well as to individuals, but its focus was on cultivating individual attention, compassion and humility, or self-effacement, while Confucius focused on ritual acts and traditions being properly carried out to ensure public order and a sense of mutual respect for one's family, community, and governing region or state—but also to fulfill one's humanness. Confucius called these ritual acts and ceremonies "holy rite." Though Simone Weil does not look to Confucianism to support her own interest in tradition, there is certainly reason to believe that, given her views on custom, solemn occasions, special meals (feasts), and family reunions, she might have had more to appreciate in Confucius had she given his *Analects* the same "meditative" reading she gave to Taoist writings. The following reading of Confucius focuses on the importance of tradition and "holy rite."[7]

Confucius, in the late sixth and early fifth century B.C.E., in the principality of Lu, saw that the truly, distinctively human in life had "a magical quality," but that such a quality went unnoticed. To reveal this quality is our human task, thought Confucius, and requires "a new way," the *tao*. This new way involved learning *li*. *Li*, in its root meaning, is close to "holy ritual" or "sacred ceremony." If we submit to *li* and act according to *li*, human virtue will prevail and harmonious community will be realized. We become truly human when we allow our "raw impulses" to be shaped by *li*. The emphasis is on living a common, reciprocal life without losing a sense of one's self. In so doing the "magical quality" of life emerges.[8]

This Confucian idea of "holy rite" or "sacred ceremony" is at the heart of the "right way" of living. Fingarette writes: "My gestures are coordinated harmoniously with yours—though neither of us has to force, push, demand, compel or otherwise 'make' this happen. Our gestures are in turn smoothly followed by those of the other participants, all effortlessly."[9] Furthermore, the self-disciplined following of *li* when embedded in life provides a path or channel that will create a smooth continuous way of life. There is nothing mechanical about this way; it involves each person's full and attentive participation: "Beautiful and effective ceremony requires the personal 'presence' to be fused with learned ceremonial skill. This ideal fusion is true *li* as sacred rite."[10] Thomas Merton in the introduction to his book *The Way of Chuang Tzu* discusses the links between Taoism and Confucianism. Merton says of the Confucian notion of *li*: "*Li* is something more than exterior and ritual correctness: it is the ability to make use of ritual forms to give full outward expression to the love and obligation by which one is bound to others. *Li* is the acting out of veneration and love, not only for parents, for one's sovereign, for one's people but also for 'Heaven-and-earth.' "[11]

Perfection in *li* for Confucius "is aesthetic as well as spiritual"; it requires that all the human, sensible (aesthetic) features of a ceremony be carried out with style and grace and, through this, the holy or sacred emerges in the performance. This ideal is not, however, for just royal occasions or rites of passage that mark special times in a community's or individual's life. It is intended for ordinary and everyday practices. What is really unusual about the Confucian account is that its form and value are recognizable by human beings in every culture, even though some cultures, like our own, have yielded their way of life to individual pursuits and have shunted communal ceremony and ritual reciprocity to the side, or even destroyed it altogether.

Consider this everyday example:

> I see you on the street; I smile, walk toward you, put out my hand to shake yours. And behold—without any command, stratagem, force, special tricks or tools, without any effort on my part to make you do so, you spontaneously turn toward me, return my smile, raise your hand toward mine. We shake hands—not by my pulling your hand up and down or your pulling mine but by spontaneous and perfect cooperative action. Normally we do not notice the subtlety and amazing complexity of this coordinated "ritual" act. This subtlety and complexity become very evident, however, if one has had to learn the ceremony only from a book of instructions, or if one is a foreigner from a non-handshaking culture.[12]

Fingarette concludes: "The examples of handshaking and of making a request are humble; the moral is profound. These complex but familiar gestures are characteristic of human relationships at their most human: we are least like anything else in the world when we do not treat each other as physical objects, as animals or even as subhuman creatures to be driven, threatened, forced, maneuvered. Looking at these 'ceremonies' through the image of *li*, we realize that explicitly sacred rite can be seen as an emphatic, intensified and sharply elaborated extension of everyday *civilized* intercourse."[13] Like Simone Weil's "reading," the meaning of these shared actions is given by all that surrounds them. We cannot ignore the importance of shared practices.

Confucius' idea of realizing *yen* (compassion or "human hearted-ness") in *li*, brings to our attention a sense of the sacred embedded in secular life or the holy in the ordinary of our existence; it suggests that what is sacred in our life has, indeed, become shrouded, but it need not be so if we act toward one another in a dignified, responsive, and recip-rocal manner. What is spiritual or holy in our lives comes most alive *in* ceremony, and ceremony requires some human community.

Simone Weil's last remark in her "London Notebook" of 1943, in the midst of retelling folktales from many cultures which focused on the importance of custom and on the sensible qualities of ritual acts, was praising the value of *experiencing* something in order to learn its truth. This remark complements Confucius' point about holy rite:

> From this alliance between matter and real feelings comes the significance of meals on solemn occasions, at festivals and family or friendly reunions, even between two friends, and so on (also sweets, delicacies, drinking together . . .) And the significance of special dishes: Christmas turkey and marrons glacés [plum pudding]—Candlemas cakes at Marseilles—Easter eggs—and a thousand local and regional customs (now almost vanished).
>
> The joy and the spiritual significance of the feast is situated *within* the special delicacy associated with the feast. (FLN 364)

In such activities and practices one experiences "transferences of attention," an alliance of thought and deed: "Think Christ with one's whole soul.—And while one is in this state the intelligence, the will, etc. and the body, perform acts" (FLN 362). The joy and the spiritual significance of such acts are *within* the feast or the deed; they transfer God's love and beauty and justice through them.

In ceremony we act most publicly and avoid secrecy; we become most transparent and least obscure to one another. In our communal ceremonies, tailored though they are to our different cultures around the globe, we can see others as most like ourselves. This community in *li* is the Confucian analog, says Fingarette, to Christian fellowship (*koinonia*);[14] it is the complement to an African sense of community or *Ujaama*; it is an extension to what we see as most valued in a shared meal (communion and silent listening so central to the meal in Jewish life)[15] or in a sacrament; it is what happens when prayer and liturgy bring human beings and God together to meet each other. We must not underestimate this aspect of life for opening us all to a greater sense of holiness in life and to the importance of human hospitality and the spirit of welcoming found in community.

Confucius taught that there is a spiritual and moral dimension to life and both of these find expression in the context of ceremonial acts. This idea was not new then nor is it now. It stood in contrast in Confucius' time to a spiritual sickness found in the breakdown of moral development and increased individual greed, just as his teaching stands in contrast to a similar moral breakdown in our society with its emphasis on the individual, on money, and on consumer fixations.

Confucius' response to his time was not that of a traditionalist; it was imaginative and creative—"visionary" Fingarette calls it.[16] Fingarette bolsters this point with the following two remarks: "[Confucius] saw that the dignity peculiar to man and the power associated with this dignity could be characterized in terms of holy rite, of ceremony. For ceremony is a conventionalized practice in which are emphasized intrinsic harmony, beauty and sacredness"; and "[Confucius taught] to seek inspiration in one's own traditions in such a way as to reveal a humanizing and harmonizing interpretation for the conflictful present. 'He who by reanimating the Old can gain knowledge of the New is indeed fit to be called a teacher'(2:11)."[17] It was a philosophical vision that "revealed humanity, sacred and marvelous, residing in community, community rooted in the inherited forms of life."[18] Compare this notion of "reanimating the Old" to build a civilized future with Simone Weil's remark:

> The future brings us nothing, gives us nothing; it is we who in order to build it have to give it everything, our very life. But to be able to give, one has to possess; and we possess no other life, no other living sap, than the treasures stored up from the past and digested, assimilated, and created afresh by us. Of all the human soul's needs, none is more vital than this one of the past.

> Love of the past has nothing to do with any reactionary political
> attitude. Like all human activities, the revolution draws all its vigor
> from a tradition. (NR 51)

Not only must we stir a sacred center, "spiritualize" our ordinary life as Simone Weil might say, to re-root ourselves within community, we must find those traditions or ceremonies that reveal our humanity and show our human respect and love toward one another. Such stirrings are essential in a continual struggle for justice. There is a difference in the respective views of the sacred center for Confucius and Simone Weil. The difference is that for Confucius what is sacred or "magical" arises from within our humanness and our humanness when truly lived in *li* expresses the sacred, while for Simone Weil the sacred enters into human relating from "outside" even though it, too, is shown through our practices in a richly bodily way.

In a few brief stanzas, Lao Tzu links his way with both Confucius and Simone Weil, bringing full circle the interdependence of the individual and her community, words and deeds, and concern for a sense of place and the common good:

> In a home it is the site that matters;
> In quality of mind it is depth that matters;
> In an ally it is benevolence that matters;
> In speech it is good faith that matters;
> In government it is order that matters;
> In affairs it is ability that matters;
> In action it is timeliness that matters.
> It is because [true goodness] does not contend that it is never at fault.[19]

In a manner not unlike Confucius', Simone Weil also stressed the importance of ceremony and tradition that was timely and ordered, dynamic and not static—static traditions became for her dead "orthodoxy," not much different than propaganda, which stood in the path of truth. "What we need," she says, "is for the forms of social life to be so devised as to remind people incessantly in the symbolic language most intelligible to it, most in harmony with its customs, tradition[s] and attachments, of the sacred character of this fidelity, the free consent from which it issues, the rigorous obligations arising from it" (SJ 8). Both Confucius' "sacred rite" and Simone Weil's "forms of social life" have the central purpose of "reminding people incessantly in the symbolic language most intelligible" to them of the ways that they can sustain inspiration and develop harmony in their public life. For both, keeping as the public aim faithfulness and obedience to community and country is a high priority. For Simone Weil consent was perhaps the *sine qua non* to remind us of our obligations. She gives two examples "for France" in her time as "indispensable" for maintaining a minimal balance of power: universal suffrage and an independent trade union movement—not to mention those many small shared acts, celebrations, meals with friends and family, treasures from our past made vital for our future. One can see the importance of each of these for consent and obedience within a community and country. Other communities than those in France, or industrialized or highly technological cultures, may have different symbols and customs that would contribute to order and harmony. The Confucian examples of simple customs like a greeting, a tea ceremony, an act of welcoming are even more basic than her examples and serve as incessant reminders of a life in common in all cultures. Both kind of examples are important for maintaining a meaningful social fabric and in preserving "the treasures stored up from the past."

NEIGHBORHOODS, PROFESSIONAL ASSOCIATIONS, AND COUNTRY

In *Oppression and Liberty*, selections from *Gravity and Grace*, and elsewhere, it might be easy to conclude that Simone Weil rejects all "collectivities." A collectivity is a "great beast" which can "devour souls"; a collectivity is unable to "think." But we also know how she was careful to ground certain terms in less abstract ways and see them in more ordinary contexts of use where they find their meaning. In *The Need for Roots*, the term "collectivity" surfaces in a less derogatory way, and suddenly is near synonymous with "country" or "family." She says "*we owe our respect to a collectivity*, of whatever kind—country, family or any other—not for itself, but because it is food for a certain number of human souls" (NR 7, emphasis added). Here collectivity means simply a social unit where people ordinarily find "food," or meaning, in their relations to one another; a social unit where "spiritual treasures" may be preserved and where one generation can show respect for its forebearers—a collectivity is the context where "the dead can speak to the living" (NR 8). It is not, she says, that collectivities are "superior to human beings," but they do provide the "natural environments" for humans to share in the meaning of their lives. It is in such environments that traditions and many ritual practices have their life. Throughout *The Need for Roots* she sees the inseparability of the individual from her social and political contexts; the moral and political are inextricably woven together in a multi-planed relationship.

There is for Simone Weil a certain "texture of social relationships" that cuts across different planes. This she calls "order" and order is "the first of the soul's needs" (NR 10). What does she mean by order? She does not mean a power-based, hierarchical order, nor a positioning of individuals by some abstract criteria like wealth, color, or gender. Order is for her that texture of social relations that allows a person to freely carry out essential obligations and not be "compelled" to abrogate their obligations or responsibilities (NR 10). The first paring of the needs of the soul in *The Need for Roots* is order and liberty—our social life needs the tension found in these together. Thus, order is a kind of "stasis" or "balance" in human relating that minimizes hindrance of action that might deny respect to any human being. If a woman, for example, is threatened with sexual abuse and does not resist for fear of greater physical harm, then there is no social order. If one takes steps to fulfill a filial obligation, as Antigone set out to do, and is hindered by a law that prohibits such a primary obligation, then Simone Weil says, "spiritual violence" is inflicted on the soul. As we all find ourselves in human social relationships and they invariably imply some measure of authority and subordination, the principle that keeps those relationships from becoming oppressive or a hindrance to essential obligations is that they are "textured" in an orderly fashion. Words like "trust," "obedience," "authority," "cooperation," and "mutual care" are what give relationships their texture. The idea of a human order and our need of it she likens "to that of a man traveling, without a guide, through the night, but continually thinking of the direction he wishes to follow. Such a traveler's way is lit by a great hope" (NR 11). This human order assumes no coercion; it is lit by an implicit trust and the fulfillment of obligations; it is the path toward a common good.

This order is less an external order than an internal one; less a mandated order than a working order; and less an abstract order than a relational one sensitive to persons and their contexts. It is the order of the soul rather than that of the state, though the latter can recognize and honor such forms of order. In short, it is an alternative order to what we are accustomed to think.

This order for Simone Weil should ideally operate within what she calls "natural human environments," and she explicitly identifies these as families, countries, historically and culturally based communities, professional associations similar to guilds, and neighborhoods. All of these natural environments should be highly textured with mutual attention, love, friendship, consent, obedience, and obligations woven at different levels into the patterns of relating. They should be composed on many planes like poetry, music, and politics. The composition of these environments interplays at many levels at once through the different kinds of relationships and the actions and practices of their participants. Let us look at the textures of some of these human, ordered environments.

Neighborhoods are the smallest social environment of a real public nature for Simone Weil (families are social environments more closely related to the private sphere of life although they do involve social relationships). Neighborhoods serve a very important role in the whole of the fabric or social order. They are where, daily, practices of "sacred rite" take place; where greetings and coffee or tea breaks, weddings and funerals, and a host of welcoming ceremonies reaffirm communal bonds; where children may be seen almost as community property under the watchful eyes of neighbors.

Neighborhoods, for Simone Weil, are not simply geographically proximate residential groupings or random housing tracts or projects. Neighborhoods could not develop because of commercial convenience such as their proximity to freeways or shopping malls. She envisioned neighborhoods to be based on the kind of ritual practices and social engagement that is so frequently foreign to our world—a world in which jury duty is evaded, crime unnoticed, and education viewed as an unnecessary tax burden. Neighborhoods, for Simone Weil, are something seen as more intimate and more intentionally entered into by their residents. They are ordered for the well-being of all—the children, the elderly, the infirm, single people, couples, and extended families. She might favor ethnically cohesive neighborhoods for their common language and traditions, but as has become increasingly apparent in our highly pluralistic society there are dangers in these and they are most likely to flourish only in rural areas. In our more urbanized culture, in urban environments, she might well see cross-class neighborhoods preferable to class-stratified ghettos, whether the latter be made up of rich or poor or in-between. Cross-class neighborhoods would more nearly mirror the larger society and would have to continually embrace the struggle for justice more clearly than single-class neighborhoods. Although single-class neighborhoods may have more traditions in common, today they are more likely to see themselves in relationship to other neighborhoods in terms of power. Power would reign as a means of stability, and its residents would be less likely to work out differences among its neighbors and between neighborhoods. Thus in the dominant urban society in which most people now live, she might see neighborhoods as preferably microcosms of the larger society and be less inclined to want to ghettoize people along lines of class or religion.

With respect to race or ethnic origin as a basis for neighborhoods, there are complex reasons to both favor and object to them. On this point there is room for disagreement, and varying interpretations of Simone Weil's views could be developed. But given the list of causes of uprootedness and the dominance of power on the social level of our lives, and given her desire that we face the difficulties of human life and give undivided attention to the face of the other in cultures, she might argue that the morally preferable way of establishing neighborhood-based communities and trying to "order" them into a country or state would be to try and integrate them thoroughly.[20] This is not so much an argument growing out of the values of a form of liberalism, but out of her view of justice as compassion-based and her desire to regard each human being as sacred and to keep one's country out of harm's way. It is true that, in some ways, this interpretation goes against her strongly expressed views about the importance of a common language, symbols, and traditions for a community. We would have to work particularly hard to preserve elements of our past, weaving traditions and ceremonies together into new fabrics. There are ways, however, in which the latter values might be worked out within her multiple-planed composition for community.

Let us suppose that we are best "ordered" in mixed class and mixed racial or ethnic neighborhoods, particularly in an urban culture. This would not keep us from entering into more professional or ethnic and religious voluntary associations, which may revolve around our work or the desire to preserve certain beliefs and traditions. Thus, another plane of social order is possible both within and between neighborhoods. Certain issues revolving around maintaining traditions tied to history or religion may be more easily cultivated in these professional, civic, or religious associations. Whatever clarity and conviction are confirmed and affirmed in these voluntary associations may help in discussions that will take place in the workplace, in neighborhoods, and in larger civic forums. In unions or guilds, literary or sports clubs, or other professional organizations, for example, issues that relate to what Simone Weil calls the wider civilization of work may get thrashed out in a setting of mutual trust, and some things that undermine the dignity or spirituality of work may become focused enough to carry back to the workplace or even over the back fence in one's mixed neighborhood to be taken up in a new "civilized" dialog. William M. Sullivan comments that it is in such "associational life that civic culture is formed," that these are contexts "for the realization of positive goods," and that it is in these associations that "individuals consider common concerns and interests."[21] Here we see the importance of place or environment for sustaining a deliberative and reflective life as a citizen.

The important thing to remember about neighborhoods and voluntary associations is that whether they be racially or ethnically diverse or not, they must be communal—that is, they must enhance the environment for social relationships. We do have many success stories of diverse associational communities in certain institutions, some churches and schools, sports activities, Boy Scouts and Girl Scouts, neighborhood watch organizations, even at many levels of the military establishment. The danger in forming communities that have no diversity is that their roots to the past may be narrow or dogmatic, and they may form exclusionary characteristics based on wealth or single race or single religion criteria. Although Simone Weil does not address this possible danger head on, there is enough she has said about "respect," "essential obligations," and "compassion crossing frontiers" to be concerned about the kind of community that develops when associations become too exclusive.

While neighborhoods and professional associations are relatively small natural environments, a country for Simone Weil (as distinct from a modern state) is the largest of natural environments. This is true particularly since she believes that virtually all states in their "modern" configuration are not "natural" entities and have little or no legitimacy. A country for her is likely to have a language historically in common with the majority of its people that is not legally imposed.

In our current situation, many neighborhoods have a language different from that of the country, but this does not exclude people in such neighborhoods from participating and sharing the dominant language of the country. This, of course, is more characteristic of countries that have been consciously and historically composed of immigrant communities such as the United States and Canada, South Africa, and Australia, and which are becoming more characteristic worldwide as economic and political uprootedness force waves of immigrants to more promising shores.

Colonialism was passionately condemned by Simone Weil, and she wrote forcefully about French policy in North Africa and Southeast Asia. The "states" carved out by Europeans were created with little regard to roots and often systematically destroyed or supplanted local traditions. Andrea Nye says, "The loss of human environments that such development brings was for Weil a 'supreme tragedy.'" Nye observes that some traditional environments are particularly fragile for women, and alien (colonial) cultures jeopardize indigenous ways of life. When these environments are destroyed "the only answer is centralization because the 'living intercourse between diverse and mutually independent centers' is impossible. Something infinitely precious and frail is lost, 'the living warmth of a human environment, a medium which bathes and fosters the thoughts and the virtues' (SE 79), the beauties of daily life: 'home, country, traditions, culture' (GG 133) which nourish and warm the spirit."[22]

In addition to those things that are destructive of the natural balances within a country by the creation of artificial states, the legacy of leadership spawned by colonial rule has generally been a disaster—especially in African nation-states. At the heart of a country is the need for legitimacy in those who govern. For Simone Weil legitimacy is claimed by a government and its leaders if it embraces three essential things: "dignity," a "concern for justice" and a concern for "the public good." These three things are, of course, related to each other, but she says that "as long as the people retain this confidence [that dignity, justice and the public good are being served]: that is legitimate government" (LPG 93). "Legitimacy," she says, "is not a primitive notion. It is derived from justice. Relative to power, justice requires above all else an equilibrium between power and responsibility" (LPG 94). It is this lack of equilibrium between power and responsibility that feeds increasingly injustices in a state. Let us look at a contemporary case where the equilibrium between power and responsibility has broken down.

Witnessing the injustices and unravelling of his own nation-state, Nigeria, Wole Soyinka is forced to ask himself "What is a nation?" When can a modern state so artificially created be said to have achieved conditions closer to that of Simone Weil's country? To this point he sees so-called Nigerian nation-building to be "nothing but a cameo of personalities, a series of transparencies of distortion, each laid over the last" with no "purpose or direction."[23] Nigeria has become what some have called more than one postcolonial African state, a "modern kleptocracy" or a "poli-thug state."[24] Soyinka sees his homeland as "the open sore of the continent." Soyinka argues that no one can find their personal identity in any terms that "relate to the existing or historical definition of that space."[25] There is no remaining focus such as language or traditions that mean anything anymore—no one is allowed any meaningful work or associations and once viable neighborhoods (village life) have been systematically destroyed by "the opportunism and adventurism of power." There has been a total breakdown of any interactive structures that might "enhance the daily quality of life," or in Weil's terms, enhance "the living warmth of a human environment." Africans have become victims of their own postcolonial states. In our listing of sources for uprooting, Simone Weil said regarding a state that it eats away a country's moral substance; it "lives on it, fattens on it, until the day comes when no more nourishment can be drawn from it, and famine reduces it to a condition of lethargy" (NR 120). It is this scenario of moral malnourishment found too often in Africa and elsewhere that breathes new life into Simone Weil's more conservative instincts about a country and what gives legitimacy to a state. The ends of these conservative instincts are, however, toward a more civil order where all humans are given equal regard and any concept of the individual ego is subsumed by justice and love.

So what do we learn from Simone Weil on community and politics and on justice and public life? Legitimacy of any nation-state is derived from justice, and there is no justice without consent of the governed. Those governing, too, must know something of the balance between power and responsibility. Above all, individual human dignity must be respected, those who are in need must be listened to, and sufficient structures or natural human environments must be cultivated and sustained to enhance the public good. All these things depend on recognizing something common to the human spirit. Andrea Nye summarizes these points as follows:

> What allows just and balanced human relations is that there is something at the core of each person which is the same, not a common nature or essence, not a common way of thinking or conceptual scheme, but something that speaks, not venting pain as an animal might, but calling out for needs to be met. What is the same in each person is the aspiration to Weil's divinity, to that illusive social balance and harmony in which no one is hurt, crushed in spirit, humiliated. That balance is only achievable, Weil thought, when there is a particular relation of communication between government and people.[26]

For natural human environments to flourish and for just and balanced human relations to be sustained, textures and different planes of human relationships must interact in an ordered manner, arts and traditions must be allowed to sustain a past and enrich a future, and education must function both to enhance attention and love toward human need and to further public trust and mutual care. Only thus will the human community be rooted.

Community and politics are vital to an individual's rootedness. Simone Weil never loses sight of that fact. One sees in the workplace, in neighborhoods, in a variety of human associations that bonds are formed by what is made vitally present in the human environment from its past. The quality of the present community depends on the order and vitality of its past creatively carried forward by present generations. In summary, we repeat this remark of hers:

> The future brings us nothing, gives us nothing; it is we who in order to build it have to give it everything, our very life. But to be able to give, one has to possess; and we possess no other life, no other living sap, than the treasures stored up from the past and digested, assimilated, and created afresh by us. Of all the human soul's needs, none is more vital that this one of the past. (NR 51)

NOTES

1. For an analysis that echoes many concerns expressed in Simone Weil's "*Iliad*," and that clearly shows how the meaning of war and the moral debates about war have changed in a nuclear age, see Jonathan Schell, *The Fate of the Earth* (New York: Alfred A. Knopf, 1982). No book since Schell's has stated the issues with as much clarity and as convincing an argument.

2. Of an estimated two hundred million landmines manufactured and distributed by all producers between 1969 and 1992, there are approximately one hundred million uncleared and unexploded mines that remain planted worldwide. Details may be found in *Landmines: A Deadly Legacy* (New York: Human Rights Watch, 1993).

3. She gives examples of how in poetry there are "at least five or six different planes of composition." This is both a "law of artistic creation"—that it is so complex and multilayered—and also "its difficulty" (NR 216).

4. This "means of expressing" would be something like a First Amendment right in the American Constitution, whereby leaders could be criticized and judged. Simone Weil, however, has limits on tolerance and has few qualms in repressing certain kinds of speech and almost anything one could classify as propaganda.

5. "The sacred majesty of the laws." Théophile de Viau was an early-seventeenth-century poet.

6. Lin Tung-chi has said that Confucianism and Taoism are often thought of as the *yin* and *yang* of Chinese life. See his essay "The Chinese Mind: Its Taoist Substratum," *Journal of the History of Ideas* 8, no. 3 (June 1947). In D. C. Lau's "Introduction" to his translation of the *Tao Te Ching*, he writes: "Almost all ancient Chinese thinkers were concerned with the way one should lead one's life, . . . Politics and ethics, for the Chinese as for the ancient Greeks, were two aspects of the same thing, and this the Chinese thinkers called the *tao*" (32). As noted earlier, Lao Tzu and Confucius were thought to be contemporaries and were said to have met one another. See Lao, *Tao Te Ching*, 8–12.

7. This is a summary following the reading given to Confucius' *Analects* by Herbert Fingarette, *Confucius: The Secular as Sacred* (New York: Harper & Row Publishers, 1972), 6–10.

8. Ibid., 6–10.

9. Ibid., 8.

10. Ibid.

11. Thomas Merton, *The Way of Chuang Tzu* (New York: New Directions, 1969), 18.

12. Fingarette, *Confucius*, 9.

13. Ibid., 11. There are interesting parallels in this example of Fingarette's with examples found in Simone Weil's "Essay on the Notion of Reading."

14. Fingarette, *Confucius*, 16.

15. See Franz Rosenzweig on the importance of "silent listening" during a Jewish meal: *Franz Rosenzweig: His Life and Thought,* ed. Naham Glatzer (New York: Schocken Books, 1953), 316–18.

16. Fingarette, *Confucius*, 59f.

17. Ibid., 63 and 68.

18. Ibid., 69.

19. Lao, *Tao Te Ching*, 64.

20. I can only say here, echoing words of Rush Rhees almost forty years ago, "in all this I am interpolating, and perhaps Simone Weil would not have said anything of the sort." *Rush Rhees on Religion and Philosophy*, ed. D. Z. Phillips (Cambridge: Cambridge University Press, 1997), 366. Springsted, in a note commenting on an earlier draft of this book, thought that my "construction of a Weilian neighborhood" was "an Enlightenment project itself." This may be a fair enough criticism which I defend by saying that it is precisely such "interpolation" that Simone Weil's thought cries out for, especially as we read it almost sixty years later.

21. William M. Sullivan, "A Public Philosophy for Civic Culture," in *Rooted in the Land: Essays on Community and Place*, ed. William Vitek and Wes Jackson (New Haven: Yale University Press, 1996), 236f.

22. Nye, *Philosophia,* 120.

23. Wole Soyinka, *The Open Sore of the Continent: A Personal Narrative of the Nigerian Crisis* (New York: Oxford University Press, 1966), 65.

24. Kwame Anthony Appiah discusses this problem in his *In My Father's House: Africa in the Philosophy of Culture* (Oxford: Oxford University Press, 1992). See his discussion on page 150. Also, Soyinka, *Open Sore*, 65ff. I also discuss this sad fact about postcolonial states in Africa in my "Understanding African Philosophy from a Non-African Point of View: An Exercise in Cross-cultural Philosophy," in *Postcolonial African Philosophy: A Critical Reader*, ed. Emmanuel Chukwudi Eze (Oxford: Basil Blackwell, 1997), 206–8.

25. Soyinka, *Open Sore*, 109.

26. Nye, *Philosophia,* 112.

8

EDUCATION AND CIVILIZATION

The first duty of a school is to develop the power of attention in children, by school exercises to be sure, but by reminding them ceaselessly that they must learn to be attentive in order to be able, later on, to be just.

Simone Weil, *Ecrit Londres*

"GREAT HOPES" AND "POSSIBLE DREAMS"

As we have seen in the previous chapter, Simone Weil gave great value to *experiencing* something in order to learn its truth, and that there be "real, active and natural participation in the life of community." The experiencing or participating for her was itself a critical process, the reanimation of "treasures stored up from the past—digested, assimilated, and created afresh by us" (NR 51). In this manner we build a future and give it "our very life." Another metaphor given us by Simone Weil that relates to how we build a future is that of a traveler in the night "lit by a great hope"—"continually thinking of the direction he wishes to follow" (NR 11). The great hope of our traveler, in Simone Weil's scheme of things, becomes *a* multiplicity of hopes cultivated in a human community, ideals held before us for which we must continue to struggle, dreams that arise in human hearts that good and not evil will be realized in both our individual and civic lives. This multiplicity of hopes, our ideals and dreams, is what David McLellan had in mind in calling Simone Weil "utopian," but which he neutralizes with the accompanying term "pessimist." It is easy to read Simone Weil's personal life as the dark side of what may be an otherwise critical, but hopeful, philosophy of life. Is it not possible, however, to set aside from time to time some of her self-negating, self-annihilating, and destructive personal diminishment to see the more constructive aspects of her philosophy? Whatever she finally thought of herself—and it was very little—she never wavered from setting for herself and all humanity the highest moral standards and doing all in her power to realize them. Her ideas on education are among those from which her darker reflections can be suspended.

In her vision of education and of civilization, it is her hopes, ideals, and dreams that prevail. Andrea Nye notes that for Simone Weil, as with Rosa Luxemburg in Germany, "Marxism had lost its moral compass."[1] Furthermore, with continued depression and recession, terrible working conditions, the rise of fascism, and "the masses of women and men . . . reduced to various degrees of *malheur* [affliction], apathy, and impotence," Nye asks:

> Where, then, is the compass that can find the lost path toward liberation, the compass based neither on the subjective, self-interested projections to which standpoint moralities, socialist or feminist, are always in danger of being reduced, nor on absolutes and universal principles in whose name violence can be done?
>
> What is missing from social theory, Weil thought, is an aspect of reality lost back in the modernist split between mechanical nature and subjective desire: the ideal. . . . An ideal must be real and at the same time "a standard for the analysis and evaluation of actual social patterns"(OL 100). An ideal must point, not to a real state realizable in fact, but to a real measure by which to judge what is better or worse.[2]

The key, says Nye, is not to engineer social order with all its contradictions of good and evil, but to draw one's ideals from a different light—a light outside this world. Simone Weil's ideals emanate from the divine and come down to us as "real measures," asking for our consent and that we live "madly" and "justly" *in* this world according to them. The ideals, as we have seen, are expressed in those concepts central to her moral and political thought: attention, passion for the truth, humility, order, love, and compassion—all those things that add up to the way of justice as compassion. Her conception of education and civilization operates within this framework of ideals "lit by a great hope."

Before looking at some of Simone Weil's ideas about education and civilization, we will sketch some of the pedagogical ideas of the Brazilian thinker, Paulo Freire.[3] This will provide us with a contemporary framework in which to place Simone Weil's views on education and civilization. Once again, it is not because Freire was influenced by Simone Weil that we draw him into our discussion, but because he, like Havel and others, sought the truth under conditions of oppression in a way that tied his life and thought to his work and actions. Freire, like Simone Weil, was an attentive observer of the human condition in a time and place of oppression and totalitarian rule, though his active work of rebellion against them was between the 1950s and the 1980s on a different continent. With a particular vision of justice and truth he sought to re-educate the poor of his beloved country.

Freire's ideas have had an enormous impact on education theory in the second half of the twentieth century. His ideas on teaching adult literacy have been particularly effective in bringing about social and economic change among urban and rural poor in South America and Africa. Freire's ideas, along with those of Ivan Illich, Jonathan Kozol, and Robert Coles, constitute a body of pedagogical literature reflecting similar moral and political concerns and projecting a set of educational ideals that are a contemporary reflection of the fragmentary ideas on education to be found in Simone Weil.[4]

Freire's central idea is education for human liberation inspired by a unity between democracy and socialism. Freire distinguishes between what he calls "realistic socialism," the failed authoritarian systems that had restricted human freedom and truth-telling in Eastern Europe and the former Soviet Union, and "socialism," which holds a "hope of utopia." He says that education for liberation is forged in "the democratic struggle for the possible dream of a fair society, one more human, more decent, and more beautiful for those reasons."[5] The ideal of "a possible dream" is important to Freire's theory. "The possible dream" entails "a good democracy [which] warns, clarifies, teaches, and educates. It also defends itself from the actions of those who, by offending their human nature, deny and demean democracy."[6] This dream establishes a horizon of hope in which all pedagogical struggles take place. All social transformation must have this horizon of hope and human liberation to be truly effective. What he calls the "fight for liberation" is

one of all human beings toward being more. It is a fight to overcome obstacles to the humanization of all. It is a fight for the creation of

structural conditions that make a more democratic society possible.
. . . The fight is for the creation of a society capable of defending itself
by punishing with justice and rigor the perpetrators of abuse; it is for
a civil society capable of speaking, protesting, and fighting for justice.
The final struggle is not to satisfy men and women, but to recognize
them as finite, incomplete, and historically bound people who are
capable of denying goodness and becoming evil, but also of knowing
goodness and becoming loving and fair.[7]

Like Simone Weil, Freire understood power and how those who
possess it will do anything to retain it, and his critiques of capitalism and
authoritarian forms of socialism are equally clear and severe (though he
does have a more favorable view of Marx than did Simone Weil). Freire
developed a method that he calls "the reading of the world." There are
naive, fragmented ways of reading the world which he calls "consciousness"—an immediate awareness of objects in the world and an account-
ing of them as facts. A more critical and deeper reading of the world he
calls an act of "conscientization"—a term he develops in *Pedagogy of the
Oppressed*—where we perceive not only facts but "the relationships
among objects and their reason for being." For example, with respect to
the fact of hunger, he says that illiterate communities, having suffered
injustice, naively read or

attribute the hunger that destroys them to destiny, fate, or God. Only
in the struggle for survival do they begin to overcome the naive and
magical perception of phenomenon. Conscientization changes one's
perception of the facts, based on a critical understanding of them.
    A person who has reached conscientization is capable of clearly
perceiving [reading] hunger as more than just not eating, as the manifestation of a political, economic, and social reality of deep injustice.[8]

Freire calls his pedagogical method of reading the world "progressive,"[9]
believing in a struggle for equal rights to overcome injustice, thus enabling human beings to "become more" by transforming their social
condition.

Finally, three ideas are central in Freire's educational method: the
importance of "pedagogical space," respect for the learners' culture, and
commitment to the task of "democratizing education." A brief look at
these, along with the ideas just discussed of a critical "reading of the

world" and the "fight for social transformation" through conscientization, provides us with a picture that reflects a number of key ideas to be found in Simone Weil's views of education and civilization.

The idea of "pedagogical space" for Freire is of crucial importance. His writings echo those of Kozol in *Death at an Early Age,* where we see the physical learning environment to determine the educational life or death of the child.[10] There must be a sense of place where a child feels comfortable, where a child is respected and her dignity restored. This must be a healthy and nonoppressive environment where a child feels a balance between freedom and authority. The physical space and the emotional space must be maintained, says Friere "as a happy and pleasant place."[11]

Incorporated into the "pedagogical space" must be respect for the learners' culture. In most educational systems teachers impose the mores and ideology of the dominant culture on its learners. In the case of Brazil, the dominant culture came from a minority of the population and was authoritarian and elitist in nature, reinforcing the oppressive experiences that rural and urban poor children already knew. Furthermore, in this environment the learners became unwitting "hosts" of the oppressor's culture. Freire insisted that the learners' culture be respected and that their "popular" experience be the starting point in their education. Their informal knowledge, language, social class, festivals—what they brought to school in their being—should be drawn forward from the learners and incorporated into the learning environment itself. One of the stated objectives of his pedagogical method was the preservation of popular culture traditions. By looking at the local people's lives, their "festivals, their stories, their mythic figures, and their religiousness," Freire discovered "not only the resigned expression of the oppressed but also their possible methods of resistance."[12] These became important tools for teaching and subsequently for the learners' own "fight for social transformation" and liberation.

Lastly, Freire had a deep commitment "to the task of democratizing education." This process was not just between teacher and pupil, but as he says, "we wanted to democratize the relationships among educators, learners, parents, custodian, school, and community."[13] His critical reading of the human condition found people "reduced to an almost thing-like status" and that those responsible for their education had an "indifferent attitude toward people." To illustrate this, Freire provides a story from an early training seminar he organized in the late 1950s to heighten awareness of education officials to human relationships in their workplace. Freire invited coworkers (educational supervisors), teachers, and custodians to participate in the seminar. He asked a senior janitor to speak first. Here is some of what "Francisco" said: "I am only a janitor doing my job, cleaning rooms and desks, buying cigarettes for the professors, serving their coffee, taking documents from one office to another." Francisco then recounts the humiliation he experiences in buying cigarettes and serving coffee to his school officials:

> I am happy with my day-to-day life. I am humble. But there are some things that I don't understand and should mention to all of you. For example, when I enter a director's office with the coffee tray and he is in a meeting with other professors, no one looks at me or answers when I say good morning to them. They only grab their coffee cups and never once say, even to be different, thank-you. Sometimes I am called in by a director and he gives me money to buy him a pack of cigarettes. I go, I go down the stairs if the elevator is taking too long, I cross the street, I buy the cigarettes, I return, I give the cigarettes to the director. "Here," another director will tell me, giving me some change, "bring me some matches." Why don't they discuss what they want so I can take care of it in one trip? Why go up and down, down and up, just to buy a little bit each time?
>
> I hope that those who never said good morning or thank-you don't become angry with a humble janitor. I told these stories because they are part of my day-to-day routine as a janitor here at the [regional office].[14]

There was a "silence" and "discomfort," Freire reports, after Francisco's comments. No attention had been paid to him. He had not been given respect and thus his dignity was harmed. This "object lesson" was not rehearsed, but shows the power of democratizing education.

"LEARN TO BE ATTENTIVE IN ORDER . . . TO BE JUST"

The remark by Simone Weil about school exercises, attention, and justice with which we began this chapter could be read as a concise summary of Paulo Freire's "possible dream" for a good educational system and a good society. Freire's goal in his pedagogical theory is, as was Simone Weil's, to help people "know goodness and become loving and fair" and to do so in the full awareness of the contradictory character of our personal and public lives. While many people know of Paulo Freire's educational pedagogy, very little has been made of Simone Weil's. But she, also, presents a radical vision of education. Moving back to Simone Weil and the multiplicity of hopes she had for a good society, we will look at the role of the many ideals she held that would be central to the education of women and men.

It should not be surprising to see her say that "the first duty of a school is to develop the power of attention in children." The importance of attention runs from attention to the smallest items in school studies ("Latin prose or a geometry problem" in grammar school), in the natural world ("the sky, the stars, the moon, trees in blossom"), right through to the "human spirit" in the way we educate technicians, lawyers, and judges. We saw the importance of attention explicitly discussed in chapters three and five. In chapter three we saw the illustration that to "win the prize" or "attain the Grail" we must be able to ask the question of its "painfully wounded" guardian: "What are you going through?" In the same essay from which this illustration is drawn, she says:

> Although people seem to be unaware of it today, the development of the faculty of attention forms the real object and almost the sole interest of studies. Most school tasks have a certain intrinsic interest as well, but such an interest is secondary. All tasks that call upon the power of attention are interesting for the same reason and to an almost equal degree. (WG 105f. Her most celebrated essay on education is this one collected in WG, entitled "Reflections on the Right Use of School Studies with a View to the Love of God.")

And she says again:

> Students must therefore work without any wish to gain good marks, to pass examinations, to win school successes; without any reference to their natural abilities and tastes; applying themselves equally to all their tasks, with the idea that each one will help to form in them the habit of that attention which is the substance of prayer. (WG 108)

Thus as we cultivate a greater capacity for attention early in school stud-ies we grow in our regard for and our ability to be receptive to beauty in nature, the cries of those who are hurting, and stirrings of the good we desire in our heart—even enhancing our capacity to consent to God's love.

She is very much aware of how this goes against the grain of how students usually understand their education, that is, to fulfill immediate goals and win good marks, never looking back at errors that may have occurred along the way. She would have all students attend equally to errors as to successes:

> In every school exercise there is a special way of waiting upon truth, setting our hearts upon it, yet not allowing ourselves to go out in search of it. There is a way of giving our attention to the data of a problem in geometry without trying to find the solution or to the words of a Latin or Greek text without trying to arrive at the meaning, a way of waiting, when we are writing, for the right word to come of itself at the end of our pen, while we merely reject all inadequate words. (WG 113)

She also gives us some tips on how to pay attention rather than just "contracting our muscles" as if we are "getting serious." This only, in the end, makes us tired: "Twenty minutes of concentrated, untired at-tention is infinitely better than three hours of the kind of frowning appli-cation that leads us to say with a sense of duty done: 'I have worked well!'" (WG 111). Nor will good intentions and willpower achieve the right ends. In this "waiting" and "untired attention" we see why she found such resonance in Taoism.

Finally, with the right kind of attention she says that "the intelli-gence only grows and bears fruit in joy. The joy of learning is as indis-pensable in study as breathing is to running. Where it is lacking there are no real students, but only poor caricatures of apprentices who, at the end of their apprenticeship, will not even have a trade" (WG 110).

In chapter five we saw that a judge should first be taught to see the suffering in the vagrant that stands before her. To have both the capacity and the freedom of expression should be a goal of education, stretching from the most illiterate soul to the most intellectual. She says: "Nothing . . . is more frightful than to see some poor wretch in the police court

stammering before a magistrate who keeps up an elegant flow of witti-
cisms" (SE 11). "What is needed," she continues,

> is a system of public education capable of providing it [a suffering and
> mute heart] so far as possible, with means of expression; and next, a
> régime in which the public freedom of expression is characterized not
> so much by freedom as by an attentive silence in which this faint and
> inept cry can make itself heard; and finally, institutions are needed of
> a sort which will, so far as possible, put power into the hands of men
> who are able and anxious to hear and understand it. (SE 11f.)

This she understands to be a "spiritual" education. For judges and lawyers this is as important as any purely "legal" education. They should
learn to distinguish between the two cries: Why am I being hurt? And
why has somebody else got more than I have? Here, too, the point of
serving justice and truth is to be able to attend to or discern where an
injustice has occurred.

Thus, prerequisite to any effective education, and essential to a
good and just civilization, is that we learn to be attentive to our world
and to the human spirit, and build a public education system that en-
hances full freedom of expression to all human beings, a government
that gains its legitimacy by listening to its public, and institutions that
provide a kind of leadership that shows a capacity for compassion: "The
education of the attention—that is the chief thing" (N 545).

Related to attention is Simone Weil's concept of "reading"—
especially reading the circumstances of life that give rise to injustice. To
ask someone "Why are you hurting?" is already to have read the situation of the suffering, to have attended to nuance, and to have shown
some level of compassion. What gives us motive for helping here is to
have seen (i.e., read) the hurt in the context in which it takes place and
in this seeing to recognize that we have an obligation to help. This
reading and acting restores "a just balance." In the end, education's aim
is no more than to restore a just balance between the good that humans
have in them and the cruelty that surrounds them. This is surprisingly
close to what Paulo Freire calls a critical "reading of the world" or
"conscientization"—we see the hurt or hunger as it is related to the
"political, economic, and social reality of deep injustice," which then
inspires a human being to "become more" and want to liberate herself.

The source of the inspiration for liberation, however, is different in Freire than in Simone Weil. For Weil, the inspiration is from an eternal source while Freire, although acknowledging the importance of his Christian upbringing, seems to believe that inspiration naturally arises when humans see and understand their particular condition from a position other than that of the oppressor, i.e., see it from their own human situation as the oppressed. (This sounds very similar to Noddings' caregiver drawing inspiration to care from the one being cared for.) Both Simone Weil and Freire see the need to build environments to enhance such liberating capacities into all aspects of public life.

This leads us directly to another central idea in Simone Weil's view of education. In *The Need for Roots* she writes:

> Education—whether its object be children or adults, individuals or an entire people, or even oneself—consists in creating motives. To show what is beneficial, what is obligatory, what is good—that is the task of education. Education concerns itself with the motives for effective action. . . .
>
> To want to direct human creatures—others or oneself—toward the good by simply pointing out the direction, without making sure the necessary motives have been provided, is as if one tried, by pressing down the accelerator, to set off in a motorcar with an empty gas tank. Or again, it is as if one were to try to light an oil lamp without having put in any oil. (NR 189f.)

The task in education is "to show what is beneficial, what is obligatory, what is good." To do this we must create the right motives and clarify what obligations follow from the motives. I would, for example, have no motive to act in any other way than in my self-interest if I did not have an aspiration that was *more than myself* or have a motive *that went beyond self-interest*. To act toward another human being out of pure friendship or in a compassionate way does not seem to be a "natural" instinct humans have—or at least if there is any benevolent streak in humans, there seem to be too many obstacles in our way to realize it. This is why she believes the values that our educational system tries to give us—which have a concrete presence in our educational system—are based primarily on the incentives of punishment and reward, forms of friendly coercion. Or, if not by threats and promises, then by suggestion (see NR 190)—a form of propaganda—of those in power. Such values, she argues, continue to convince the populace how well off they are under this "best of all possible" regimes. This is one way an oppressor stays in power. Simone Weil writes:

> The recognition of human wretchedness is difficult for whoever is rich and powerful because he is almost invincibly led to believe that he is something. It is equally difficult for the man in miserable circumstances because he is almost invincibly led to believe that the rich and powerful man is something. (GG 110)

In this way our motives and incentives for self-improvement are to want to be just like the rich and powerful—the oppressor. Here the parallel is clear between Simone Weil and Freire's idea of wanting the learners' culture to frame the learning and not the culture of an oppressor.

In response to this situation, she says: "The word aspirations suits us much better than that of values. For values involve a presence, an aspiration an absence, and our good is absent." How are we to unravel this mysterious saying? Given the gravity or oppression of the human condition which favors power over benevolence, goodness (the good or God) seems all but absent. Thus if I am to aspire to anything other than balancing my life through power, I must conceive of something outside of my life. She also notes that "the aspiration toward the good that is in us is exposed to wounds from the [world around us]"—so much so that the good has almost diminished completely. I must, however, go on hoping and desiring the good—aspiring for what is absent. In this way I may discover it. "Evil," she says, "becomes an operative motive far more easily than good." So I must be ever alert to the kind of motives I may possess and judge them by the resultant actions of the motives: "But once pure good has become an operative motive in the mind, it forms there the fount of a uniform and inexhaustible impulsion, which is never so in the case of evil" (NR 212f.). The source of this "inexhaustible impulsion" is from God, "arising in a man's soul . . . as a source of inspiration" (NR 284). "Pure good" as a motive is simply, as hard as this seems, to do no one harm and to love the other in a compassionate way.

Thus I must critically attend to what results in love and justice in all that I do, so that I can discern and enhance purely good motives over evil ones. It is here that Andrea Nye's idea of a new compass returns—

ideals that serve as standards to measure or judge what is better or worse. These ideals are linked to what is absent: they come down to us and provide motives for action; they are a "source of inspiration" linked with the supernatural. We identified some of these ideals as the measures "lit by a great hope" for our actions: absolute attention, passion for the truth, renunciation and humility, love and compassion. I can aspire to justice insofar as I can measure my actions by these ideas. In this way I am engaged in a kind of pedagogical practice which may lead to the way of justice as compassion.

So we have these aspirations, ideals, and dreams, "lit by a great hope" which creates motives to show us what is beneficial, obligatory, and good: "Education concerns itself with the motive for effective action." Cultivating attention and creating purely good motives are the two highest aims of education for Simone Weil. They are foundational for "breathing an inspiration into" (NR 187) all aspects of education, into reading and writing, solving problems and engaging in experiments, learning a skill that embraces a capacity for reflection and not just utility. She says: "An educational method which is not inspired by the conception of a certain form of human perfection is not worth very much" (NR 218). I understand her to mean by "a certain form of human perfection," that form of perfection which draws its motive from what is absent from it—a motive given by God and inscribed in life by the degree of compassion expressed therein: "The inspiration for such an education must be sought, like the method itself, among the truths eternally inscribed in the nature of things" (NR 219).

In a list of methods or "means of education" discussed in *The Need for Roots* (pages 190–92), Simone Weil lists five:

1. First, fear and hope, brought about by threats and promises.
2. Suggestion.
3. Expression, either officially or under official sanction, of some of the thoughts which, before ever being publicly expressed were already in the hearts of the people, or in the hearts of certain active elements in the nation.
4. Example.
5. The modalities themselves of action, and those of organization created for purposes of action.

Of these, she says, the first is the "grossest" and most prolifically used. The second is the one that Hitler shows a genius for; and "the other three are unknown." She then tries to show how the unknown three might serve as a better means for educational practice. Number three goes along with breathing inspiration into education—publicly forming *ideals* that echo what are "in the hearts of the people" already, touching their aspiration to good and even some desire to help as they would want others to help them. This would draw out more benevolent practices. Here the practice of enhancing someone's capacity for freedom of expression is crucial—giving articulate speech to the silent and afflicted. This means is also like Freire's respect for learners and their culture. The fourth means, example, makes appeal to individuals and public officials to be both "thoughtful" and "truthful" in making public policy, to create safe and happy environments for education, and for all to practice reciprocity of "little virtues" as well as the "mysterious ones," as Philip Hallie noted these, to show mutual respect and compassion for one's fellow human beings. Finally, the goal—the ultimate test as to whether we are "truly madly" struggling for justice—is to put as many of our ideals into practice as is possible, both publicly and privately. In his own way, what Paulo Freire calls *praxis*—putting into practice all those elements in his pedagogical method to realize human liberation—reflects these last three methods of education found in Simone Weil.

EDUCATING FOR CIVILIZATION

With order as the first need of the soul—order meaning the texture of social relationships which provides a framework for obligations to one another—educational institutions are an important public way of enriching and serving this first need. Simone Weil believed that education and its institutions were paramount to sustaining community in both urban and rural areas. Schools of all sorts—public and private schools, professional schools, adult training centers for industrial and agricultural workers—were the training grounds for being rooted. "Every human being needs to have multiple roots," she says (NR 43). Schools are one important environment for such rooting. She lamented the poverty of education in many ways, how it watered down culture and promoted thoughtless action. In the last chapter we noted how our modern "stovepipe atmosphere" was rapidly producing "a culture very strongly directed toward and influenced by technical science, very strongly tinged with pragmatism, extremely broken up by specialization, entirely deprived both of contact with this world and, at the same time, of any window opening onto the world beyond" (NR 45). Pedagogy in primary schools had fallen to a "parrotwise" repetition, reciting facts—"the earth moves round the sun"—without actually looking up at the heavens. Of all these weaknesses she writes:

> What is called today educating the masses is taking this modern culture, evolved in such a closed, unwholesome atmosphere, and one so indifferent to the truth, removing whatever it may still contain of intrinsic merit—an operation known as popularization—and shoveling the residue as it stands into the minds of the unfortunate individuals desirous of learning, in the same way as you feed birds with a stick. (NR 46)

She has plenty to say about both rural and urban education and how life needs to be breathed into them. Like Paulo Freire she stressed the importance of place—that "education in the villages should be to increase the feeling for the beauty of the world, the beauty of nature" (NR 87). Also like Freire, she believed that "rural school teachers should know the peasants and not look down on them" (NR 88). Teachers should be trained from the local villages. Finally she says, a point also echoed by Freire, that "a very large part of [teachers'] training ought to be devoted to the folklore of all countries, presented not as an object of curiosity but as something superb. . . . They should be made to read peasant literature—Hesiod, *Piers Plowman* . . . the few contemporary works which are of authentically peasant inspiration" (NR 88f.).

With respect to the training of industrial youth in urban centers, she stresses that they must be made to "feel at home . . . in the world of thought" (NR 65). Their culture is different from that of the villager and their particular culture must be respected and brought into their education. A constant effort must be made by teachers to find ways to "transpose truths." To convey this to workers "one has to have placed oneself at the center of a truth and possessed it in all its nakedness" (NR 68). Again regarding the connection between thought and action, she provides this concrete pedagogical example:

There is quite a simple way in which geometrical necessity could be introduced into training schools, by associating theoretical study and the workshop. One would say to the children, "Here are a certain number of tasks to be carried out [constructing objects fulfilling such and such requirements]. Some of them are possible, others impossible. Carry out the ones that are possible, and as regards the ones you don't carry out, you must be able to force me to admit that they *are* impossible." Through this crack, the whole of geometry can be made to pass into the sphere of practical work. (NR 69f.)

In addition to the necessary math and technical science necessary for the tasks they will have to undertake, Simone Weil wants these youth to have a general literary education as well. There should be "contact between the people and Greek poetry, the almost unique theme of which is misfortune!" She believes this is important because "a workman who bears the anguish of unemployment deep in the very marrow of his bones, would understand the feelings of Philoctetus when his bow is taken away from him, and the despair with which he stares at his powerless hands. He would also understand that Electra is hungry" (NR 70). She made several practical efforts to confirm this belief about the tie between Greek literature and urban workers. She taught evening courses in Le Puy and Saint-Etienne to miners and factory workers using texts of the Greek classics, *Electra, Antigone,* and some of the Greek poets. The same link should be shown between science and practical work. Andrea Nye notes that "In a Weilian revolution, the very subject matter of the sciences is transformed so that scientific theory is understood as ways of acting in the world."[15] In terms of technical scientific education she recommends combining school work with mixed apprenticeships starting at a young age (NR 76).

Simone Weil experimented in other ways—for example, on how best to teach "methods in science" as part of a philosophy course. In her first teaching post in the Lycée for Girls at Le Puy, at age twenty-one, she wanted to help her students bypass or overcome textbook learning and see the connections between sciences (for example, between mathematics and physics). She wrote to a colleague: "I offered to give a few supplementary lectures on the history of science. They [her students] agreed, and all of them attended the lectures voluntarily." She goes on to discuss what she was able to do in "six or seven extra hours," starting with early Greek science up through the infinitesimal calculus and the application of mathematics to physics. This, she said, "was followed by all of them, even those most ignorant in science, with passionate interest." It seemed a great success. The students said "it was the only method which could make [them] see science as something human, instead of a kind of dogma which you have to believe without ever really knowing why" (SL 2).

This form of education has as its aim promoting what she called a "civilized culture"—last purely seen, she thought, in the culture of Languedoc. Any civilized culture must develop the highest level of attention and find ways to hand on from generation to generation the knowledge of good and evil it has struggled to discern, its treasures in poetry and story, its science and traditions; it must come to understand the meaning of love and friendship, order and obligation, and how these are all connected with civic responsibilities and love of country.

Given her own experience of work in factories, on farms and in vineyards, her lifelong sympathy for manual laborers, and the anticipated long comeback to be made following the destruction of the war, she was particularly keen on physical labor as forming the core of any civilization. Physical labor should be the "spiritual core" or any "well-ordered social life" (NR 302). Work for her was the companion of reflection or thought; thus its importance went hand in hand with all forms of education. Two of her well-known remarks on this subject are: "Our age has its own particular mission, or vocation—the creation of a civilization founded upon the spiritual nature of work" (NR 96), and "The contemporary form of true greatness lies in a civilization found upon the spirituality of work" (NR 97). This idea she believed was "the only original thought of our time;" the only one not "borrowed from the Greeks" (NR 96). The word "spirituality" doesn't imply any particular affiliation or religion, though it does relate to what we have discussed as "motive" or "ideal" that inspires action. She writes: "A civilization based upon the spirituality of work would give to Man the very strongest possible roots in the wide universe, and would consequently be the opposite of that state in which we find ourselves now, characterized by an almost total uprootedness. Such a civilization is . . . the object to which we should aspire as the antidote to our sufferings" (NR 98f.).

We will say more about how we might aspire to a civilization rooted in the spirituality of work in our last chapter. Here it is enough to conclude that if the object of any civil society is justice, then, first of all, work roots a citizen in nature and gives a purpose or motive to life itself (toiling with nature, physically and bodily involving oneself in creation of some product for survival and for civilization), and education for civilization requires a new awareness ("attention" or "conscientization") of the very human condition in which one works and a sense of place and responsibility so that the work itself can transform suffering to hope. Education for civilization also requires the art of "transposing truths." To do this, one must possess the truth, consent to it, and place oneself at its center, then transpose what you possess into a continual struggle for justice in the world through the practice of compassion.

NOTES

1. Nye, *Philosophia*, 90.
2. Ibid., 91.
3. Paulo Freire was born in 1921 near Recife, Brazil, and died May 2, 1997, in Sao Paolo. He lived in exile from 1964 to the mid-1980s in Chile (working with UNESCO), in Cambridge, Massachusetts (as a consultant at Harvard's School of Education), and in Geneva, Switzerland (as a special consultant on education for the World Council of Churches). During this period he never lost touch with his people in Brazil and their struggle against the tyranny of their government. He is considered by many to be the most important educational philosopher of our century. Among Paulo Freire's most interesting works are *Pedagogy of the Oppressed*, trans. Myra Bergman Ramos (New York: The Seabury Press, 1968); *Pedagogy of Hope*, trans. Robert Barr (New York: Continuum, 1994); and *Letters to Cristina: Reflections on My Life and Work*, trans. Donaldo Macedo with Quilda Macedo and Alexandre Oliveira (New York: Routledge, 1996). The last of these summarizes his life and work and shows the evolution of his thinking. All the quotations to follow are from this most recent work, *Letters to Cristina*.
4. These educational theorists, all influenced by Freire, have interesting works in their own right. See Ivan Illich, *Imprisoned in the Global Classroom* (London: Writers and Readers Publishing Cooperative, 1976), *Gender* (New York: Pantheon Books, 1982), and *Deschooling Society* (New York: Harper Torchbook, 1988); Jonathan Kozol, *Death at an Early Age* (Boston: Houghton Mifflin, 1967), *Illiterate America* (New York: New American Library, 1985), and *Amazing Grace: The Lives of Children and the Conscience of a Nation* (New York: HarperCollins, 1995); and Robert Coles's five-volume *Children in Crisis* (Boston: Atlantic-Lit-

tle, Brown, 1967, 1972, 1978), *The Moral Life of Children* and *The Political Life of Children* (Boston: The Atlantic Monthly Press, 1986), and *The Spiritual Life of Children* (Boston: Houghton Mifflin Company, 1990). Robert Coles also wrote *Simone Weil: A Modern Pilgrimage* (Reading, Mass.: Addison-Wesley Publishers, 1987), which has a number of insights on her educational views and which explore some psychological motives for her ideas.

5. Freire, *Letters to Cristina*, 120.

6. Ibid., 156.

7. Ibid., 160.

8. Ibid., 182f.

9. This is a term that Simone Weil did not particularly like. She associated it with the nineteenth- and early-twentieth-century liberal idea of "progress," a kind of forward or upward historical movement (popular Marxism). This was an obstacle to the central notion of divine incarnation as a motive for "a just balance" in life.

10. Kozol chronicles his experience as a young teacher in an inner-city Boston school with an appalling physical environment—no heat, broken windows and plumbing—all contributing to a debilitating learning environment. Freire and Kozol held regular discussions while Freire was in exile in Cambridge, Mass., in 1969. Freire said of Kozol's book, *Death at an Early Age*, that it was "one of the first books in which I found myself. . . . As I read, everything in the book touched me strongly, demanding my total focus, not letting me put it down" (*Letters to Cristina*, 124).

11. Freire, *Letters to Cristina*, 124–27.

12. Ibid., 117.

13. Ibid., 90.

14. Ibid., 96f.

15. Nye, *Philosophia*, 90.

9

SIMONE WEIL, POST-HOLOCAUST JUDAISM, AND THE WAY OF COMPASSION[1]

I believe in the sun even when it is not shining, I believe in love even when feeling it not; I believe in God even when he is silent. [An inscription on the wall of a cellar in Cologne where a number of Jews hid themselves for the duration of the war.]

SIMONE WEIL'S JEWISHNESS

Implied in the story by Zvi Kolitz, "Yossel Rakover's Appeal to God," is this question: Can someone born of Jewish heritage be released from being a Jew? We pose this question of Simone Weil: Can she be released from being a Jew? In Kolitz's story, Yossel Rakover is one of the last survivors in the Warsaw Ghetto and with petrol bombs in hand he is prepared to die and hopes to take as many of his German enemies as possible with him. Waiting for his final hour he writes his last testament. In it he says:

> I believe that to be a Jew is an inborn trait. One is born a Jew exactly as one is born an artist. *It is impossible to be released from being a Jew.* That is our godly attribute that has made us a chosen people. Those who do not understand this will never understand the higher meaning of our martyrdom. If I ever doubted that God once designated us as the chosen people, I would believe now that *our tribulations have made us the chosen one.*[2]

165

Simone Weil took strong objection to the notion of "being a Jew." If she was born of Jewish parents who never practiced the Jewish religion and if she never went to a service in a synagogue or kept any Jewish holy days, can she be released from being a Jew? Like many European free thinkers born with some Jewish background in the late nineteenth and early twentieth centuries, she answered this question with a firm, though disquieting, "Yes." In her rational mind, as one de-cultured of her "Jewishness," she attempted to argue her case in several ways. But consider Yossel Rakover's view that "One is born a Jew exactly as one is born an artist." If a born artist does not practice their art, then they never blossom *as* an artist. So, too, if a born Jew does not practice their religion, then they never blossom *as* a Jew. Does their lack of practice, however, "release" them from their birth heritage?

In her famous letter to the Minister of Education regarding his si-lence on her request for a new teaching appointment in 1940, presum-ably because "the new statute on Jews" would prohibit her appointment if she were a Jew, she feigns not to know "the definition of the word 'Jew.' "[3] There begins an argument that is both characteristic of one aspect of her philosophical instincts—to ask for the meaning of a word so she can get clear on its applications[4]—and uncharacteristic of her in that it shows a certain moral blindness to what is going on around her with respect to Jews in France and elsewhere. We will return to the point of her moral blindness. She claims not to fit the statute definition and, furthermore, shows how irrelevant that definition is to being a religious person. Although she makes her point about the ambiguity of the government's statute and even its "lethal absurdity," her argument does not come close to the heart of the matter of what it means to be a Jew![5]

Can one be released from one's ethnicity or birth environment, or from one's being a Jew, by an argument? Certainly not. Where are we, then, in thinking about being a Jew and more specifically about Simone Weil's Jewishness? We are about where Rush Rhees often found him-self! How "hard it is," he said "to understand some of Simone Weil's notions"—there seems no adequate "explanation." We must keep prob-ing, asking questions, trying to gain some illumination.[6]

But why are we concerned at all with this issue of Simone Weil's Jewishness in a book about her moral and political thought? There are two main reasons for this. First, we must try to get clear on just how much her denial of her Jewishness shapes her thought as a whole—whether this point of blindness, in fact, undermines her moral integrity and diminishes the authority from which she speaks. Second, it is important to ask if it makes a fundamental difference if Simone Weil, or anyone for that matter, is a Jew, a Christian, a Muslim, etc., with respect to uncovering matters of truth and justice. Of course, the view of the faithful in these religions may lay claim to understanding *all* that is true, or true just *as* a matter tied to their particular doctrinal lenses. If, however, you have no particular lens, or you accept truths from all the lenses in search of truth and justice, then it is of less value that you stand *with* any of the given religions—or if you do stand with one, that you have a capacity to see that other religious beliefs may also reveal something of the truth of your own belief. What has been argued all along, and which we hope will be further shown in this chapter, is that in her moral and political philosophy, Simone Weil is the inheritor of several religious traditions and limits herself to no single religious point of view. Drawing from the language of classical Greek philosophy, Christianity in a very selective way, from parts of post-exilic Hebrew writings (Psalms and Job, for instance), from ancient Egyptian, Chinese, and Indian wisdom, Simone Weil develops her moral and political thought in a framework of spirituality that both crosses traditions and gathers up the seeds of truth in all these. Having said this, it remains particularly troubling, because of the nature of the Jewish persecution in Europe in the 1930s through World War II, that Simone Weil should have so many negative and often ill-informed opinions about Jews and Judaism. So, we must probe further.

Stronger charges against Simone Weil concerning her remarks against Judaism and being a Jew are that she represents a classic example of the Jewish "self-hatred" shown by other late-nineteenth- and early-twentieth-century Jewish intellectuals.[7] "Self-hating Jews," says Sander Gilman in his brilliant study, *Jewish Self-Hatred*, "respond either by claiming special abilities in the discourse of the reference group or by rejecting it completely and creating a new discourse, uncontaminated, they believe, by their exclusion from it."[8] Simone Weil certainly claims no special abilities in the discourse of the Jews, but some might argue that she manifests self-hatred in her complete rejection and in "creating a new discourse." There is no question that her originality as a philosopher is to have created a new discourse, but it would be wrong to imply that her new discourse was a self-conscious—even subconscious—rejection of her Jewish heritage. She never really knew, let alone understood, a Jewish heritage to reject. Her French language, her education, her political struggles arguably removed her from the kind of "Jewish environment" that prevailed in Germany and Eastern Europe from the late 1800s into the 1930s.[9] If she was repressing her Jewishness, it was not by inventing a new discourse.

By her use of such notions as the "impersonal," which is her mark of a human being, she is avoiding some of the worst features found in literature which discuss self-hatred. She does not avoid being a Jew, however, by assigning a new definition to herself—a different other to the otherness of being a Jew. She rather attempts to transcend all types—personality or ethnic or religious—in favor of the impersonal, of all humans' being *anonymous*.[10] This is an important point to which we will return.

Since to adequately scrutinize this issue of her "self-hatred," as George Steiner himself admits, "is (as perhaps, in the case of Wittgenstein) . . . immensely complicated, requiring . . . the most scrupulous delicacy of inquiry" and provisionality,[11] we must pursue some different lines of investigation—probe in other directions.

In her highly original, though rather speculative thesis, Rachel Feldhay Brenner argues that a "significant subtext" of Simone Weil's death and resistance writings were her denials and rejection of her ethnicity, her baptism, and her womanhood. I have commented earlier on Brenner's point of "Weil's complete silence regarding women's social oppression and exploitation" and her "dissociation from gender identity."[12] On both these points I believe Brenner's arguments to be shortsighted and lacking in their larger understanding of Simone Weil's overall moral point of view. Regarding the denial and rejection of Simone Weil's Jewishness and baptism into the Catholic Church, however, Brenner's case is both complex and interesting. On these points we will survey a few of Brenner's key arguments; then we will look at Simone Weil's position in two further ways.

First of all, Brenner rejects both extremes found in the literature: those that seek to either "attenuate the extremity of her anti-Jewish pronouncements" but nevertheless claimed "she was more Jewish than she believed she was,"[13] and those who portray Simone Weil as "a pathologically imbalanced, deeply disturbed, self-hating Jew."[14] Seeking a middle ground, Brenner explores the thesis that Simone Weil "almost deliberately" chooses to remain ignorant of Jewish life, and in so doing, adopted a course of resistance to the crises of her times which ignored the specific persecution of Jews, but nevertheless pursued a course of self-renunciation to her death for the sake of France. Part of her course of self-renunciation was cloaked in her insistence that her religious life had always been Christian. Even her denial of baptism into the Catholic Church is construed by Brenner as part of her deliberate denial of her Jewishness, for to acknowledge certain doctrines that "membership" in the church entails would imply acceptance, by inference, of "her kinship with the Jewish community."[15] Her choice was to be alone in her spiritual journey, not a sojourner with either the Jewish or Christian communities. Brenner cites a letter to Father Perrin where she says: "I feel that it is necessary and ordained that I should be alone, a stranger and an exile in relation to every human circle without exception. . . . To be lost to view in it is not to form a part of it, and my capacity to mix with all of them implies that I belong to none" (WG 54f.). Brenner concludes:

> In a paradoxical way, Weil's defiance of the forces of terror complied with the oppressors' plan for eliminating the Jewish people. By constructing a life of loneliness and solitude, Weil attained a tragic state of self-liberation from all human contact. Her self-imposed alienation allowed her to ignore the fact that, as a Jew, she had become the object of destruction. At the same time, her social exclusion corroborated the despotic decree that set Jews apart from human society.[16]

There is a second, more speculative level in Brenner's analysis. She believes that Simone Weil not only "almost deliberately" denied her Jewish identity, but at the same time consciously chose to deny her physical needs as a self-sacrificial act: "The desire to obliterate her Jewishness therefore emerges concomitantly with the desire to destroy her body as an offering for the general good."[17] Brenner then proceeds to tie Simone Weil's rejection of her Jewishness with her controversial death through her understanding of "de-creation" and her "Example of Prayer" where she prays for complete physical disfunction and that she be "devoured by God, transformed into Christ's substance, and given for food to afflicted men" (see FLN 243–4). "Could it be," queries Brenner, "that Weil's pleading for deafness, blindness, and muteness actually communicated the desire to neither hear, see, nor acknowledge her identity mirrored in the unfolding affliction of the Jews?"[18] This desire is corroborated by her last desperate pleas to be literally thrown— "parachuted"—into the front lines with her "suicidal" nursing scheme (see SL 145–53). The strong suggestion is that Simone Weil's Jewishness is "the main source of her affliction," from which she alienates herself and seeks martyrdom for another cause, France.[19] To make this argument plausible, one would have to show connections between Simone Weil's frequent discussions of affliction, along with the fact that it can be a condition of any and all human beings, and specific denials of her Jewishness. Those connections are not concretely in the literature— especially before 1940.

In her analysis Brenner seems to have lost sight of a larger view of Simone Weil's thought—her central moral and political view which runs consistently through her thought from the earliest essays to her last writings—*that is, her devotion to the other, to the anonymity of each individual without losing sight of their particularity as human beings.* Thus Jew and non-Jew, Frenchman and German, Gypsy or suffering guardian are all to be regarded with an equal degree of attention and compassion. Simone Weil's view is not nearly as self-serving as Brenner's argument assumes.

Brenner's analysis is one of the boldest attempts so far to account for Simone Weil's death and her denial of her Jewishness. The available evidence from her own life and writing, however, evoke a plethora of possible readings. There is in the last three years of Simone Weil's life enormous upheaval and frustration which she masked by plunging herself into intense study and writing. She was in flight from the invading Germans largely because of her Jewish background while, at the same time, trying to figure out how to return to the fray and resist the fascists. While in Marseilles and New York City she wrote intensely about her relationship to Christianity. Her study of "Oriental wisdom" at this time made it clear that there was no room for her within the Catholic Church, and that her faith was one that spread across and beyond practicing within a single tradition. Her *Letter to a Priest,* written in New York, is her most comprehensive critique of religion and most sustained case for a broadly based spirituality consistent with her view of God's relation to nature and the human condition. We will comment further on this below and in our last chapter.

We will draw attention to one last theme of Brenner's interesting analysis—the larger context into which she places her four women re-sisters: Edith Stein, Simone Weil, Anne Frank, and Etty Hillesum. In the conclusion to her book, Brenner writes:

> The women's standpoints with regard to their persecution, their religious beliefs, their destiny, and their art were infused with em-pathic concern about the world in crisis, and this concern manifested itself at three levels.
>
> As individuals, they demonstrated solidarity, sympathy, and iden-tification with the suffering victims of the war (Weil identified with the suffering French people; the other women's sense of solidarity, as "catastrophe Jews," was with the persecuted Jews). As post-Emanci-pation, assimilated Jews, all four were deeply distressed about the dis-integration of the warring world's humanistic, enlightened image. And as adherents to the humanistic ideal, they were preoccupied with envisioning and planning for the postwar world—which they knew they would not live to see.[20]

The background for Brenner's whole thesis is that all these thinkers fit the mold of enlightenment thinkers, following a path of other mod-ern humanists. But this merely describes a milieu into which these women were born. In Simone Weil's own personal political and spiritual instincts, as we have seen, she was far from being a humanist. In fact, she criticizes humanism and any idea of progress as a perversion of a true Greek Renaissance, and her political and spiritual views, though not easily classifiable, are more conservative than any to be found in the liberal humanist tradition. Thus, of the three levels expressed, Simone Weil only clearly fits the first, i.e., she "demonstrated solidarity, sympa-thy, and identification with the suffering victims of the war." But even if we place her into the category of "post-Emancipation, assimilated Jew," Simone Weil never grieved over the collapse of the "world's hu-manistic, enlightened image," and though she was "preoccupied with envisioning and planning for the postwar world," she did not do so from "the humanistic ideal." Her ideal was far more radically centered in the notion of divine incarnation as the motive for all good action in the world: "Compassion is natural, but it is stifled by the instinct of self-preservation. It is only the possession of the entire soul by supernatural love that revives the activity of compassion" (FLN 318). Very few, if any, humanists would embrace such a remark.

There is no doubt that contradictions and paradoxes abound in Simone Weil's own understanding of Jews and her Jewishness, and explanations are hard, if not impossible. Still in search of illumination let us explore two further lines of argument. The first will be to look at the tension between her view of "Jews" and how she understands the Old Testament's place in her list of authentic texts that reveal some divine inspiration. The second will be to pursue a course suggested by Anna Freud, and engage in some speculation of our own about Simone Weil's possible response to the Holocaust had she survived the war.

In a notorious entry near the end of her notebooks, Simone Weil does not mince words about her hatred of Jews, calling them "the poison of uprooting personified." I will quote the remark in full because it embraces her attitude toward virtually all she believes uprooting and evil: Rome, Christendom, the failed Renaissance, her distrust for the eighteenth-century enlightenment with its "lie about progress," the uprooting of colonialism, capitalism and totalitarianism:

> The Jews—that handful of uprooted individuals—have been responsible for the uprooting of the whole terrestrial globe. The part they played in Christianity turned Christendom into something uprooted with respect to its own past. The Renaissance attempt at a rerooting failed, because it was of an anti-Christian inspiration. The trend of "enlightenment"—eighteenth century, 1789, laicization, etc.—increased this uprooting to a still infinitely greater extent with the lie about progress. And uprooted Europe went about uprooting the rest of the world by colonial conquest. Capitalism and totalitarianism form part of this progressive development of uprooting; the Jew-haters, of course, spread Jewish influence. The Jews are the poison of uprooting personified. But before they began uprooting by spreading this poison, Assyria in the East and Rome in the West had already started doing so by the sword. (N 576–77)

One can only speculate how she thought "Jews" played a role in all this uprooting, but the common denominator is the use and abuse of a will to power and the absence of any "spiritual life" or a discernable "inspiration" toward the good in each of these "beasts."

Curiously, at about the same time she made the above notebook entry, she was working out for herself a very elaborate and complex hermeneutical scheme for understanding the Old Testament and what divine inspiration it may contain. In a letter to Jean Wahl in late 1942, just before sailing from New York to London, she writes the following (this among "thoughts hastily set down in no order or sequence" which filled "notebook after notebook"—including all those thoughts collected in N and FLN). What does this following long entry tell us? She had her list of those sources in which would be found divine inspiration and truth—many of which we have noted before, but this list is particularly comprehensive:

> ancient mythologies, in the philosophies of Pherekydes, Thales, Anaximander, Heraclitus, Pythagoras, Plato, and the Greek Stoics; in Greek poetry of the great age; in universal folklore; in the Upanishads and the Bhagavad-Gita; in the Chinese Taoist writings and in certain currents of Buddhism; in what remains of the sacred writings of Egypt; in the dogmas of the Christian faith and in the writings of the greatest Christian mystics, especially St. John of the Cross; and in certain heresies, especially the Cathar and Manichaean tradition. (SL 159)

Following this list comes what she says is the contribution that "the Jews" have made to this inspiration:

> As regards the Jews, I think that Moses knew this wisdom and refused it because, like Maurras, he conceived religion as a simple instrument of national greatness; but when the Jewish nation had been destroyed by Nebuchadnezzar the Jews, completely disoriented and scattered among many nations, received this wisdom in the form of foreign influences and introduced it, so far as was possible, into their religion. Thus it inspired, in the Old Testament, the book of Job . . . most of the Psalms, the Song of Songs, the sapiential books . . . and what is called the "second Isaiah," and some of the minor prophets, and the books of Daniel and Tobias. Almost all the rest of the Old Testament is a tissue of horrors. (SL 160; see also WG 160 where she repeats this list which "contain[s] an incomparable expression of the beauty of the world.")

There is here for all of us to see, "wisdom" or "truth" to be found in some of the Hebrews' writings—particularly in the post-exilic writings. We could say that she is not totally insensitive to these writings; she did draw some personal inspiration from some Old Testament texts. But at the same time she surely is abusive and ignorant in her reading of what she calls the more historic books, the "impure" parts of the Old Testament.[21] On the side of inspiration, for example, she believed there is no greater source of divine inspiration than the words of the Psalmists sung in Gregorian plainchant. These few Hebrew writings, if they could be culled out from the "tissue of horrors" found in those texts which served as instruments of "national greatness," would find their way into her canon of great sacred texts to be taught in schools. She believed that religions were a treasury of human thought that should be part of any curriculum; that "religion has at all times and in all countries, save quite recently in certain parts of Europe,[22] played a dominant role in the development of human culture, thought, and civilization. An educational course in which no reference is made to religion is an absurdity" (NR 92). She even goes so far as to suggest that eternal wisdom is like the "Ark of the Covenant, the Covenant, the visible and palpable promise here below, the sure basis of hope. That is the truth which bites at our hearts every time we are penetrated by the beauty of the world. That is the truth that bursts forth in matchless accents of joy in the beautiful and pure parts of the Old Testament, in Greece . . . in China with Lao-Tse, in the Hindu scriptures, in Egyptian remains." This wisdom lies hidden, but will appear to us, "before our very eyes, clothed in our own knowledge, if one day God opens our eyes, as he did Hagar's" (NR 285).

Levinas has real trouble with Simone Weil's selective hermeneutic, with her taking only what he says are the "digestible" parts for her purposes. He bristles at the idea that she thought the digestible parts are "exceptions" and were shaped by "foreign influences."[23]

What seems most disturbing to Simone Weil is that the eternal "wisdom" that runs through all these different sources has come under periodic threat of destruction from the spiritless "brutes" whose "pride and will to domination" seen in "the Spartans, the Romans, the Hebrews *before Nebuchadnezzar,* and probably the Assyrians. . . . [and] today, Hitler and many others . . . trying to abolish [the truth] throughout the whole world" (SL 160f., emphasis added). With, however, less than six months left in her life and with the intense pressures of her final political writings in London, the details of neither the above hermeneutic nor how the Jews were such a poisonous uprooting force in history were to be worked out. One suspects she may have only dug herself into a deeper hole. On the other hand, in his critical reflections, Rush Rhees had this to say:

I imagine that if she had lived longer she might have forced herself to see more of what was good in Israel. Jesus interpreted the supreme commandments differently from Moses (and he could be more bitter in his criticisms of the Scribes and the Pharisees than Simone Weil was towards the Jewish faith), but he does seem to have thought that in some sense the word of God was to be found there; and I imagine that this might have made her try to find more favourable readings of some of them. But I think the main part of her criticism would have remained.[24]

And, of course, what would follow her imminent death were the mountains of varied polemics and interpretations we have today regarding her Jewishness.

We have only glimpses of how words from the Old Testament "bite at her heart." For example, words from Isaiah haunt her right at the point where her self-inflicted starvation began. Probably in January 1943 in London she wrote a rather desperate letter to Maurice Schumann, "begging" to be sent into France—"I cannot help being shameless . . . like a beggar . . . I have no argument except to cry my needs" (SL 179). She believed that only such a mission to France would save her life— even if the mission meant certain death. She wanted to be a witness to a love she believed she lacked but which might flow through her "like a continual fountain of supernatural energy." She says, "There are some words in Isaiah which are terrible for me: They that love God 'shall run and not be weary; and they shall walk and not faint.' This makes it physically impossible for me to forget, even for a moment, that I am not of their number" (SL 170). She later connects these words of Isaiah with a comment on "saintliness." She continues, "I don't want you to do me the injustice of imagining that I affect saintliness—you once seemed to say something to that effect. Above all I don't want at any price that you should think better of me than the truth allows" (SL 175). Saintliness, she believes, is the minimum for a Christian and that most Christians place it as a virtue above and beyond any expectations they may have for their own religious life. Much interior struggle is involved in everyone to try and restore the notion that what God wants is for us to express God's sanctity. Thus "I" must withdraw and allow this sanctity to flow through me. This is what is meant by "running without being weary and walking without fainting." But it is only if she is released to run that she will not die; otherwise she sees her imminent demise due to the "moral, intellectual and physical limits" that being in London has placed upon her. When this "triple limit" is reached, she says, I shall report that I have nothing more to contribute" (SL 178). Thus a Jewish prophet presses in on her near her death with words that she struggled to give expression to all of her life; that the madness of love is the only true way to run and not be weary. Without such a race she had only to die. Without such an opportunity for God to flow through her in a final mad act, she would not meet what for her was an obligation. There is no denying the tension, even the contradiction, that flows through her words about Jews and the inspiration that might be taken from the holy word of the Jews.

Lastly, we will take up a more speculative line in our search for illumination and understanding of her Jewishness. We take our lead from a remark of Anna Freud. Freud says: "I suspect that if Simone Weil had lived she might have found other matters to preoccupy her than this one of her Jewishness, or she would have altered the way she thought of that part of herself. I hope so! . . . She couldn't simply walk away from it [her Jewish ancestry]."[25]

We agree that just as she could not *argue* her way out of her Jewishness, neither could she "simply walk away from it" as she seemed to want to do. We are left to speculate on how she might have "altered the way she thought about that part of herself."

Simone Weil clearly is a person of spiritual substance, but not easily categorized as a Jew or Christian, or something else, even though she said "if there is a religious tradition which I regard as my patrimony, it is the Catholic tradition."[26] This is said in the same essay she denies being a Jew, but her reasons for saying she is Catholic no more make her a Christian than her denials release her from being a Jew. She does have some specific things to say about what it is to be a religious person, and we will see in what ways these are compatible with "being a Jew" as expressed by some post-Holocaust Jewish thinkers.

In the end, Simone Weil did not wish so much to be something other than a Jew as much as she wanted to be regarded simply as a human being—as "her" in an "impersonal" way—not as a Jew or a Christian, and to regard others in the same way. "Every man," she writes, "who has once touched the level of the impersonal is charged with a responsibility towards all human beings" (SE 16). What is sacred in a human being is, she says, "him" or "her," "the whole of him [or her]. The arms, the eyes, the thoughts, everything" (SE 9). Furthermore, each human being has an inherent passion, identified deeply with their very soul. In this sense of being human, she transcends any particular religion, as those are characterized by various traditions.

In her sense of the "impersonal" she is neither Jew nor Greek, Christian nor Buddhist, Platonist nor Cathar. What is essential to being a human being could never be realized within any of these specific forms—all bear the cloak of a bad collective. She could only be one of these or all of these in an anonymous way. If, indeed, she is none of these and possibly all of them anonymously, then the question of release is not a meaningful question. But before we close off our speculations with such paradoxical conclusions, let us explore several issues germane to her thinking about being a human being, and to thinking about being a Jew as that is understood in the context of post-Holocaust Judaism. We return to where we began this chapter, to Yossel Rakover's Jewishness.

YOSSEL RAKOVER'S JEWISHNESS

"Warsaw, April 28, 1943.

"I, Yossel, son of David Rakover of Tarnopol, a Hasid of the Rabbi of Ger and a descendant of the great, pious, and righteous families of Rakover and Meisel, inscribe these lines as the houses of the Warsaw ghetto go up in flames."[27] There is no doubt about his claim to his Jewish heritage! Through the darkness he and his family suffered and the "spiritual level" to which he had sunk—"Life is a tragedy, death a savior;" he says, "man a calamity, the beast an ideal; the day a horror, the night—relief."[28]—he still writes: "I cannot say that my relationship to God has remained unchanged after everything I have lived through, but I can say with absolute certainty that my belief in Him has not changed a hair's breadth."[29]

What has changed in Yossel Rakover's relationship to God is his awareness of God's absence from him and his people. He says: "It is a time when God has veiled His countenance from the world, sacrificing mankind to its wild instincts."[30]

He will die "forsaken by the God in whom he believed unshakeable."[31] Before his death he wishes "to speak to [his] Lord as a living man, a simple, living person who had the great but tragic honor of being a Jew.''[32] In his last appeal he sees his Jewishness as a source of pride.

> I should be ashamed to belong to the people who spawned and raised the criminals who are responsible for the deeds that have been perpetrated against us. . . .
>
> I am happy to belong to the unhappiest of all peoples of the world, whose precepts represent the loftiest and most beautiful of all morality and laws.[33] In the midst of his forbearance, with great presence of mind, he asks God:
>
> O Lord—and this question burns in me like a consuming fire—*What more, O, what more must transpire before You unveil Your countenance again to the world?*
>
> You should—You must—forgive those members of Your people who, in their misery, have turned from You.
>
> I tell You this because I do believe in You, believe in You more strongly than ever, because now I know that You are my Lord, because after all You are not, You cannot after all be the God of those whose deeds are the most horrible expression of ungodliness.
>
> If You are not *my* Lord, then whose Lord are You? The Lord of the murderers?
>
> If those that hate me and murder me are so benighted, so evil, what then am I if not the person who reflects something of Your light, of your goodness?[34]

Yossel Rakover's last lament is against those who remained "silent in the face of murder . . . those who express their sympathy with the drowning man but refuse to rescue him"; those are the ones who deserve God's punishment—the indifferent and hypocritical.

He ends his appeal: "I die peacefully, but not complacently; persecuted, but not enslaved; embittered but not cynical; a believer, but not a supplicant; a lover of God, but no blind amen-sayer of His."[35]

Simone Weil would understand Yossel Rakover's Appeal to God. She would understand his awareness of God's absence.

She would understand his belief that suffering is a sign of God's favor.

She would understand his belief that God is on the side of the victim.

She would understand his clarity about the silence, indifference, and irresponsibility of those who are accomplices to violence.

She would understand his view that those who are silent deserve punishment more than "warriors" or those involved in battle.

And she would understand what he means when he says he is a "person who reflects something of [God's] light, of [God's] goodness"—one through whom God's energy passes.

LEVINAS ON YOSSEL RAKOVER'S APPEAL

Emmanuel Levinas recognizes in Yossel Rakover's appeal "the true spirit of traditional, mature Judaism," but uses the story as an occasion for a "polemical" response.[36] For Levinas and other Jewish thinkers who survived the Holocaust, Judaism requires some fundamental reinterpreting for generations whose "Hebrew learning has faded" and who "have lost touch with our sources."[37] But Levinas's polemic has a barbed edge for a wider audience of French intellectuals. He says that Yossel Rakover's appeal conveys an "attitude that reflects something better than the reading habits of intellectuals—something superior to the handful of concepts borrowed, for instance, from Simone Weil, who, as everyone in Paris knows, is the latest fad in religious terminology. What this text provides is Jewish learning modestly understated, yet full of assurance; it represents a deep, authentic experience of the spiritual life."[38] Levinas reserves special scorn for Simone Weil and her particular ignorance of Judaism later in his talk.

The most important question that this story as an expression of post-Holocaust Judaism provides an answer for is: What is the meaning of the suffering of the innocent? Levinas concurs with Yossel Rakover that, first and foremost, such suffering as the Jews experienced implies the absence of God, but this does not spell the end of religion for a mature Jew. What a Jew finds as "deep and authentic"—as truly spiritual—in such an experience is "mediated by teaching, by the Torah."[39] Levinas says:

> It is the hour when the just person has nowhere to go in the outside world; when no institution affords him protection; when even the comforting sense of the divine presence, experienced in a childlike person's piety, is withdrawn; when the only victory available to the individual lies in his conscience, which necessarily means: in suffering.

> This is the specifically Jewish meaning of suffering—one that never takes on the quality of a mystical expiation for the sins of the world. The condition in which victims find themselves in a disordered world, that is to say, in a world where goodness does not succeed in being victorious, is suffering. This reveals a God who, while refusing to manifest himself in any way as a help, directs his appeal to the full maturity of the integrally responsible person.[40]

The focus for being a mature Jew, then, rests with "the integrally responsible person"—not with God unveiling God's self to a person or to Israel. God's revelation is already known in the teachings. Thus to follow Torah takes primacy over love of God especially when God is absent. Levinas says that what makes Judaism so profound is that it does not depend on "direct contact with the sacred." If that were the case, then in the wake of God's absence all would be lost. Being a Jew depends, as Levinas says, on "a trust not based on the triumph of any institution, but on the inner clarity of the morality conveyed by the Torah. A difficult journey, this, already being undertaken in spirit and truth, and which has nothing to prefigure! [He then exclaims:] Simone Weil, you have never understood anything about the Torah!"[41]

If this is true and central to what it means to be a Jew, then it is clear why Simone Weil could not understand her Jewishness—she had "never understood anything about the Torah!" In fact, says Levinas, she had "ignored [Judaism] in a right royal way."[42] We must look once again at just what is involved in understanding the Torah or the "authentic experience of the spiritual life" for the Jew and whether such an understanding might be framed in terms independent of understanding the Torah.

In going back to Levinas on Yossel Rakover, Levinas says: "The spiritual becomes present not by way of palpable presence, but by absence; God is concrete, not by means of incarnation, but by means of the Law; and his [God's] majesty is not the felt experience of [God's] sacred mystery. [God's] majesty does not provoke fear and trembling, but fills us with higher thoughts."[43] We have here a direct challenge to Christian conceptions of the incarnation as well as the larger notion of God's direct revelation—ethics replaces immediate experience of God. If, however, God is absent for Simone Weil as it is for Yossel Rakover and Levinas, then the very notion of incarnation needs some revision.

We will try to show later that Simone Weil gives us such a revisionary account. The ethical perspective of Levinas's Jewish spirituality, his "higher thoughts," relate to such commands found in Torah as: Love your neighbor, be a just and righteous human being, remember to keep the Sabbath . . . and these no matter what or however difficult the task may seem. We must become, as Levinas says,

> capable of trusting in an absent God. . . . Matured by a faith derived from the Torah, [Yossel Rakover] blames God for his unbounded majesty and excessive demands. He will love him inspite of God's every attempt to discourage his love. But Yossel . . . cries out, "do not put the bow under too much strain" . . . God must unveil his countenance, justice and power must find each other again, just institutions are needed on this earth. But only the person who recognized the veiled God can demand his revelation. . . .
>
> To love the Torah more than God—this means precisely: to find a personal God against whom it is possible to revolt, that is to say, one for whom one can die.[44]

There is perhaps no more forceful statement of what is called post-Holocaust Judaism than Levinas's summary of Yossel Rakover's appeal. Post-Holocaust Judaism must be "capable of trusting in an absent God," live a faith derived from Torah, and continue steadfast in love even when discouraged to do so. Only then is humanity prepared for God, in God's own way, to "unveil his countenance." We have here a "personal God against whom it is possible to revolt."

SIMONE WEIL AND POST-HOLOCAUST JUDAISM

Just as Simone Weil noted that Hector in the *Iliad*, already slain, lay "far from the hot baths" prepared for his return, so all humans who suffer are far from the "hot baths" of their home (IL 4). She recounts a "force" so devastating in the *Iliad*—with its intended parallels to those who suffer under Hitler's tyranny and to all who "bow [their] neck to force" in wars—that it exhausts the capacity for reflection, justice, and prudence. In such conditions of oppression, both victim and those who victimize fail to see their relations with other human beings; their sight for others is blinded, all sense of limit lost, their souls are near annihilation. This is what she calls "affliction"—"a device for pulverizing the soul" (SE 27). Such violence, she says, "obliterates anybody who feels its touch" (IL 19, and see SNLG 171f.).

Where does Yossel Rakover find the strength to endure such "pulverizing," even to love an absent God? It is a sense of human dignity, an ethic born of reflection on and practice of Torah, that carries Yossel forward. And where does Simone Weil locate a strength to endure in the *Iliad's* desolate "picture of uniform horror"? She locates strength to endure in a "few luminous moments" when a human momentarily "possesses his soul" and finds room for "courage and love." These "luminous moments" are not contingent on "palpable" divine revelations. These come with those "intervals of hesitation, wherein lies all our consideration for our brothers in humanity"; they are found in attention to the enormity of the suffering. Love and justice remain possible only if the affliction has not totally annihilated the soul and if what is human can still cry out "why am I being hurt?" The cry is a revolt against God (SNLG 196f.).

Simone Weil says that the great enigma of human life is affliction (SNLG 171). She says, "It is not surprising that the innocent are killed, tortured, driven from their country, made destitute or reduced to slavery, put in concentration camps or prison cells, since there are criminals to perform such actions. . . . But it *is* surprising that God should have given affliction the power to seize the very souls of the innocent and to possess them as sovereign master" (SNLG 171f.). God forsaking the innocent and allowing their souls to be crushed seems too much for many survivors of the Holocaust—God's absence seems unequivocal, and the enigmatic feature of this is how to even imagine that God would or even could "unveil God's countenance again." She writes:

> Affliction causes God to be absent for a time, more absent than a dead man, more absent than light in the utter darkness of a cell. A kind of horror submerges the whole soul. During this absence there is nothing to love. What is terrible is that if, in this darkness where there is nothing to love, the soul ceases to love, God's absence becomes final. The soul has to go on loving in the void, or at least to go on wanting to love, though it may be only with an infinitesimal part of itself. Then, one day, God will come to show himself to this soul and to reveal the beauty of the world to it, as in the case of Job. (SNLG 172)

What enables the soul "to go on loving in the void"? For Levinas and Yossel Rakover it is possible because of the practiced ethic of Torah. For Simone Weil some form of grace (supernatural intervention) is necessary combined with what hope remains in an afflicted human soul—that "infinitesimal" desire, a "wanting to love." It is at the point she calls the "greatest distance from God," out of the silence, that this desire to love arises:

> He who is capable not only of crying out but also of listening will hear the answer. Silence is the answer. This is the eternal silence for which Vigny bitterly reproached God; but Vigny had no right to say how the just man should reply to the silence, for he was not one of the just. The just man loves. He who is capable not only of listening but also of loving hears this silence as the word of God. (SNLG 197)

Yossel Rakover is such a "just man" and, as he loves Torah in the absence of God, he is demanding God's revelation. As Levinas says: "God must unveil his countenance, justice and power must find each other again." But Simone Weil has no Torah to love, and she must find other sources wherein "justice and power find each other again." One of those sources for her is at the "foot of the cross," the furthest distance from God, in the affliction of Christ. There is this deep Christological strain in several of her last writings, but equally strong in her later writings is a less Christological, more universal moral strain that has a greater compatibility with Torah and with the compassion of the Buddha or as found in Taoist writings. To this latter strain we now turn.

The epigram to the Zvi Kolitz story with which this chapter begins reads: "I believe in the sun even when it is not shining, I believe in love even when feeling it not; I believe in God even when he is silent." This epigram could serve as a credo for Simone Weil's moral philosophy.

I believe in the sun even when it is not shining: *The sun* and its power of illumination is the great metaphor of Plato that resonates throughout her work. There is, a priori, a horizon of grace, a periphery of light—always ready to dawn—even when not remotely in sight. It is because of this dawn, somewhere in the horizon, that a "few luminous moments" are possible.

I believe in love even when feeling it not: *Love* coupled with *justice*—or the way of justice as compassion—is the single most dynamic principle in her moral thought. These two terms form one concept which she says "bathe the work [of the *Iliad*] in their light," even though this epic is one "of extremes and of unjust acts of violence." Love and justice "bathe" all her works; they are "accents" that resound in darkness and heighten the tension continually at play between the divine and the human. An enigma, however, in Simone Weil's understanding of love is that although a powerful and dynamic moral principle, it is also a notion that is singularly ambiguous in her own personal life.

I believe in God even when He is silent: *God* is a more concrete image of the sun, antecedent to and uniquely embedded within the human world. As we have seen, God is known only in God's absence, or in silence, or in the beauty of this world, or in praise or through compassion. She says that "Praise to God and compassion for creatures . . . is the same movement of the heart" (FLN 102) and that "God is absent from the world, except in the existence in this world of those in whom His love is alive. Therefore they ought to be present in the world through compassion. Their compassion is the visible presence of God here below. . . . Compassion is what spans [the] abyss which creation has opened between God and the creature. It is the rainbow" (FLN 103).

For the Jew to love the Torah goes beyond a strictly "law-based morality." As so many recent Jewish philosophers remind us: to love the Torah places responsibility for being a Jew on *deeds*, on love and compassion, and on justice and gratitude in worship. For Abraham Heschel being a Jew means "to bring God back into the world, into our lives. To worship is to expand the presence of God in the world. To have faith in God is to reveal what is concealed."[45] Torah for a Jew must embrace the tradition of *kavanah*—a principle that combines law and love, or in Heschel's words, like Torah it is "the art of setting a deed to inner music" or "intoning" God into our hearts.[46] God will arise, God's countenance will be unveiled, says Levinas, when one mediates one's relationships through one's neighbor: "The justice rendered to the Other, my neighbor, gives me unsurpassable proximity to God. It is as intimate as the prayer and the liturgy, which, without justice, are nothing."[47]

Simone Weil to her discredit had *no* understanding of Torah as did a practiced Jew like Yossel Rakover. But as a moral philosopher she did understand human suffering and compassion in the form of love and justice. Her moral philosophy was premised on a compassion-based morality as opposed to either a law-based morality or a rights-based morality. It is in this compassion-based morality that her moral philosophy and post-Holocaust Jewish morality connect; they enter into conversation with one another. Both emphasize practice, the practice of love and justice, of praise and compassion. Both are keenly aware of human suffering and affliction in the face of God's absence. Yet, curiously, both find God in the neighbor, as the true *other*, and both also find their true humanity there. Like Levinas, Simone Weil finds "unsurpassable proximity to God" through love and justice toward her neighbor. It is here, however, that the question of her moral blindness returns to haunt us. If she sees God in the face of the other, in love of one's neighbor, why did she not see her neighbor in the Jews being deported to death camps? Her own compassion-motivated morality leads us to expect more from her about what she knew was happening to Jews. This surely is a moral failing.

For the Jew and for Simone Weil, creation has room for both success and failure, good and harm-doing. If God appears absent or withdrawn to us, it is because we are seeking our own way and not struggling hard enough to love our neighbor and establish a relationship with God. We must, as Levinas says, establish our wisdom and goodness and holiness as creatures of God; we must retain our own being as well, especially in the face of God's absence. Rabbi Joseph Soloveitchik says our task is "to bring down the Divine Presence to the lower world, to this vale of tears." This, he says, is "the mystery of *Tzimtzum*. . . . [where we] reside together with [God] in this world, and it is only through cultivating that togetherness in the here and now that [we] can acquire a share of the world to come."[48] In the mystery of *Tzimtzum*, God created the world then withdrew into God's self in order to leave a creation that could of its own will establish a relationship with God. Simone Weil's notion of "decreation" and a human's "willing to love" even in affliction is a variation of this "mystery" (see FLN 297).

Strains of the view of the spiritual life we have been discussing in these last few paragraphs are found in some post-Holocaust Judaism and in Simone Weil. In Yossel Rakover's appeal to God and in Simone Weil we have what might be called an *apophatic spirituality*. Neither can envision God definitively; their religious speech is never finished. But in silence, in rebellion against God, in attention to the *other*, and in praise and compassion are the recognizable forms of a genuine spiritual life.

Even if Simone Weil had not understood the Torah —in part because it was not a part of her practiced life and in part because she associated it too closely with other forms of oppressive religious and political ideologies—she had moved past both Judaism and Christianity as both seemed manifest to her in her world. She may never have come to understand Torah as did Yossel Rakover and Levinas, but for her that was irrelevant as she *apophatically* struggled toward discovery of love, justice, and the silent compassion of God.

Many of the moral ideas that Simone Weil develops in her own inimical way, burdened as they are at times with an overzealous Christology, may be found differently in the very tradition that was her heritage at birth, which she denied—even vehemently rejected—but from which she may never be released.

NOTES

1. About half, mostly material found in the second half, of this chapter was previously published under the title "Simone Weil and Post-Holocaust Judaism," *Cahiers Simone Weil* 20, no. 1 (March 1997): 48–63.

2. In Frans Jozef van Beeck, S. J., *Loving the Torah More than God? Toward a Catholic Appreciation of Judaism* (Chicago: Loyola University Press, 1989), 22, emphasis added.

3. Weil, "What is a Jew? A Letter to a Minister of Education," in *The Simone Weil Reader*, ed. George A. Panichas (New York: McKay, 1977), 79f.

4. In her 1937 essay "The Power of Words," she had written: "Words with content and meaning are not murderous. . . . But when empty words are given capital letters [like she believed the Statute's definition of 'Jew' to be], then . . . men will begin shedding blood for them" (SE 156). The term "Jew" as it was then being used had become what she called a "lethal absurdity." As noted in chapter one above, she concludes that "to clarify thought, to discredit the intrinsically meaningless words, and to define the use of others by precise analysis—to do this, strange though it may appear, might be a way of saving human lives" (SE 156).

5. Her arguments in this letter have been discussed in several sources and shown to be not only weak, but perhaps even not very serious. See Coles, *Simone Weil*, 43–62.

6. Rhees, *Discussions of Simone Weil*.

7. This charge is made strongly by George Steiner in "The Self-hatred of Simone Weil," *Times Literary Supplement*, 4 June 1993: 4, when he says: "In

Weil's detestation of her own ethnic identity, in her strident denunciation of the cruelty and 'imperialism' of the God of Abraham and of Moses, in her very nearly hysterical repugnance in the face of what she termed the excess of Judaism in the Catholicism she, finally, refused to join, the traits of a classical Jewish self-loathing are carried to fever pitch. In that uncomely respect, Weil is of the family of Marx, of Otto Weininger and, at passing moments, of Karl Kraus." Robert Coles cautions: "I don't think we do Simone Weil justice by glossing over this dark hour of her life, by failing to give it thorough scrutiny. [And asks:] Had she succumbed to the self-hatred of the victim?" (Coles, *Simone Weil,* 49). See also Thomas Nevin, *Simone Weil, Portrait of a Self-Exiled Jew* (Chapel Hill: University of North Carolina Press, 1991), especially chapter nine. For a comprehensive study of Jewish self-hatred, see Sander L. Gilman, *Jewish Self-Hatred: Anti-Semitism and the Hidden Language of the Jews* (Baltimore: The Johns Hopkins University Press, 1986), especially chapters one, five, and six.

8. Gilman, *Jewish Self-Hatred,* 19.

9. There is little evidence of the kind of "self-hatred" linked with the familiar "hidden language of the Jews" in Simone Weil; no background of Hebrew or Yiddish is spoken at home; and she was never cast as the Other by her French friends except by virtue of her political leanings and perceptibly different sexual habits, until the statutes forced a "difference" upon her.

10. There are lapses in Weil's behavior, to be sure, especially with the rising tide of fascism beginning to affect daily life in France. This is evident when she advised the baptism of her only niece, Sylvie, so Sylvie might avoid the stigma of being "classified" a Jew. (See Coles, *Simone Weil,* 46.) One might also argue that to the degree that she sidled up to Catholicism she was trying to define herself as something other than a Jew. But even on this latter point she was scrupulous about not wanting to be identified with just another "religion." Such lapses seem only human in a time of such vicious anti-Semitism. These, I believe, are the exceptions given the larger moral direction of her literature. Such exceptions, however, are not easily defended.

11. Steiner, "Self-hatred," 4. There remain some troubling arguments that support an affirmative answer to Coles's question about whether she had "succumbed to the self-hatred of the victim."

12. See Brenner, *Writing as Resistance,* 158–63. See, above, chapter four, second section.

13. Brenner, *Writing as Resistance,* 69f.

14. Ibid., 71.

15. Ibid., 73.

16. Ibid., 74.

17. Ibid., 88. This is a somewhat speculative link, admits Brenner, but she says that the "likelihood" of such linkage "deserves attention."

18. Ibid., 93. This prayer itself is the subject of much derision by Weil interpreters. The most illuminating reading of this prayer I am aware of is in Rush Rhees's chapter on "Love" in the forthcoming *Discussions of Simone Weil*. He reads it as both "a flight from responsibility" and as a reflection on her unreserved consent to the love of God and her belief that she is unworthy of that love.

19. Brenner, *Writing as Resistance*, 95 and 127.

20. Ibid., 175.

21. See Emmanuel Levinas's critique of Simone Weil's view of the Old Testament in his "Simone Weil against the Bible," in *Difficult Freedom: Essays on Judaism*, trans. by Seán Hand (Baltimore: The Johns Hopkins University Press, 1990), 133–41. A harsher and more sustained criticism of Weil's interpretation of the Old Testament and her alleged anti-Semitism can be found in Hans Meyerhoff's 1957 essay, "Contra Simone Weil: 'The Voices of Demons for the Silences of God,' " in *Arguments and Doctrines: A Reader of Jewish Thinking in the Aftermath of the Holocaust,* ed. Arthur A. Cohen (New York: Harper and Row Publishers, 1970), 70–85. Meyerhoff sees Simone Weil's understanding of the Old Testament as a "slander upon her own people . . . a last desperate measure of defense against total despair."

22. This would no doubt include the German Christian church whose membership was in tacit complicity with the Third Reich.

23. Levinas, *Difficult Freedom*, 135f.

24. Rhees, *Discussions of Simone Weil*.

25. Coles, *Simone Weil,* 57f.

26. Weil, "What is a Jew?" 80. Her claim to Catholic "patrimony" is itself problematic, but not an unreasonable weapon in her "word" arsenal against the Minister of Education.

27. van Beeck, *Loving Torah*, 14. Simone Weil was lying in a hospital in Middlesex, England, just months before her death, while the Warsaw Ghetto was going up in flames.

28. van Beeck, *Loving Torah*, 15.

29. Ibid., 17.

30. Ibid.

31. Ibid., 20.

32. Ibid., 21.

33. Ibid.

34. Ibid., 23.

35. Ibid., 25.

36. Ibid., 32. This was a radio talk entitled "To Love the Torah More than God" given by Levinas in France on April 29, 1955, twelve years after the Warsaw Ghetto rebellion.

37. van Beeck, *Loving Torah*, 36.

38. Ibid.

39. Ibid., 39.

40. Ibid., 38.

41. Ibid., 39.

42. Levinas, *Difficult Freedom*, 134.

43. van Beeck, *Loving Torah,* 39f.

44. Ibid., 40.

45. As found in *Seeds of the Spirit: Wisdom of the Twentieth Century*, ed. Richard H. Bell with Barbara L. Battin (Louisville: Westminster John Knox Press, 1996), 8.

46. *Seeds of the Spirit*, 131 and 8.

47. Levinas, *Difficult Freedom,* 18.

48. Joseph Soloveitchik, *Halakhic Man* (Philadelphia: Jewish Publication Society of America, 1983), 52. *TzimTzum* (or Tsim Tsum) is a concept associated with the Jewish mystical tradition of the Kabbalah. See also H. L. Finch's discussion of Weil's idea of "decreation" and the Kabbalah in his "Simone Weil: Harbinger of a New Renaissance?" in *Simone Weil's Philosophy of Culture*, especially pages 299–304.

10

SIMONE WEIL'S WAY TOWARD A "WORTHY" CIVILIZATION: A LEGACY FOR MORAL AND POLITICAL PRACTICE

LISTENING TO SIMONE WEIL

S imone Weil's account of love and justice "turns downward," not upward. Even with all her talk about the supernatural and the spiritual, she does not offer a transcendent escape-oriented love or morality, nor is her view of justice and political philosophy "other-worldly" in orientation. As we have discovered, her view of love and justice is cast in terms of particularity, of a way of justice as compassionate love toward each and all human beings. It is inspired by a certain understanding of God, true, but it is so even though—and perhaps because—God is more often absent in our world and in our human moral consciousness than God is present.[1]

Even her own death was not an escape, but a sacrifice to her agony of not being able to "be in the fray," to engage in the human struggles taking place on the battlefields of Europe. Nor was her death a martyrdom "for her beloved France." Rather it was a sustained cry to be heard as the cry of any afflicted human being should be heard. No one was listening to her—least of all her "Free French" leaders in London.

Is it possible that today we might listen a bit more carefully to what she was saying, and that having heard her in some of the above chapters we might seek for a more just balance in our moral, economic, and political lives? Should not we have been listening when she said: "We are living in a world in which nothing is made to our measure"; where there exists "a monstrous discrepancy" between our body, our mind, and the things that make up our current human condition; where everything is in "disequilibrium" (OL 108). Should this not bring out the rebel in us as it did in her? Should we not be struck immediately by how the concept of justice has been diminished by our niggling over rights? Are we not sufficiently aware of the violence that takes place in our everyday lives or that results from abuse of power? When will our attention be sufficiently focused on the shallow, litigious nature of our legal system so that once again we will be able to discern injustices? Is it not self-evident that we are rapidly losing all sense of community and tradition in our public lives? Are we not able to see the discrepancy between what our children learn in our educational system and a vision of education that might help us build a worthy civilization? Have we lost sight of human longing for the good, or have we come to expect only harm? These questions and more reverberate from the pages of Simone Weil's moral and political writings. They should be echoing in our ears and our hearts today.

What are we to make of such wholesale indictments, which seem to ring as true of our time as they did in hers, as this: "Our age is so poisoned by lies that it converts everything it touches into a lie. And we are of our age, and have no reason to consider ourselves better than our age" (NR 97). We have seen on numerous occasions that Simone Weil's thought is no stranger to hyperbole! She can as easily condemn a whole "age" as she can a single tyrant like Hitler. Such indictments, however much a reader may wish to exempt him or her self, force each of us to take note of our own lives. We inveigh: How much am 'I' a part of this age of lies? Why should I be made to feel guilty? The poison is not of my making.

The strategy of such hyperbolic talk, of such talk about discrepancies in our lives, for Simone Weil is always aimed at helping us "to dwell wholly in the truth" (NR 253), to breathe an inspiration in us that comes from outside our selves. To see clearly our own limits we must see them "against a genuinely spiritual way of life" (NR 91)—a way that embraces a notion of the good or God and which practices justice as compassion. We must have an ideal, an inspiration before us, based on eternal truths and not on ourselves.

OBSTACLES TO A WORTHY CIVILIZATION

As we have seen, Simone Weil's last works, especially *The Need for Roots*, focused intensely on outlining what was needed for a new civilization complete with a legal and educational system, and a public, political consciousness, all enabling individuals to live freely but with a deep sense of obligation toward one another. But, as early as 1934 (and perhaps earlier), the idea of preparing for a "new civilization" was clearly in her mind. She wrote to a young pupil of hers who sought advice on whether to leave school before taking her exams that she should "make full use" of opportunities given her for learning and that she should do all she could "towards preparing for that new civilization." Simone Weil outlines the immediate future as follows. She was convinced there would be a war with a Franco–Russian alliance against Germany and Japan after which we would have to rethink the very meaning of our existence. She writes:

> Briefly, I foresee the future like this: we are entering upon a period of more centralized and more oppressive dictatorship than any known to us in history. But the very excess of centralization weakens the central power. One fine day (perhaps we shall live to see it, perhaps not) everything will collapse in anarchy and there will be a return to almost primitive forms of the struggle for existence. (SL 8; this whole letter is very revealing, even prophetic, see SL 7–10)

The war did come much as she described it and we did see a period of more centralized and more oppressive dictatorship in Central and Eastern Europe and in China and southeast Asia. And though there was not anarchy, we saw the veneer of stability burst toward democracy due to all those who "loved liberty."

What Simone Weil envisioned and wanted was not so much a new society as "a form of civilization likely to be worth something." This form of civilization must find its inspiration "among the truths eternally inscribed in the nature of things." In *The Need for Roots*, writing within the war she "foresaw," she goes on to describe what, given the human condition, inhibits the development of such a worthy civilization:

> Four obstacles above all separate us from a form of civilization likely to be worth something: our false conception of greatness; the

degradation of the sentiment of justice; our idolization of money; and our lack of religious inspiration. We may use the first person plural without any hesitation, for it is doubtful whether at the present moment there is a single human being on the surface of the globe who is free from the quadruple defect and more doubtful still whether there is a single one belonging to the white race. But if there are one or two, which, in spite of everything, is to be hoped, they remain hidden. (NR 219)

Again, for her to indict the whole of "the white race" with the first person plural is nothing—particularly as nearly the "whole" of that race are locked into a horrendous war with one another at the time of her writing. For her the important issue is to look at why we are in such a terrible fix and to examine the obstacles to forming a better civilization. She is calling, as noted in "The *Iliad*," for one of those "intervals of hesitation, wherein lies all our consideration for our brothers in humanity." It is one of the paradoxical qualities of her thought that although she talks of the "obstacles" to a worthy civilization, to expose the obstacles has the effect of seeing one's way through them or overcoming them. To see what stands in the way of a good civilization exposes and projects the very forms that would make it a worthy one. Let us look at each of these obstacles.

Our False Conception of Greatness

We would all like to be part of a civilization that is "worth something." Simone Weil's "inspired" or "genuinely spiritual" civilization would respect meaningful work, embrace justice, have a sense of a common good, offer a "perfect liberty" among its citizens, and have a compassionate heart. This is a "worthy" ideal; it is the form of civilization she believes is "worth something"—it is the lure to the development of her entire moral and political thought. We are, however, burdened by our own selves which deter the fulfillment of her ideal. Uprooted in so many ways, we have few clear markers to follow. Rather than "struggling for justice," we are seeking a share of power and place in willful ways, both as individuals and as collective nation-states in the world.

It is perhaps easiest to see our false sense of greatness at the level of the nation-state. So let us start there. In our century, driven by more than seventy years of ideological competition between communism and democracy, and jolted by the rise of fascism and the surge to empire of Japan, virtually the entire globe was uprooted and destabilized. As we have seen, Simone Weil saw this danger early in our century—easily in the early 1930s and documented in *Oppression and Liberty* — and warned of its devastating consequences for building a worthwhile civilization. For her the national integrity of each people deserved as much respect and autonomy as is practical for its functioning without building armies or being uprooted by an external power. She believed there must be "a balanced compromise" between the wills of people of different nations—a cooperative spirit as she writes in her "Thoughts on the Colonial Problem." She clearly says: "There is no divinely ordained international hierarchy any more than there is a political one; and to recognize this truth is not inconsistent with the most ardent patriotism" (SE 210). Where the problem begins is in what former American statesman William Fulbright called "the arrogance of power," that is, in creating hierarchies by "might," either economic or military, or by some inflated sense of "manifest destiny" or claim to some "divine" Right (with a capital R).

Simone Weil says that "great nations" should set their minds toward trying "to conceive the world's destiny. Not to decide it" (SE 210). It decides itself in the course of its behavior. No one has authority to "decide" another's destiny. If, however, we try to conceive—to imagine or project new possibilities—then an ideal may come into view. This, she believed, "would perhaps be the best stimulant, the best way towards recovering our self-respect" (SE 210). To "conceive" the world's destiny is to imagine a world against the standard of justice—to project an ideal that can help shape a country and *allow* it to nurture its past and chart its own path into the future. Too often, governments and corporations have been busily "deciding" the world's destiny, and in willful, arrogant ways have imposed those decisions on others—hence "the colonial problem" with all of its economic and political ramifications. Now, in what is called a "postcolonial" era, there is more insidious "deciding" going on (rather than open governmental and political oppression of one nation over another), which only extends the "colonial problem" in a different form.

Of course, another insight gained through Simone Weil, what appears as "collective" decision making, is nothing more than the extension of the arrogance of individual human beings and seeing that the responsibility for such behavior rests with our own wretchedness and our unwillingness to expose the lies and deceit in ourselves. As "thoughtful" creatures, we should be engaged in greater "conceptual" activity, not to mention humility, with regards to the world's destiny. This would invite "inspiration" and "ideals" into the discussion.

The Degradation of the Sentiment of Justice

No concept has been given more attention in this book than has the concept of justice. It is at the heart of Simone Weil's moral and political thought. An obstacle to a worthy civilization is the degradation and diminution of justice. We have seen that one way in which justice has been degraded in our enlightenment culture is by reducing it to rights discourse—a thin conception at its best.[2] I will not review our discussion from chapter three, but when this confusion is understood, then Simone Weil believes that attention can be turned toward justice. Justice would entail that we not ignore the human condition where people cry out for the injustices done to them and that we pay attention to the affliction suffered from the injustice. A just person never turns a deaf ear to a particular injustice in a particular human being. What arises from the kind of unconditional attention to the afflicted is some sense of obligation or responsibility to the other. It arises not in a natural way but as an operation of grace—as the manifestation of God's love through acts of human care for others. In Václav Havel's terms, it is only when one comes "face to face with one's neighbor" that the human heart can be opened and responsibility in love can be exercised; this is how divine love enters into human relationships. This action is what Simone Weil calls a "change in the direction of justice." As long as we are in the realm of "rights talk" we will never move in the direction of justice. Contention and self-interest rule in a rights-based morality. The diminishment of justice is in our failure to create conditions for it where it is absent (SJ 5). Most significantly, justice seeks the consent of others and respects their refusal. "Real justice," says Springsted, "is a matter of taking another's will and projects seriously." This causes us to make adjustments in our own lives and plans to accommodate another's reality.[3] It also raises awareness of new obstacles, allows for a pause, and opens us to the needs and concerns of others.

There is one final stage in overcoming the degradation of the sentiment of justice. We need, Weil says, "for the spirit of justice to dwell within us," and "the spirit of justice is nothing other than the supreme and perfect flower of the madness of love." It is this madness that "turns compassion into a far more powerful motive for any kind of action"; it compels one to abandon everything for compassion, which in turn brings God down to the one cared for (SJ 9). This, of course, is so difficult that Simone Weil believes that we yield such madness to reason and "the instinct of self-preservation." In so yielding, justice does not dwell within us; we stop struggling for justice and its sentiment begins to disintegrate.

Our Idolization of Money

Money, more than anything, has turned us away from community-building. A public culture turns inward, becomes a private pursuit, once the possession of money gives an individual a taste of power and self-sufficiency. Numerous needs of the soul fall away when a person acquires private means to achieve what once required a cooperative effort.

Although Simone Weil does not develop her critique of money, she does see it as holding urban workers hostage. The wage-earning class, especially when the work is by the piece—to which her own factory experience is testimony—"obliges each workman to have his attention continually taken up with the subject of his pay" (NR 44). This is uprooting because a worker can never feel at home, being always under pressure that the pay will not be enough or the threat of unemployment will become real.

This same experience of "homelessness" and feeling hostage to the workplace is a growing reality in our present time; it is tied to the increasing pressure from industry to hire part-time employees with reduced compensation and benefits. Business and industry leaders argue that this downsizing strategy is the only way that they can compete in the global market. With part-time work, the same anxiety arises, and a worker is unable to feel secure. No, or fewer, benefits accompany most part-time employment. To have enough money to cover essential medical, pension, and insurance costs, one needs several part-time jobs. This fragmentation multiplies the workers' restlessness and anxiety and contributes to a greater uprootedness in the society as a whole. More people are working for more hours and less pay with less security, undercutting the dignity of the worker and undermining what Simone Weil thinks crucial to make work itself meaningful. The issue of the calculated increase in part-time work today is one that would have drawn Simone Weil onto the picket lines, as would the practice whereby full-time industrial jobs have been "farmed out," so to speak, to developing countries where poverty quells rebellion.

This is what money does in uprooting those who have little of it. At the other end, Simone Weil sees idolization of money to be one of the evils of unbridled capitalism. Money, she believed, corrupts the rich as well, leading to a different kind of inward spiral again—now forcing those who have wealth to protect their right to the property and things they have gained by it, and the interests that draw their attention away from justice. Everyone works fiercely either to earn enough to stay afloat or to hold onto what they have. In both conditions the spiral leads to an atomized social condition and greater contention between classes and moves us further away from communal pursuits. Public life suffers and social values diminish.

Finally, Simone Weil believes that money strikes at the heart of justice. As we have discussed, justice requires mutual consent and she says clearly:

> Consent cannot be bought or sold. Consequently, whatever the political institution, in a society where monetary transactions dominate most of social life, where almost all obedience is bought and sold, there can be no freedom. Just as oppression is analogous to rape, so the dominance of money over work, pushed to the point where money becomes the prime motive for work, is analogous to prostitution. (SJ 6)

It is not a very big step to draw the analogy from prostitution to politicians "bought" by large contributions to political campaigns and party coffers or in return for special favors to interest groups.

Our Lack of Religious Inspiration

By now it should be clear that by "religious" Simone Weil does not simply and only mean "Christian," even though the notion of God coming down to this world in the form of a human being and suffering may be the single most compelling symbol for her. There are manifold ways, in virtually every religious tradition, in which the divine is "drawn down" into our human world. She rejected the idea of one and only one incarnation: "At all events, we do not know for certain that there have not been incarnations previous to that of Jesus, and that Osiris in Egypt, Krishna in India were not of that number" (LTP 19). Remarking on an idea from Zen Buddhism, she writes: "It is Buddha who makes flowers grow from the branches of trees, to make men look upward. It is he who makes the moon sink below the waves, so that the afflicted may know that God comes down" (FLN 181f.). Simone Weil's deep worry, obsession even, is that we continue to turn a blind eye to every form, present and past, of the spiritual in life—that we draw no inspiration from anything other than ourselves.

Simone Weil might agree with Martha Nussbaum in identifying Christianity as "a protean religion": it has many forms and some of these forms seem compatible with other religions or spiritual systems, ancient or modern.[4] Her own version of Christianity is closer to ancient Greek thought, or the religion of the Cathars, or to what she found in "Oriental Wisdom." This may be why, in her version of Christianity, she wants to stick closely to the story of Christ's life and death with the central imagery of suffering and the cross. In this way she avoids some major theological disputes. "The Gospel," she says, "contains a conception of human life, not a theology" (FLN 147). Her faith was what she called an "implicit faith" tied to a long-standing "agnosticism," on the one hand, and the spirituality of many traditions, on the other hand (WG 94f.). Her objections are aimed at a Christianity of dogma—one "guilty of an abuse of power" and its totalitarian use of "those two little words: *anathama sit*" and one too closely bound to the institutional church that she refused to embrace (WG 80, 82, 85).

Simone Weil might also have agreed with Nussbaum's saying that "many of [Christianity's] forms have, in fact, begun from an idea of human helplessness that lies closer than Augustine's does to ancient Greek thought."[5] This idea of human helplessness is very close to Simone Weil's understanding that Chrisianity is pre-eminently a "religion of slaves." This idea of human helplessness, in both Nussbaum and Weil, is not the same as a notion of "original sin." What we have seen Simone Weil say is part of all human beings—their limitations, helplessness, even wretchedness—is not the same as saying that humans were born that way. This is more of a "gravitational" condition of the world and not of individuals by heredity. At its best her view of human helplessness could only be said to be, using still another phrase of Nussbaum, "a secular analogue of original sin," underscoring our imperfection and also guilt which may result from failure to fulfill our obligations to others.[6] This points again to the "protean" nature of religion and its potential compatibility with multiple religious traditions as long as we are not too doctrinally specific. This point was also discussed earlier.

There is, finally, one more point about our lack of religious inspiration that stands in the way of a worthy civilization. As we saw in chapter seven, tradition and ritual practices are important for any meaningful sense of community. This is even more true of a religious community. Simone Weil says that "it is only *the radiance from the spiritual treasures of the past* that can induce in a soul that state which is the necessary condition for receiving grace. That is why there is no religion without a religious tradition, and it is so even when a new religion has only just appeared" (SE 207, emphasis added).

As much as she saw the Greek concepts of love and justice to be similar to those found in her view of Christianity, she also saw the ideas of the Greeks to be found in and influenced by ancient Egyptian culture and by science coming out of the East (Persian culture).[7] For her, no religion or culture or civilization arises without a past, and its past is the source of its "spiritual treasures." This means that the practices (prayers and liturgies), stories, and sacred texts of religions everywhere draw their inspiration from a common source of grace. If one attentively engages in the practices of any particular religious tradition and draws inspiration from its sacred stories and texts, one will be in a position to receive grace. In *Letter to a Priest*, written in the autumn of 1942, she says:

> Every time that a man has, with a pure heart, called upon Osiris, Dionysus, Krishna, Buddha, the Tao, etc., the Son of God has answered him by sending the Holy Spirit. And the Holy Spirit has acted upon his soul, not by inciting him to abandon his religious tradition, but by bestowing upon him light—and in the best of cases the fullness of light—in the heart of that same religious tradition. (LTP 29)

Without a past and its traditions we lose, or at least seriously impair, our capacity to call upon God and receive the fullness of this eternal light.

This is evidence in support of an argument that, although Simone Weil often identified herself with what she called in her "Spiritual Auto-biography" "the Christian attitude" or "the Christian inspiration" (WG 62), her "Christianity" truly *meant* a "universal" acceptance of God's light and truth as it *enters into* the human world. Rush Rhees takes this a step further and simply says: "She was far from the Christian tradition. But how much more reverent (or so it seems to me), how much more an attempt to see the *world* in its relation to God, in contrast to the traditional Hebrew and Christian views—which seem to narrow every-thing and refuse to recognize the world about them at all."[8]

It was her hope, and one we should bear in mind even more firmly today, that French colonial influence in the East (which largely meant French Indochina—Cambodia, Laos, and Vietnam) has not totally cor-rupted its "spiritual treasures." The same could be hoped for French and British (and Belgian and Portuguese, etc.) colonial interest in Africa, but the uprootedness there seems more complete than in the East. Also, she believed the colonial interests were motivated primarily by the "prestige of money and . . . arms" (SE 207) and, given today's global economic colonialism, that same motivating force seems stronger and even more dangerously uprooting than ever. The "spiritual treasures" everywhere seem under siege and religious inspiration is retreating fast. This, of course, provides us with one plausible explanation for the rise of "reli-gious fundamentalism" worldwide—Islamic, Jewish, Christian, and Hindu—which lays claim to trying to halt the retreat. Although she did not address this problem, she would most likely have reacted to the religious fundamentalists just as she did to the Old Testament Hebrew Nation, the Roman Empire, and the Catholic Church, that is, as "col-lective" voices of dogma, militant and intolerant of the other, and be-cause of that, lacking in a true inspiration.

Today we need to identify, name, and publicly resist all false collec-tive voices among religious, secular, and state organizations which retard religious inspiration and destroy "the radiance from the spiritual trea-sures of the past." Simone Weil is always very clear that in both politics and religion, in community and nation-building, "love of the past has nothing to do with any reactionary political attitude" (NR 51). Even when she appeals to "beautiful medieval things"—the treasures of Lan-guedoc or St. Francis, for instance—she says, "The public . . . should relate and attach to the middle ages both the conservative idea and also what is authentic in the revolutionary idea—that is to say, the part of it which is neither fantasy of progress nor will to power but is simple desire for justice" (FLN 173). What we give to the future generations can be nothing more than "the treasures stored up from the past and digested, assimilated, and created afresh by us" (NR 51). The key point here is not that the past is sacred in itself, but that whatever we take from the past must be "digested, assimilated, and created afresh by us" to inspire a "simple desire for justice" and create a worthy civilization.

JUSTICE AND THE WAY OF COMPASSION

I will begin this section with a brief discussion of reflections made by Simone Weil on America's past and its "spiritual treasures." She made only a very few remarks about America and its potential influence following the war. They were, however, very provocative ones— provocative enough to cause us to pause and reflect on what she said, especially as America has become *the* dominant economic and military power in the globe just fifty years after her remarks. In her "Thoughts on the Colonial Problem," she says the following, almost in the manner of a parable:

> There is perhaps no way by which Europe can avoid being disin-
> tegrated by the American influence except through a renewed contact
> with the East on a really profound level. At the present day, when the
> American, the Englishman, and the Hindu are together, the two for-
> mer will fraternize on the surface, each of them secretly thinking him-
> self much superior to the other, and the Hindu will be left out. To re-
> create by degrees an atmosphere in which the reactions of the three
> will be different may well be, from the spiritual point of view, a matter
> of life and death for Europe. (SE 205)

To Simone Weil, America's weakness is not to have a coherent past. What past it may claim is a European past. (Today, of course, because of the wholesale uprooting nature of our century and massive migration of human populations, America's past increasingly reflects an African, Latin American, and Asian past, along with some new consciousness of its Native American past.) America's "pasts" are now plural—a fact in which Simone Weil might not take a great deal of new hope. Still, what is called the American "spirit" is fabricated by the sheer strength of will and words—forged from a few European enlightenment ideas—and, of course, she believed "efforts of will are illusory" (FLN 316). By contrast, she believed "the East clung tenaciously to its past until our [French and British] influence half uprooted it [partly through money and arms]. But it is not yet more than half uprooted" (SE 207). She sees a unique "pivotal" role that a recovering Europe can play after the war. It must, however, avoid becoming "Americanized" and can do so by turning "Eastward" for inspiration. The inspiration she sees still "half" alive resides in the cultures of the East with their rich "spiritual treasures" found in Hindu and Buddhist texts, Taoist literature, and Ancient Egyptian writings. Although "half" alive in mid-century, fifty years later these spiritual treasures have spread further into Western consciousness and may be a more viable rescource for spiritual renewal today.

Simone Weil writes:

> If, without turning our eyes away from the future, we try to revive our contact with our own millennial past ["beautiful medieval things"]; and if we seek a stimulus for this effort in genuine friendship, founded on respect, with everything in the East that is still securely rooted, then we may succeed in saving the past from almost total obliteration, and thus also save the spiritual vocation of the human race. (SE 208)

In this she draws us back, once again, to Languedoc as part of her "millennial past," to justice and love in the forms of genuine friendship and respect for the other, and to the way that embraces compassion still found to have some breath of life in the East. We must also underscore that it may be "a matter of life and death" that we be able to stand together, Hindu, Christian, Jew, Muslim, Frenchman, American, Arab, Englishman, Asian in "an atmosphere" of peace and justice (SE 205). One of our global civilization's great challenges is to find a way to create an atmosphere in which citizens from all countries and of all religious traditions on this earth can "fraternize" in a way that shows their mutual respect and trust.

Is there any reason to suppose that her advice for European moral and political reconstruction after the war is not good advice for the development of any worthy civilization? All of America's pasts should be mined for their treasures, digested and re-valued in the light of our current situation.

One of Simone Weil's most profound remarks which may help us think about how we may use her thought to help us think about ourselves, our past, and our future is found in *The Need for Roots*. She believes that compassion is a spiritualization of the suffering that one goes through. If we simply try to take in the dimensions of human suffering that this century has endured, then there should be a vast reservoir of spiritual motivation that can transform any civilization into a worthy one. She says that *"this same compassion is able without hindrance, to cross frontiers, extend itself over all countries in misfortune, over all countries without exception; for all peoples are subjected to the wretchedness of our human condition"* (NR 174, emphasis added). This is one of those "great hopes" discussed in chapter 8. A hope that may be carried from one family member to another, from one worker to another, from one community to another, from one country to another—all frontiers are open to compassion. It is a way of justice visible to anyone, in every culture East and West, North and South, who has looked injustice in the face: "Whereas pride in national glory is by its nature exclusive, nontransferable, compassion is by its nature universal" (NR 174). Or remember the *Tao Te Ching*: "The whole world says that my way is vast and resembles nothing. It is because it is vast that it resembles nothing. If it resembled anything, it would, long before now, have become small." National pride is small, and the three treasures that the *Tao* cherishes are compassion, prudence, and humility—vast treasures that can be taken anywhere. To forsake these treasures "is sure to end in death."

"Compassion is the rainbow," she said, reaching across any frontier, respecting no boundaries, multicolored to show its embrace. One frontier that compassion crosses is the frontier from the supernatural to the natural, not the other way around. "God is absent from the world," she said, "except in the existence in this world of those in whom God's love is alive. Therefore they ought to be present in the world through compassion. Their compassion is the visible presence of God here below" (FLN 103). Simone Weil is clear that whether one professes a religious faith or not, one need only possess compassion in the form of "two virtues": "All those who possess in its pure state the love of their neighbor and the acceptance of the order of the world including affliction—all those, even should they live and die to all appearances atheists, are surely saved" (LTP 36). Making God present in a world that does not see God, has forgotten God, or even cursed God for God's absence is a function of compassion toward another particular human being. "Whoever is capable," she says, "of a movement of pure compassion towards a person in affliction (a very rare thing anyway) possesses, maybe implicitly, yet always really, the love of God and faith" (LTP 36).

Isn't this idea, this way, large enough for us? Can't we find in it enough light to illumine the darkness of our times? There is no more public notion in Simone Weil's moral and political vocabulary than that of justice as compassion. This is one of those concepts that she brings back to us in a startlingly fresh way; it is presented to us as a whole new way to think about justice. It unmasks the shallow and self-serving nature of our "cultural translation" of justice into "rights" discourse. The way of justice as compassion "keeps both eyes open on both the good and the bad and finds in each sufficient reasons for loving. It is the only love on this earth which is true and righteous" (NR 173). "Compassionate love," she says, "is the only just love" (FLN 95).

Simone Weil reminds us that in the *Symposium*, the origins of love are described as being born of "poverty" and "the Way (*Poros*)" (SNLG 131). If we keep before our eyes the moral and material poverty of our century, as well as humility, and try to set a new course characterized by the way of justice as compassion, perhaps the third millennium could begin to take a different form from the last. To be realistic, we must also be prepared for the criticism that such a course setting would be viewed as "mad." She gives us constant reminders which also serve as encouragements to keep on the way: "To the extent to which at any given time there is some madness of love amongst men, to that extent there is some possibility of change in the direction of justice: and no further" (SJ 5). What we need, she says, "is for the spirit of justice to dwell within us" (SJ 9). If we can discern such a spirit dwelling in our political spaces and our moral actions, then we are on the way and "struggling for justice."

PROSPECTS FOR THE NEW MILLENNIUM

Simone Weil talked of "saving the spiritual vocation of the human race." Hyperbole again? Perhaps. But for her, having a spiritual vocation is not just some religious idea. It is to understand "the lay of the land" in our world; it is to root our lives in the spiritual nature of work that reconciles our humanity with the natural order; it is to see our human life complete with its ideals and aspirations grounded in an inspiration that is not limited to our finite selves. It is fair to say that modern political and public life has lost all sense of a spiritual vocation, and therein lies the problem. How are we to revive a spiritual vocation? What are some aspects of such a vocation that we can learn from her and put into practice? How are we to conceptualize our life for the next millennium rather than allowing the visible and present pariahs of our uprooted culture to decide our future for us by default?

A crucial aspect of this new vocation is to learn how to practice politics "on a multiple plane"—to see it as multifaceted and not simply a one-dimensional exchange of power between parties or persons. Politics without a "spiritual vocation is basically an exchange of power between two or more parties on a more or less equal basis—the more or less being relative to the advantages or disadvantages of the exchanging parties. Politics as spiritual vocation understands such exchanges to result in a "just balance." Simone Weil says that all who have political responsibility must, in their hearts, "hunger and thirst after justice" on a multiple plane (NR 217, also SJ 4). That is, justice must be in play on every plane—among citizens, between civic employees, with political rivals, and crossing frontiers to other municipalities and countries. Some just balance must be struck with respect to needs and economic interests among citizens and between nations. Justice must also be understood to derive its legitimacy not from one political or economic ideology or another, but from the eternal in time, from some incarnation of truth, from the play of the supernatural virtue of justice as compassion.

Politics itself and a political philosophy have to do with how we enter public space and dwell there.[9] It is in the manner of the dwelling that the quality of the spiritual enters in. If we dwell to usurp power and enhance our interests, we abdicate responsibility and become an obstacle to justice. If we dwell with a compassionate heart, all our public spaces will be transformed by the spirit of justice. Dwelling spaces are not just physical spaces; they are living spaces, public and private, where human interactions constitute the nature of the "dwelling." For Simone Weil, real political, public dwelling spaces must be understood in terms of their spiritual qualities, i.e., how the dwelling therein reflects God's love and justice in the actions of those dwelling there. In chapter five we discussed the importance of Simone Weil's remark that "earthly things are the criterion of spiritual things." Extending that concept to political space, we see that the value of spiritual things can only be verified as an illumination projected on our physical dwelling places (FLN 147). And we said earlier that Simone Weil's new virtue of justice rooted in her compassion-based morality provides all human beings with a means of restoring their political voice—a voice that has a capacity within the human realm of drawing God "into the fray."

Another aspect of a spiritual vocation within the public sphere is to build communities that will ensure individual liberty. The current key to doing this is to encourage practices that promote and secure democracy. From very early in Simone Weil's writings she believed, following the democratic example of Athens and the spirit of the revolutions of the eighteenth century, that we should be lovers of liberty. "What would prove decisively that we love liberty," she says, "would be our support for any measure that guaranteed at least a little liberty to those whom we have deprived of it. By doing this we should convince not only other people but also ourselves that we are truly inspired by an ideal" (SE 202). There have been a number of dramatic examples of lovers of liberty, inspired by an ideal of equality and human dignity, who have led recent democratic movements in their countries: Václav Havel and Nelson Mandela immediately come to mind. Both men are living examples of the spirit of justice dwelling in their countries. To sustain the inspiration for this ideal, current major democracies with wealth and power must be vigilant of any colonial tendencies they may have and act with attention, contrition, and a generous spirit toward poorer democracies and in support of lovers of liberty within countries under repressive regimes. They must also be more attentive to the double standards used in policy making that too narrowly serve only their self or national interests.

Short of encouraging democracy at the level of nations, another aspect in saving the spiritual vocation in public life is to encourage and cultivate more natural human environments that build a culture. Here is where all that we discussed about the value of tradition and friendship, of shared language, of voluntary associations and neighborhoods comes into play. In the chapters on "Community and Politics" and "Education and Civilization" we discussed the importance of "spiritual treasures" from a culture's past that need to be reanimated and created afresh for the flourishing of local communities.

Both individual liberty and a devotion to community are necessary for a democratic society. Also, for Simone Weil both individuals and communities must turn attention toward the natural order. Without a balance in the natural order, there is little to inspire social and political order. Simone Weil says that the love of God is implicit in the order of the world. This is a "complement to the love of our neighbor" (WG 158). God created the universe but does not command it. God leaves two other forces to rule in God's absence: "On the one hand there is the blind necessity attaching to matter . . . and on the other the autonomy essential to a thinking person" (WG 158). Thus being thoughtfully in the world we must attend to its beauty and labor to reconcile ourselves with it. This sense of nature's sacredness is what is at the heart of all ecological or environmental movements. The world is there for us to eat, but also to look at (WG 166). These two things must be placed into a saner balance if we are to even see the end of another century.

Reading Simone Weil inspires us to free our imaginations—to conceive a future destiny, not to decide it. Her thought helps us avoid some of the negative consequences that are the inheritance of the twentieth century. Even when we find her ideas impractical and we cannot muster enough courage to practice her "mad love" and take up her way of justice as compassion, we may be able to build upon the "great hopes" and "possible dreams" she has spawned for us.

In Simone Weil's moral and political writings there is no neat system presented to us—no Cartesian worldview. And although we are often tempted to say that Plato and Kant help us explain what she means by desiring the good and seeing the beauty of nature on the one hand, and in understanding human equality and dignity as ends in themselves on the other, her world never gets played out as either Platonism or Kantianism. She composes her world in surprising ways which in turn invite us to compose a world *with her,* tailored to our own surroundings. Today, our surroundings happen to be not too distant from her own, so her remedies often can make more or less direct sense to us. We still have strong memories of economic depression, and both the prosperity and the dark side of industrial production have not been completely outgrown. The holocausts of Nazi Germany, Hiroshima and Nagasaki, Pol Pot, and Rwanda are still more than just museum pieces to us. So her suggestions of what might be done after World War II to avoid future holocausts still have tread left on them. Even as some of her ideas seem to have outworn their sensible applications, they retain an echo of their idealism, and thus project for us a hope that we can do better than we are doing in building community and educating our citizens, and in knowing how best to deal with a criminal justice system that seems adrift and repressive.

Even if we point to our most dramatic changes since her lifetime—the sudden turn to democracy and away from communism and fascism, or to a technology that leaves the industrial revolution in a pile of rust or looking like a long-abandoned ruin, or to the effects of a smaller globe resulting from the digital revolution and the dilemmas of global economic competition on the human condition and the natural ecosystem—we are still left with the same prospects of abuse of power, of an increasing disequilibrium between rich and poor, of growing isolation and insulation of individuals wanting to escape the stresses of everyday life, and with the further destruction of our earth's natural resources and beauty. Thus we still must find better ways to upbuild and sustain human dignity in work, to remind modern states that their principal duty is "to ensure that the people are provided with a country to which they really feel they belong" (NR 167), and to preserve the earth's environment. If we could do these things, we may be able to stem the tide of massive human migrations and give less stable countries more breathing space to develop. There is no end to learning how to discern the "spiritual treasures" of our past, preserving traditions and nurturing a greater sense of natural, communal, and civic order.

Have we any less need today to learn to listen to our human condition? Can we afford to pay any less attention to the cries of those who suffer and are afflicted—to the homeless, prostitutes, growing numbers of street children, an aging humanity that are being shunted into storage facilities? Are we not daily made aware of victims of domestic violence? And what do we do with the victims of undiscriminating violence, a violence inflicted upon unsuspecting civilians by the uncontrolled production during the last fifty years of killing instruments like landmines and unstable chemical and biological weapons deteriorating towards incalculable horrors? Are we not closer than ever to massive suffering due to multiple global conflicts, environmental pollution, famine, sustained natural disasters that seem heightened in our human consciousness because of instant news images, and to the increase in population world-wide?

Is it so hard then, to conceive of a way that would help us analyze, look at, care for our present human condition? Is it so hard to conceive of a way that values the spiritual treasures of our past? Is it so hard to conceive of a way that values the virtues of compassion, prudence, and humility? Is it so hard to conceive of a way of justice as compassion that might help us begin to transform the power politics of our age to a civilization that might be worth something? To conceive of such ways is what Simone Weil's moral and political thought open up for us; they are ways that command our attention and that we may both wait upon and act upon!

POSTSCRIPT

Rush Rhees says in his cautious, probing way that Simone Weil "was far from the Christian tradition. But how much more reverent, how much more [she sees] the *world* in its relation to God." This was written well before most interpreters took to canonizing "Saint Simone." Rhees's numerous reflections on her thought which have only come to public light in his edited notes and essays in 1997 and 1998 show a remarkable grasp of the whole of her thought as it is tied to the many flaws in her person and unanswered questions in her writing. In the thirty years since Rhees meditated on her work, we have seen a particular bias surface in the literature about Simone Weil. This bias interprets her life and thought almost exclusively within or closely associated with the Christian tradition Rhees says she is far from. How has this happened?

Many interpretations simply assume that the Christian framework is the appropriate starting point for understanding her life and thought. This is, perhaps, not surprising since her religious experiences are linked to Christian festivals (in a Portuguese fishing village), to Christian saints (Francis of Assisi and John of the Cross), to a Christian poet (George Herbert), to Christian monasteries (Solesmse), and to her claim of being possessed by Christ himself. These were not minor experiences; they were instrumental in transforming her understanding of justice and truth by crystallizing their supernatural dimension. She also rejected, even scorned, her own Jewishness and condemned most pre-exilic Hebrew scripture. The episodes linked with her friend and confidant, Father Perrin, and others about baptism and the Catholic Church certainly added fuel to her veiled or tacit acceptance of Christianity short of membership. Virtually all the brief accounts of her in encyclopedias and biographical collections regard her as a religious thinker, mystic, unorthodox saint—even theologian (presumably concerned with Christian doctrines). We believe that the bulk of this secondary literature is too narrowly dependent on a few texts, for it is unduly influenced by the most readily available published texts in both French and English selected toward supporting this bias (*Gravity and Grace* and *Waiting for God*) and the momentum that has accrued from commentary based primarily on these for almost four decades. There has also been a reliance on the personal recollections of Gustave Thibon and Father Perrin.[10] Can we easily remove the encrustations that have accumulated over the decades of reading her works? Is there an alternative view that should be proffered?

On a circumstantial level, one might ask: Where in France between the wars might one find spiritual solace from physical torment? Or where might a Jew flee in a nation wholly secularized but steeped in a symbolically rich and aesthetically worthy Christian heritage? It should not be surprising that the most available—even most compatible—spiritual language for this woman in the context in which she found herself would be a largely Christian spiritual language established as it was and reflected in the beauty of Romanesque architecture and Gregorian chant, framed in words of bondage and grace, and nurtured by the lost chivalrous tales of Languedoc.

In our account we have tried to place the autobiographical material into its larger perspective and not make it the driving force of our interpretation. We have done this without losing sight of two things: 1) that Weil's thought and her life cannot, finally, be separated, for her beliefs and actions are seamless; and 2) that the religious experiences she had between 1935 and 1939 were highly formative for her mature moral and political thought, making it clear that the eternal is known only in time and that her philosophy is grounded in a spiritual way of being in the world—a way whereby the eternal enters time in the form of justice as compassion.

Let us step back for a moment and try to distance ourselves from the secondary religious readings. Simone Weil's focus was almost singularly on the social and political situation in Europe between the wars. *Virtually all* of her published writing during her lifetime had to do with political and ideological debates, workers' oppression, individual liberation, matters of legitimate authority of government or human rights and justice; or it was writing that related to her intellectual interests in classical Greek literature and science, Plato or Descartes (her doctoral thesis), and related philosophical concerns. On the scale of the whole, one finds relatively few purely religious discourses apart from her highly critical debates and correspondences with friends who saw the depths of her spiritual insights and linked them with their own religious beliefs.[11] Although one might say that many of her later writings take the form of meditations on moral and religious themes, they are not exclusive to either asserting Christian beliefs or rejecting Jewish ones. They are, as we have shown, pluralistic in their religious sentiment—that is, they embrace a number of philosophical and religious traditions in her continual quest for the truth.

Then, step back again and look at her later literature as a whole—*The Need for Roots*, "Human Personality," "Essay on the Notion of Reading," "The Legitimacy of the Provisional Government," "Are We Struggling for Justice?" and more. These are not "religious" writings tied, in any sense, to sectarian literature or doctrines, although they do have an overlay of what she calls a spiritual way of life. Her searching disposition in her last years had her *neither* just running away from her Jewishness *nor* running into the arms of the Christian church. Rather she was probing "oriental wisdom," condemning colonialism in Algeria and Indochina, learning Sanskrit, meditating on Taoist literature and Zen, on folk mythology and the *Bhagavad-Gita*, as well as wrestling with how her intense religious experiences related to her thought and personal commitments as these are reflected in her autobiographical letters and notebooks. She was forever crossing frontiers, shaping her compassion-based morality so it would both listen and speak to the human condition. She was to her death, first and foremost, a philosopher searching for the truth linked to the eternal wherever it may be found. She was not a theologian concerned to clarify and promote any particular religious doctrines. She was, as she said to Father Perrin, "a stranger and an exile in relation to every human circle without exception," and her "capacity to mix with all of them implies that I belong to none"

(WG 54f.). Too many have tried to complete her incomplete autobiographical remarks in a direction for which she was herself skeptical.

While she is acutely aware that Europe's spiritual treasures may be linked to ancient Greece and to Christianity, the contact we have with any spiritual treasure that may be our own or another's (as with her contact with the Gospels, the *Bhagavad-Gita*, and Taoist writings) could be useful in "stimulat[ing] us to seek for our own particular source of spirituality" (SE 45). She found neither her Jewish tradition nor Christianity sufficient for her own spirituality. Ideally she thought that one's spiritual vocation should be drawn from whatever sources led one to the truth of seeing justice as compassion.

Simone Weil's philosophy was intricately tied to her social actions, and its spiritual side was for the purpose of helping to reveal the truth which she believed could not be reduced to nature alone. Should we not take all these latter facts about her life and action as primary in our interpretation and understanding of her moral and political thought, rather than leaning on the secondary reflections about her saintliness or religious predilections? It is toward rebalancing our reading scales that much of this book has been oriented—toward understanding Simone Weil as the moral and political philosopher she was, as a woman who read the world through the eyes of compassion and who never once ceased in her highly focused, if continually tormented, struggle for justice.

NOTES

1. Although we have discussed on several occasions the importance of the grammar of "God's absence" and "God's presence" as used by Simone Weil, and the importance of this grammar for understanding justice and compassionate love, we have not taken up the more difficult metaphysical questions of the "existence" and "reality" of God in her thought. Her account of God's existence or necessary nonexistence related to our knowledge of God and of our love of other individual human beings is one of her most impenetrable philosophical ideas, full of paradox and contradiction. We have only brushed past this knotted issue, believing it less central, though not unrelated, to her notion of God's absence and presence. A book on her philosophy of religion would have to confront this issue head-on. Rowan Williams has tackled this issue as few have dared to in his "The Necessary Non-Existence of God," in *Simone Weil's*

Philosophy of Culture, 52–76. A different tack is taken in talking about the "reality" of God in D. Z. Phillips's essay, "God and Concept-formation in Simone Weil" in the same volume, 77–92. Also see J. P. Little, "Simone Weil's Concept of Decreation," in the same volume, and Miklos Vetö, *The Religious Metaphysics of Simone Weil,* trans. Joan Dargan (Albany: State University of New York Press, 1994).

2. Springsted attaches the notion of "thin" justice to Martha Nussbaum's view of justice as developed in her *Love's Knowledge: Essays on Philosophy and Literature* (New York: Oxford University Press, 1990). He calls her view a kind of "procedural liberalism, simply improved." See Springsted, "The Politics of Perception," a paper given at the Simone Weil Colloquy, The College of Wooster, April 1997, and again in Prague, the Czech Republic, August 1997. Unpublished manuscript, 11–14.

3. Springsted, "The Politics of Perception," 20.

4. Nussbaum's notion of "a protean religion" is discussed by Fergus Kerr in his *Immortal Longings*, 5f.

5. Kerr, *Immortal Longings*, 6.

6. Ibid., 10. Kerr discusses Nussbaum's link to Henry James's and Marcel Proust's idea of our "human finitude as marked by guilt" and how we become "finely aware and richly responsible"—"a flawed complex self," but not one born with this condition (12 and 14). I think it is clear from passages like those found in FLN 295–99, 303, and elsewhere, that Weil avoids anything like a doctrine of original sin.

7. Her point is often lost on Western ears by those who believe Greek culture to be unique and the West's principal, if not only, cultural predecessor. She writes: "Herodotus makes it as clear as it could be. In prehistoric times there was a Mediterranean civilization, whose inspiration came chiefly from Egypt and to a lesser extent from the Phoenicians. . . . Greek culture arose perhaps as a result of this assimilation by the Hellenes or perhaps through the persistence of the earlier non-Hellenic populations. In the Trojan war one of the two sides represented civilization, and it was the Trojan side; the accent of the *Iliad* reveals that the poet was aware of this. Greece as a whole always showed towards Egypt an attitude of filial respect" (SE 204).

8. Rush Rhees, *Rush Rhees on Religion and Philosophy*, 371.

9. Development of this idea can also be found, with some variation, in Springsted, " 'Thou Hast Given Me Room': Simone Weil's Retheologization of the Political," *Cahiers Simone Weil* 20, no. 2 (June 1997): 87–98. Springsted characterizes Simone Weil's political philosophy as "a 'retheologization' of the space in which we dwell"—"that politics and political space needs to be understood in the light of the supernatural" (94–95). The term "theologization" I think is misleading. It points in the direction of a more systematic or doctrinal position in ways that Weil's concept of "spiritual" or "spiritualization" does not.

10. The introduction to and the selections made by Gustave Thibon to *Gravity and Grace*, and the personal recollections of Thibon and Perrin, *Simone Weil As We Knew Her*, trans. Emma Craufurd (London: Routledge & Kegan Paul, 1953), have heavily influenced the reading lore. They did have some "special authority" in that they knew her intimately during her time in Marseilles and were given many of her notebooks to deal with at their discretion when she left.

11. The few formal essays most closely connected with the Christian faith were "Concerning the Our Father" in WG, "Forms of the Implicit Love of God" (though this essay moves far beyond just a Christian focus) in WG, and "The Love of God and Affliction" in SNLG.

Appendix

THE SPIRIT OF SIMONE WEIL'S LAW[1]

Ronald K. L. Collins and Finn E. Nielsen

> It is the aim of public life to arrange that all forms of power are entrusted, so far as possible, to men who effectively consent to be bound by the obligation towards all human beings which lies upon everyone, and who understand the obligation.
>
> Law is the totality of the permanent provisions for making this aim effective. (SE 223)

S till wrestling with the philosophic side of existence, Simone Weil tried in the last year of her life to discover how "the eternal and unconditional obligation 'descends' or incarnates in this world" (PR 245). Could human obligation be expressed in a legal text? Could law—constitutional, statutory, and judicial—actually rearrange power without perpetuating its inhumane force? Could law serve the pursuit of truth in some authentic sense? Could penal laws ever be more than retaliatory? Could the keepers of the law, especially judges, be trusted to fix their attention on a notion of justice rooted in human obligation? And finally, could law be made dialectical? Essentially, these were the questions with which the Free French philosopher grappled.

WEIL'S ENCOUNTER WITH LAW:
THE PERSONAL AND POLITICAL CONTEXT

"Simone Weil's encounter with law was, on the whole, late, con-jectural and finally rather brief" (PR 227). There are a handful of late

217

writings with specific discussions of law, though she did not regularly devote much ink to the subject. We shall, as we continue, identify and critique her essential writing on both the letter and the spirit of law, as well as various other law-related reports she drafted during the 1942–43 period of her life.[2]

Additionally, in her last years Weil wrote much about many things linked to law and legal systems. Consider, for example, her extended essays on liberty, rights, and obligations. Likewise, her conception of justice and her critique of oppression are practically and theoretically related to questions of law. Even her spirituality is, at some level, law-grounded insofar as the needs of the soul are, of necessity, connected to law. From this vantage point, *The Need for Roots*—with its reflections and directives on liberty, obedience, judging, freedom of opinion, truth, punishment, etc.—is a text penned in the light of law. The same holds true for her remarkable 1943 essay, "A Draft for the Statement of Human Obligations."

At one point in a discussion of justice in her "Human Personality" essay, also drafted in 1943, Weil flags the importance of law in the following grand way:

> We must learn to distinguish between [the cries of the person ("why am I being hurt?") and those of personalism ("why has somebody else got more than I have?")] and to do all that is possible, as gently as possible, to hush the second one, *with the help of a code of justice, regular tribunals, and the police. Minds capable of solving this problem can be formed in a law school.* (SE 30, emphasis added)

The "problem" to be solved here is nothing less than the puzzle of justice, in all its practical, political, and transcendent forms. This crucial and largely overlooked passage—its message curiously directed to law students—suggests many conceptual relationships: for example, between law and truth, law and liberty, law and equality, law and rights, law and obligations, law and punishment, and law and the supernatural.

Between December 1942 and April 1943, this problem became increasingly pressing to Weil as she reflected on the state of affairs in her beloved France. Working for the fighting Free French Movement in London, Weil and others debated the question "as to whether after the victory, the Vichy government, which had certain elements of legality, should be supplanted in the normal manner or should be overthrown in order to re-establish true legality. This led to reflections on legitimacy" (SP 505).[3] And it was precisely this issue, what we might call the *crisis of legitimacy*, that became increasingly important to Weil in the last months of her life. It is not enough to talk or rhapsodize about *"légitimité."* As Weil put it in her discussion of uprootedness:

> But giving a sentiment a name is not sufficient to call it to life. That is a fundamental truth that we are too apt to forget.
>
> Why lie to ourselves? In 1939, just before the war, under the regime of decree laws, republican *légitimité* already no longer existed. It had departed like Villon's youth *"qui son partement m'a celé,"* noiselessly, without any warning, and without anyone having done or said anything to stop it. As for the feeling for *légitimité*, it was completely dead. (NR 180)

During the four months she spent at the Free French office on Hill Street, a "worn out and tense" (SP 518) Weil wrote, among other things, night and day about the crisis of legitimacy. Acting in her official capacity, she focused on this problem when she reviewed and commented on various legal and political documents and reports prepared by resistance committees in France. For example, she was asked to author a report on a draft for a new constitution prepared by the Commission for State Reform, a commission established by General de Gaulle. This report, entitled "Remarks on the New Draft for a Constitution" (EL 85–92), was penned along with similar reports such as her "Essential Ideas for a New Constitution" (EL 93–97), "The Basis for Constitutional Reform" (SP 510), and "The Legitimacy of the Provisional Government" (LPG).

These reports were wide-ranging and contained numerous comments on the French Declarations of 1789 and 1793, the 1875 Constitution, and the commission's proposals for change. This work prompted Weil to direct her attention to constitutional matters such as the structure of government and the separation of powers. Still, it was not a task executed in any mere technical or formulaic sense; rather, her discussion of these and related points was enveloped in a more philosophical analysis. The immediate crisis of legitimacy was a vehicle for examining an older crisis that had plagued the country since the French Revolution.

Painting with a still broader brush, Weil dealt with the legitimacy question—often moving beyond constitutional law to statutory law, equity, and jurisprudence—on the larger canvas of the historical, cultural, philosophical, and spiritual points pertinent to the crisis of legitimacy. In her words: "Seeing that we have, in fact, recently experienced a break in historical continuity, constitutional legality can no longer be regarded as having an historical basis; it must be made to derive from the eternal source of all legality" (NR 181). Against this backdrop, she approached the question of law and laws in two notable essays ("Human Personality" and "Draft for a Statement of Human Obligations") and in *The Need for Roots*. In all of these works, constitutional and other, she was typically a stern critic of the existing French legal system.

Incredibly, maintained Weil, the political, legal, and educational systems of France had produced "the degradation of the sentiment of justice" (NR 219) in the souls of the French. The legal system of the Third Republic, for example, was one of privilege, bureaucracy, corruption, and cruelty. As if to compound the problem of a relatively weak judicial system,[4] judicial advancement was grossly dependent on currying political favor. What judicial power there was, was arbitrarily exercised. Moreover, an arcane web of procedure increased the potential for injustice. The glory of 1789 had been entirely spent on a system at odds with fundamental fairness. It was this system of government and law to which Weil responded when she sketched the outlines of her own legal thought.

Weil's writings of this period, especially on law, were daring, provocative, and always fragmented. She herself once acknowledged that they tend to sound "pretty fanciful, but [are] not" (EL 97). When Weil wrote on law for the Free French (and herself), she would not infrequently sacrifice precision for principle, clarity for commitment, and comprehensiveness for perspicacity. The strengths and shortcomings of these writings reflect the struggles that engaged the thirty-four-year-old Weil—struggles never confronted by the timid of her time.

FRAGMENTS AND COMMENTS

In what follows, we offer various fragments of Simone Weil's writings that deal with law in some explicit way.[5] A significant number of the fragments appear in *The Need for Roots*, particularly in her discussions of liberty, obedience, freedom of opinion, and punishment. Accordingly, we have patterned this part of our essay after the fragmentary structure of Weil's thought.

Law and Liberty

In the context of her discussion of liberty, Weil examines three law-related conditions necessary for liberty to be complete. They are: the forms of legal rules; the sources of the law; and the stability and number of legal rules of any political order. As to the first, the law's *forms*, she writes:

> Rules should be sufficiently sensible and sufficiently straightforward so that any one who so desires and is blessed with average powers of application may be able to understand, on the one hand the useful ends they serve, and on the other hand the actual necessities which have brought about their institution. (NR 12–13)

From this statement emerges an idea of law that is: value-purposeful and not positivistic;[6] derived from the reality of necessity though quite different from the modern jurisprudence of Legal Realism; and finally, a notion of law more akin to self-realization in the classical sense than to self-representation in the modern sense.

Beyond form, the *source* of the law is also crucial, both in origin and perception: Such rules "should emanate from a source of authority which is not looked upon as strange or hostile, but loved as something belonging to those placed under its direction" (NR 13). These rules of the regime are to be "incorporated" into one's very "being" (NR 13) and come, in time, to be accepted in much the same way that salutary habits of behavior are accepted. Accordingly, while the source of the law is external, its process is more an internal one. Because this process is largely an internal one, it is vital that citizens *understand* their laws.[7]

According to this formula, arbitrary actions (unexplainable by definition) by lawmakers, jurists and/or executive officials, whether malevolent or benevolent, can never lay claim to real legitimacy. Moreover, this notion of law is, at one level, more horizontal than vertical, if only because it depends not on the sanctions of a powerful sovereign but rather derives from a shared vision of the law that portrays superiors as symbols of the good.[8] Thus, "liberty is the power of choice within the latitude left between the direct constraint of natural forces and the authority accepted as legitimate" (SE 225). The latter regulates (in the same kind of way that we regulate room temperatures) the domain of free choice. Generally speaking, nature compels whereas law counsels. Both, however, make demands upon the individual, but in significantly different ways.

Finally, laws may neither be erratic nor innumerable if they are to serve the goals of liberty: "They should be sufficiently stable, general and limited in number for the mind to be able to grasp them once and for all, and not find itself brought up against them every time a decision has to be made" (NR 13). Laws must not be so vague and numerous as to make this goal unobtainable. This is not simply to produce a due process of results, but more importantly to produce a *deliberative process* of fairness.

If the number of laws is to be confined, and if their meaning is to remain intelligible, certain things must follow. First, the regime cannot be a mass one (or a mass-oriented one) because the number of laws is at some point proportionate to the number of citizens. Second, law cannot be premised primarily on the rule of rights, either economic or civil, for such regimes must protect a plethora of claims. Special interest legislation and perpetual litigation—two hallmarks of the regime of rights—are an anathema to Weil. Third, and related, Weil's general notion of constitutive and statutory law appeals more to principles than to particulars. That is, if such rules are to be kept limited in number, lawmakers must resist the process of micro-contextualized legislation that attempts to suit law to a myriad of events. Lastly, citizens must play an active role in the legal process rather than abandoning that process to professional rulers.[9]

There is yet another explanation, adds Weil, why the number of constitutive and statutory laws ought to be fixed: "There is no reason at all why the sovereignty of the law should be limited to the field of what can be expressed in legal formulas, since that sovereignty is exercised just as well by judgments in equity" (NR 26).

This statement seems at odds with what we have just examined. That is, why would Weil press for sufficiently straightforward laws, limited in number, and then defend the open-ended rule of an ever-changing law of equity? At least two answers are possible. First, there is indeed a contradiction here—one that simply must be accepted.[10] Writing in her Marseilles notebooks, Weil said the following about the value of contradiction and its relation to law:

> Bad union of opposites (bad because fallacious) is that which is achieved on the same plane as the opposites. Thus the granting of domination to the oppressed. In this way we do not get free from the oppression-domination cycle.
>
> The right union of opposites is achieved on a higher plane. *Thus the opposition between domination and oppression is smoothed out on the level of the law*—which is balance. (GG 91, emphasis added)

Applied to the issue at hand, the law-as-limited versus law-as-open-ended contradiction cannot be overcome on the plane of positive law. Rather, only when law becomes transcendent—when it rises above itself—can these two opposites coexist in a way salutary to the soul. Any blind and mechanical system of law, like Marx's systematic materialism, cannot resolve the contradiction, but can only give the allusion of having done so. And this, for Weil, is an illegitimate use of contradiction.

Second, perhaps the two points may be reconciled with one another, but in a slightly different way. For example, since the principles of law must be knowable to all, law's particular application, of necessity, depends on its interpretation by courts of equity. Put differently, there needs to be a certain domain (constitutional and perhaps statutory) where the principle, and maybe even the formula, of the law must typically be rendered in a clear and concise manner. Beyond that realm, however, the fair application of the law depends on flexibility, on a judge[11] seeing past law's letter to life's context. Thus, Weil was highly critical of the French Code, which she felt "stripped Justice of its majesty" (EL 152). For her, the declared law serves as a *guide*, while equity declares the law of a given case.[12] In this latter regard the judge must pay particular attention to the needs (physical and spiritual) of those before the court. That is why "human attention alone," Weil wrote in her last notebook, is essential to the legitimate "exercise [of] the judicial function" (FLN 351). This means, in Weilian terms, black-robed officials of the state suspending their thought, keeping it detached, while waiting for it to be penetrated by the reality of those who come before the bench of justice.

Law and Obedience

Obedience, both to rules and rulers, is a vital need and a corollary to liberty. Yet this need is profoundly denied whenever laws turn obedience into any form of involuntary servitude. In Weil's legal lexicon, as elsewhere, the key word here is *consent*. Obedience "presupposes consent, not in regard to every single order received, but the kind of consent that is given once and for all" (NR 14). The "sole reservation, in case of need," she added, was that "the demands of conscience be satisfied" (NR 14). Again, the consent is to principles more than to particulars.

What in some countries are called "technical" defenses have no place in this legal order. This is *not* because there is some sovereign ruler who may break the rules *carte blanche*, or because individual liberty is at the mercy of the governing mob. When the consent is to principles, the idea is constantly to reaffirm their role in life's everyday affairs. Why, in other words, does the wearer of the ring of Gyges[13] (be he president or plumber) not steal and rape? To ask this question is categorically different from asking whether there was an infraction of the letter of a given positive law or judicial precedent. Similarly, it is to reject the idea that law may be dispensed with when utility makes it convenient to do so.

Consent, the "mainspring of obedience," is not to be confused with "fear of punishment or hope of reward" (NR 14). We will turn to the topic of punishment later. As to the hope of reward, note that Weil refuses to cast law in a cost-benefit, Adam Smith-like manner; and for much the same reason she does not hold law out as a utilitarian reward mechanism. The whole idea of law as something bartered or contracted for is foreign to her.[14] Additionally, and in rather cryptic terms, Weil declared: "Those who encourage a state of things in which the hope of gain is the principal motive take away from men their obedience, for consent, which is its essence, is not something which can be sold" (NR 14).[15] Citizens need to comprehend in a full and fair sense *why* they must obey laws and not just that they must do so. Without this, one might do the right thing for the wrong reason, for example, in the same way that a jogger defeats her exercise program by taking a short cut to reach her goal, which is not really a particular site, but rather a physical state. Again, more than results count here. Law, properly realized, allows citizens to synchronize their actions with the rule of necessity;[16] hence, in a Weilian sense, obedience through law has an all-important (and unexpected) transformative quality. This in turn may suggest something akin to natural law,[17] but a natural law decisively *not* Aristotelian or Thomistic in character.[18]

Law and Freedom of Opinion

Of the fourteen needs of the soul listed in *The Need for Roots*, Simone Weil devoted the most space to the entries on "freedom of opinion" and "truth." The latter, she tells us, "is more sacred than any other need" (NR 37), whereas the former is an "absolute need on the part of the intelligence" (NR 23).[19] The need for either is not, however, synonymous with that constitutive right of freedom of expression as known, for example, in the United States. There are crucial differences. For Weil:

- Freedom of opinion is absolute, but only while in the service of a single value.
- Freedom of opinion and association are importantly different, and thus enjoy different claims to legal protection.
- There is a corresponding *duty* of the state to suppress certain kinds of expression.
- Special courts must be created to dispense justice on these matters, even though precise *judicial* definition may be impossible.

Collectively, these characteristics are far more radical than their American counterparts, both in affirming such constitutional protections and in withholding them.

Absolute legal protection for freedom of opinion has never won the approval of the high tribunals of France, Great Britain, Canada, and the United States, among others. Still, for Weil, who delighted in her Sundays in Hyde Park,[20] a certain category of speech may never be abridged by the state. For Weil, the essential reason for protecting such expression is to advance the development of the intellect. Any speech that furthers this end in a meaningful way cannot be governed by the state. Accordingly, Athens acted illegitimately when it tried and sentenced Socrates; and contemporary regimes do likewise whenever they squelch truth-seeking discourse in the name of some so-called security interest.

The key idea here is this: "There has been a lot of freedom of thought over the past few years, but no thought" (NR 33). How can this be? One answer is that modern Western culture has overemphasized *freedom* while deemphasizing *thought*. From Weil's perspective, this is explainable in two ways: First, the power of intrinsically meaningless words, as she observed in a trenchant 1937 essay,[21] has taken a free and deadly hold in the political and cultural realms. Words like "capitalism" or "communism" or even today's "feminist" or "environmentalist," for example, tend to shut off real thought; these and other "ism" or "ist" words stupefy people more than they inspire deliberation. In fact, that is exactly their political mission. Second, and related, is the problem of propaganda in all its many forms. Propaganda, as Weil explained it, was akin to expression intended to influence *action* rather than to prompt *thought*.[22] Such expression, be it in political or literary form, conveys information in such a way so as to lead its audience to believe that it can be certain about things without engaging the mind. To borrow from Weil's writings on science, we might call this "quantum" communication (SNLG 49, 58, 63).

Freedom of opinion and association were importantly different for Weil, and the penal law should treat them so. Unlike the constitutions of several modern nations, Weil urged us to separate the domain of these two rights. Again, why?

When people attempt to speak as a group or political party, which is the rule in today's society, the threat of uniformity, collective imagination, group pressure, coercion, and/or propaganda is usually so great as to close off even the opportunity for real freedom of thought (NR 27–33).[23] "In the domain of thought," said Weil, "there should never be any physical or moral pressure exerted for any purpose other than the exclusive concern for truth" (SE 225). Of course, this critique of collectivities tracks what Weil said about the corruption of language through meaningless words and propaganda. Because political parties are the prime offenders when it comes to subverting the search for truth, "no group should be permitted by law to express an opinion" and political parties should be abolished (NR 27).

Consistent with what has been presented here, the more that any expression moves away from the pursuit of truth and towards the *persuasion* of the public, the more it may be treated as conduct and regulated proportionate to any harm it inflicts on the citizenry. Most of what appears in the popular press, and some of what passes as literature, would fall into this category of limited protection. In all likelihood, publications such as Thomas Paine's *The Age of Reason* (1794) and Camille Paglia's *Sexual Personae* (1990) would be entitled to even less protection, if any. Above all, this secondary level of freedom of opinion must never, directly or indirectly, deny the "eternal obligations toward the human being, once these obligations have been solemnly recognized by law" (NR 24). Thus, "race-hate" speech, for example, would be unprotected.

In order to prevent "offenses against the truth" (NR 38), propaganda of all kinds needs to be outlawed. This would be done by injunction (prior and/or post restraints of the press) and, if necessary, by criminal sanctions. Finally, group or associational communication could be regulated depending on the extent to which the association allowed for actual freedom of opinion within its ranks, and on the extent to which the group pressed for the real *needs* of its members instead of acting as an agent for the collective appetite (NR 32–33).

And just how is all of this "repression" (Weil's word, NR 26) to be done in a manner that comports with basic fairness—especially where, as she adds, a "juridical definition is impossible" (NR 26)? The answer depends, in good measure, on Weil's understanding of judicial justice.

Law and Judging

"The faith of a judge is not seen in his behavior at church, but in his behavior on the bench" (FLN 146). This statement, entered in her New York notebook, might suggest that for Weil the divide between the judicial and the spiritual was (or should be) great. Quite the contrary. As has been said earlier, her notion of attention is inextricably linked to her idea of judicial justice (FLN 351). Thus, the members of the "special courts" instituted to protect the public from "offenses against the truth" had to be

> drawn from very different social circles; be naturally gifted with a wide, clear, and exact intelligence; and be trained in a school where they receive *not just a legal education, but above all a spiritual one*; and only secondarily an intellectual one. They must be accustomed to love truth. (NR 40, emphasis added)[24]

This represented the paradigm of the Weilian jurist. But beyond this elevated notion of the judiciary, or at least the judiciary as reflected in her special courts, Weil also saw the judicial role in more general constitutive terms. Thus, in her "Essential Ideas for a New Constitution" she envisioned a very active judiciary with a key role to play in the affairs of the state. Judicial constitutional review of legislative enactments was essential. Only by this mechanism could "governmental and citizen compliance with the Fundamental Declaration" of the country be assured (SP 506). For this reason, the requirement of a case (an actual controversy between two parties) could be dispensed with and a judge could raise a point of fundamental law on his or her own motion (SP 506). Broadly speaking, maintains Patrice Rolland, this is a "true 'government of judges' that she is creating" (PR 250). The government's primary concern is justice: "There is an office of the state whose object is justice: this is the judicial office (EL 152).

Perhaps the best single statement of Weil's thinking on the judiciary and its role in society is set out in her London report, "Essential Ideas for a New Constitution," where she noted:

> Judges must have much more of a spiritual, intellectual, historical education than a juridical one (the strictly legal domain should only be retained in relation to unimportant things); they [judges] should be much, much more numerous; they must always judge with equity. For them the law should only serve as a guide. This should also apply to previous judgments [judicial precedents].
>
> But there should be a special court to judge the judges, and it should dispense extremely severe punishments.
>
> The legislators should also be able to summon before a court chosen from among their fellow members any judge guilty, in their eyes, of having violated the spirit of the laws. (EL 95)[25]

This lone statement reveals much about Weil's conception of the judiciary and the judicial role. Her judges are hierarchical[26] public figures who serve as one of the key moral voices of the community. Thus, "they would be responsible for," among other things, "publicly condemning any avoidable error . . . in a printed text or radio broadcast" (NR 38, 39). In fact, so great is their position in this new constitutional order that she provided that they be the ones to choose the president (from among the highest judges), who would in turn select a prime minister (EL 96).

Weil's judges are certainly not restrained in a way subservient or largely deferential to majoritarian will, even when that will is expressed in direct or representative legislation. Commenting on a draft constitution prepared by De Gaulle's Commission for State Reform, she noted:

> What do the words "representation of the majority and the opposition" signify? It is the introduction of political passions in their most arbitrary form, the least legitimate, in an official capacity, into what should be the seat of impartiality. If three men are there in their quality of representatives of the majority they will consider themselves obliged to speak in terms of this quality and not according to the unique light of their conscience. (EL 88)

In Weil's legal universe the positive law is only a guide for judges. Her judges are in some ways policymakers, lawmakers, law executors, and law interpreters all in one. Accordingly, in Weil's society their number should be enhanced considerably. While judges are to assume an active role in the community's affairs, similar to the one exercised by country priests, neither their presence nor number is intended to foster excessive litigation of the kind so popular in America. For such litigiousness is born out of a regime of rights, which Weil strongly opposed. Rather, judges were to act as mediators concerned with mutual obligations, and as cultural and spiritual mentors concerned with the common good.

This middle ground is made possible by the rule of equity. For Weil, the concept of equity—as discounted by Creon in Sophocles' *Antigone*—is central. It is this vast and fluid rule of law that permits her to discount standard legal formulas, judicial precedent, and even the idea that juridical definition is possible in the abstract (NR 24, 26). What this means, at least in the context of her "special courts" presiding over speech crimes, is the possibility of partisan or even arbitrary rule.[27] Furthermore, the broad sweep of such legal power would undoubtedly have a "chilling effect" on the dissemination of all forms of public information.

How, then, does one prevent unjust usurpations of judicial power? Clearly, the need to guard against such abuses is even greater when one considers the power of Weil's judges to try the prime minister,[28] sentence the president to death once he or she is duly removed from office (SP

506), and sentence writers to "prison or hard labor for [any] repeated commission" of offenses against the truth, "aggravated by proven dishonesty of intention" (NR 38). Then there was an even more sweeping power, namely, their duty to punish[29] *"everything which is evil"* (EL 95).

Weil hoped to curb the potential for such abuses of power and coercion in three key ways: first, by the judicial selection process; second, by an oversight process consisting of a special court to "judge the judges" aided by a legislative check on judicial rule; and finally, by "severe" sanctions against any jurist who violated his or her sworn duties. As for the chilling effect on public expression, it is probably something Weil generally saw as a social good. After all, "in every area," J. P. Little reminds us, "she wanted to make people responsible for their words and actions, and the more power they exercise, the more responsibility they must show."[30]

Law and Punishment

"We have lost all idea of what punishment is" (SE 31), argued Weil. She was highly critical of the retributive form of penal justice (the rule of fear) that had long been the norm in the Republic of France. "Repressive" (SE 31), "irresponsible conduct" (NR 21) was how she characterized the penal law as formulated by the parliament and exercised by the police, courts, and prison officials. For her, they did no more than inflict meaningless suffering while failing to dispense uplifting punishment. Weil decried the inherent abuses of the system to the point that she found it virtually "impossible for there to exist among us, in France, anything that deserves the name of punishment" (NR 22). Writing in her notebooks, she could not contain her outrage:

> The apparatus of penal justice has been so contaminated with evil, after all the centuries during which it has, without any compensatory purification, been in contact with evil-doers, that a condemnation is very often a transference of evil from the penal apparatus itself to the condemned man; and that is possible even when he is guilty. . . . Hardened criminals are the only people to whom the penal apparatus can do no harm. It does terrible harm to the innocent. (GG 65)

The French penal system, as she saw it, was bankrupt in conception and corrupt in execution. Accordingly, her critique and recommendations were conceptual and constitutional in nature.

Above all, Weil said, crime is a malady of the soul (FLN 140). Unless one understands this, it is impossible to comprehend how punishment represents an essential need of the human soul. Crime is a turning away from the good (why would anyone commit a crime if not for some spiritual malfunction?) and a corresponding renunciation of one's fundamental obligations towards others. Punishment, then, is a vital "method of procuring pure good for men who do not desire it" (SE 31).[31] Because of some "affliction" (SE 32) or disorder in the soul, the desire for the good is dormant. If this condition is to be cured, punishment must awaken "in a criminal, by pain or even death, the desire for pure good" (SE 31).[32] In this way, punishment is therapeutic,[33] not retributive[34]; its value depends on attentive consent, not on passive submission. Ultimately, punishment, if truly legitimate, gives more than it takes. Without this, punishment is more than a failure—it is institutionalized terror. On this basic point Weil is emphatic: "If one judges a criminal to be incurable, one has no right to punish him; one ought only to prevent him from doing harm. The infliction of a punishment is a declaration of faith that in the depths of the guilty there is a grain of pure good. To punish without that faith is to do evil for evil's sake" (FLN 345).

But the criminal justice system is antithetical to even the idea of such a declaration. Judges, for example, preoccupied with formulaic justice (i.e., the letter of the law or the rule of precedent) or pledged to retribution, desecrate the individual in the name of some perverse sense of justice. In the hands of such a judge, punishment can no longer affirm hope in the individual; it can only deny it systematically.

In matters of sentencing, penalties should not only reflect the nature of the crime, but also the power of the person who committed it. Weil called for a "conception of punishment in which social rank, as an aggravating circumstance, would necessarily play an important part in deciding what the penalty was to be" (NR 17). This equality principle was not based on any formal equality of charges or uniformity of sentencing. Quite the opposite, for according to this principle equality recognizes the "inevitable differences between men" but never allows those differences to "imply any difference in the degree of respect" (NR 16). For Weil, the concept of proportionality is necessarily tied to the concept of equality, particularly in criminal law.

At some important level, a person's obligations correspond to that person's power. Here too, the focus is on the individual. When a member of parliament or the president of a big corporation steals, it can never be treated the same as when a factory worker or waiter steals, notwithstanding the amounts taken. The former, given their social and economic stations, have greater obligations. (Criminal law, in Weilian terms, operates as sort of an *honor* code, where punishment mirrors the extent of one's public esteem.) Therefore, the "severity of the punishment must . . . be in keeping with the kind of obligation which has been violated, and not with the interests of security" (NR 21). The last point, societal security, shows how far Weil is willing to steer away from any utilitarian conception of criminal justice and move instead towards a conception grounded in individual responsibility. Correcting crime first and foremost means striving to correct the moral disorder within the individual. Everything else is secondary (NR 6–7).

SOME PRELIMINARY CONCLUSIONS

In a larger sense, what practical and theoretical conclusions do these fragments on law suggest?

Above all, law is a means for transforming the power of arbitrary rule into a system oriented towards the recognition and realization of human needs, physical and spiritual. Integral to this idea is Weil's notion of obligation. Since her concept of obligation is two-dimensional, law serves both temporal and transcendental purposes (NR 6–7). As to the latter, law is also one means, along with education, whereby the "reality *outside* of this world" might be implanted within the reality of *this* world. From this vantage point, law is not an end in itself; rather, it points beyond itself.

What are the (inevitable?) consequences of attempting to combine these two realities? Do they pose a clear and present danger to our tolerant and liberal pluralist society? Are they perforce a formula for tyranny? Connor Cruise O'Brien's words suggest a possible answer:

A France reconstructed on Weilian lines . . . would have no political parties, no trade unions, no freedom of association. It would have had a rigid, primitive, and eccentric form of censorship—one that would permit Jacques Maritain to be punished for having said something misleading about Aristotle. . . . There would be liberty, or something so described, coming second after "order" and just before "obedience" among the needs of the soul, but the guarantees of this liberty are in no way indicated.[35]

But the specter of *this* tyranny is not the only one. That is, what of the tyranny of a tolerant and liberal pluralist society? For example, its "tolerance" incapacitates it in the face of the tyrannical power of words—those words that condemn people and nations to death. Its "liberality" allows for the image of *freedom* of thought in the absence of any genuine *thought*, or perhaps even the possibility of such. Is community possible in a regime obsessed with rights? Moreover, this pluralist society is virtually helpless to combat the tyranny of moral reductionism and moral relativism. It is precisely because of this, one might add, that the "tolerant" society unavoidably turns away from a rehabilitative ideal of penal justice to a retributive one. And ultimately, there is a deeper philosophical, political, and legal question confronting modern liberals: Can liberty, in any of these senses, *actually* amount to freedom from restriction?[36]

This latter kind of tyranny, as much as the one described in O'Brien's charge, was of great concern to Simone Weil. In her own way she declared war on the various modern forms of tyranny and likewise challenged the premise of liberty as the absence of any restraint. But in doing so she was not altogether unmindful of the potential for tyranny in her own ideal regime. That is why she stressed the importance of *attention* as an essential prerequisite for the exercise of judicial power; of *consent* as a necessary precondition for genuine punishment; and the value of a legal order rooted in a concept of *obligation*. Without these preconditions, judicial rule disintegrates into arbitrariness; punishment collapses into brutality; and law crumbles into brute force. Weil seemed astutely aware of these facts. On an even more pragmatic plane, she realized that her "pretty fanciful" ideas might only come into existence "after one or two generations" and would likewise require many "transitional stages" (EL 97, 96).

Given all of these preconditions, is the legal order Weil described realizable in *this* world? We answer "no," but with an explanation. For one thing, the obvious incompleteness of her writings in this area would alone render their application highly problematic, if not preposterous.

For another thing, since so much of what Weil wrote was paradoxical and contrary to contemporary opinion, her "foolish" message is likely to be seen as deserving not "the slightest attention" (SL 200). Still, the transformative potential of her outsider's words (about law, labor, education and politics, etc.) inheres in its generative capacity to stimulate new and bold thought while at the same time offering some conceptual criteria by which to critique the status quo. Consistent with this, Weil insisted on no more than that her readers ask always: "Is what she says true?" (SL 201).

Weil attempted to employ law so as to safeguard the individual, not by a regime of rights but by one of obligations. On this score, her thought is radically different from the conception of law advanced by modern liberals. She defended the individual in ways that today's liberals simply have not. Equally telling, since her notion of law is rooted in the individual, it is a notion far different from the one championed by contemporary defenders of civic republican rule. Moreover, Weil openly criticized the collectivity in ways that defenders of civic republican thought have not. This crossing back and forth over this ideological divide is puzzling. Combining concerns about the individual (think liberal rule) with the notion of obligation (think civic republican rule) is, from a modern perspective, more than paradoxical—it is outright contradictory.

In assessing Weil's legal (and political) thought, it is useful to reflect on how she works with, and sometimes through, this apparent contradiction. For example, on the question of freedom of opinion she calls for certain absolute protections of individual liberty. This smacks of the liberal order. But she then goes on to stress, among other things, that freedom of opinion must never, directly or indirectly, deny the "eternal obligations toward the human being, once these obligations have been solemnly recognized by law" (NR 24). This smacks of the civic republican order. Consider, by way of another illustration, her thoughts on law and obedience. On the one hand, she identifies consent (again, think liberal) as the key factor of legitimate order. On the other hand, she rejects the idea of law as bartered and links the notion of obedience with that of obligations owed to the person (again, think civic republican).

Weil's notion of *community* is rooted in the *individual*, and vice versa. Conceptually speaking, is this possible? Functionally speaking, how is this to be done? For the purposes of this essay, we can no more than sketch a few introductory and incomplete answers to these questions:

1. Dismantle the regime of rights; furthermore, arrange all forms of power so as to comport with human needs.
2. Attempt to bridge the gap between the two realms; the notion of obligation can serve as one such bridge. In principle, the idea is to establish a reciprocal relation between the individual and the community.
3. Redefine the public notion of hierarchy (for example in government, business, and social life) away from status by privilege and power and towards rank seen as a reflection of the magnitude and weight of burdens and risks assumed.
4. Formulate a structure of law compatible with rule by principles—principles that find expression at every level from the constitutional preamble down to the local court practice.[37]

Though somewhat tempered by a separation of powers principle, the judiciary is the bright star in Weil's constellation. Her judges are rather similar in practice to Plato's "custodians of the law"[38] ; and to some degree, the role of her special court judges is analogous in principle to that of the "nocturnal council"[39] in Plato's *Laws*. What does such a vision of the judiciary imply?

Potentially, the judiciary may well be the most deliberative of the branches of government. Not surprisingly, this potential accounted for Weil's preference for the judicial institution. Moreover, the judiciary is typically the least democratic of the branches. So far as an antidote to rule by the collectivity, her judges needed to be above the reach of the crowd. Beyond this, Weil's trust in rule-by-judges reflects a real skepticism of both *executive power* and *legislative capacity*. Recall that her judges are also policymakers and lawmakers. Drinking at once from the three fountains of power, her officially robed custodians possess the strength that "James Joyce and his hero meditated upon: 'to forge within the smithy of my soul the uncreated conscience of the race.' "[40] But what if actualizing their consciences means producing results comparable to Chief Justice Roger Taney's 1856 ruling legitimizing the institution of American slavery? Weil's answer moves along two tracks: first, their character and backgrounds, as discerned in the selection process,[41] would most likely prevent such occurrences; and second, such transgressions, if they did occur, would be met with "severe" punishment, presumably even the death penalty. But given their immense power, is this enough?

Neither the majesty nor fairness of the law can reside in a black letter text detached from the realities of the person. "Laws are texts," she said, "characterized by a rather large generality, with the intent of serving as *guides* . . . for the government . . . [as well as] for judges" (EL 94, emphasis added). How, then, are judges to interpret or apply or even announce the law?

Two Weilian concepts are relevant here, "reading" and "attention." As to the former, judges read not only texts, but, more importantly, persons and situations:

> Justice. To be ever ready to admit that another person is something quite different from what we read when he is there (or when we think about him). Or rather, to read in him that he is certainly something different, perhaps something completely different, from what we read in him.
>
> Every being cries out silently to be read differently. (GG 121)

Reading a code (or judge-made precedent) can never be the same as reading a man or woman entangled in the web of life. Yet there are similarities in these two realms: both kinds of reading require a certain detachment, though of radically different types. To read a codified text in a detached way means setting the person aside in the name of some abstract or formulaic rule, whereas to read a person means setting our indifference towards him aside in the name of the person himself. To apply the full force of the Napoleonic Code to punish a common thief is, for Weil, to read the lesser of two texts (i.e., codified text) as if it were of greater importance than the text of the person. This is perforce illegitimate.

Judicial detachment born out of a faith in legal texts professes justice through indifference, whereas judicial detachment born out of a faith in the person professes justice through a discernment cognizant of real needs. Detachment from the one realm must be transferred to the other. That is why "human attention alone," maintained Weil, is vital to the legitimate "exercise [of] the judicial function" (FLN 351). On this point she was unyielding: "Attempts have been made to find mechanisms for the maintenance of justice which would dispense with the need for human attention. It cannot be done" (FLN 351).

The notion of equity is most compatible with Weil's view of law. Of course, this also means, contrary to the evolving Western practice, that neither Weil's criminal laws nor her restraints on freedom of opinion are narrowly written. What is clear and concise are the principles of law set out in the Fundamental Declaration. Statutory laws help to sharpen the focus of these principles, but are likewise written with a relatively high level of generality. Equally telling, her notion of equity is not (contrary to English common law) bound to judicial precedent.

Equity, for Weil, is contextual (the realities of this world) and normative (i.e., the reality outside of this world). Practically speaking, her equitable "system" of law is essentially ex post facto oriented. That is, where laws are not particularized, where they are not concise, they take on meaning only *after* the fact, after a judge has breathed life into them. Looking at the legal system from the "front end," such rule by equity cannot put the citizenry on actual notice of exactly what conduct is, or is not, prohibited. Yet, for centuries ex post facto laws, at least in the case of penal matters, have been deemed synonymous with tyranny. How would Weil respond to such a charge?

Weil might have answered somewhat along these lines: Law should not be, either in formulation or application, static. The more that it tends in that direction, the more it will defeat the high purpose of justice. Citizens, government officials, and judges are not unaware of the law; that is, they are abundantly cognizant of its declaration of principles. Living *in* the law means living *out* these principles, always attentively applying them to a myriad of situations. Always thinking; always reading. In living out the law, what is most important is the process of continually orienting oneself towards the good. Written laws, seen as "guides," point citizen and judge alike in this direction. In this sense, then, law may take on a concrete meaning after the fact, though it is imbued with meaning from the beginning. Conversely, when the legal realm of right and wrong is neatly packaged in black letter in a code or case, law (seen as a dialectical process) is sapped of its meaning.

"One finds in the *Écrits de Londres* a vocabulary of punishment that is particularly abundant and which did not exist in the earlier writings of Simone Weil" (PR 245). In reading her post-1942 writings, one cannot help but notice the presence of punishment. Why? What does this tell us about her legal thought?

Recall that for Weil the purpose of punishment is therapeutic. It is an inclusive concept (bringing people in), not an exclusive one (sending them out).[42] Punishment removes "the stigma of . . . crime" (NR, 21). Punishment, she tells us, can reveal one's mistake, much as a teacher does when helping a pupil to understand an error in geometry. Finally, punishment is redemptive.

Not surprisingly, Weil found it salutary to introduce her concept of punishment into an idea of law for at least two reasons: first, to make possible the dialectical process in the law; and second, to infuse law with an overtly moral purpose. As to the former, punishment operates as an essential corrective device in the process of "working out" the law. That is one reason why it represents "a vital need of the human soul." As to the second point, Patrice Rolland has offered the following comment on Weil's notion of punishment and its operation in the political process:

> Political responsibility, by abandoning all thought of a penal judgment of political acts, gives up judging them in moral terms, that is to say it gives up believing that it possesses the ultimate truth about historical and political acts. Penal sanctions define acts as wrongs, acts which themselves are defined on the basis of moral values. (PR 247)

In this context, Weil's notion of punishment reintroduced moral questions into politics and thereby *rejects* the idea that there are no truths in this realm. Punishment compels us, and especially our leaders, to face up to the moral matter. If there are no political truths, then there can be no punishment. The converse is equally true. Nuremberg-type political trials cannot be confined to the horrors of a single kind of inhumane behavior. Of course, utility—namely, the relative practical costs of identifying such truths—may counsel against punishment. Here again, Weil wanted these hard questions confronted, not evaded. So committed was she to this point that she was prepared, *if necessary*, to punish even her beloved General de Gaulle (EL 72).

Simone Weil left much incomplete. Yet, in her writings we can discern an ideal of law laboring to be born—an ideal at once unbending and unbound.

NOTES

1. This essay originally appeared in Bell, *Simone Weil's Philosophy of Culture*, 235–59. In addition to the standard abbreviations used throughout the text of this book, the following abbreviations will also be used in this essay: SP, Simone Pétrement, *Simone Weil: A Life*; and PR, Patrice Rolland, "Simone Weil et le Droit," *Cahiers Simone Weil* 13, no. 3 (Sept. 1990): 227.

2. These reports dealt with: 1) "responsibilities and sanctions for the mistakes committed by the French before the war, during the war, and under the Occupation"; 2) the "bases for a statute regarding French non-Christian minorities of foreign origin"; and 3) the formation of a future party and the structure of government (SP 507–10).

3. The immediate, but by no means sole, cause of this crisis was the question of whether or not the constitution of the Third Republic was still in force in light of the changes wrought by the Vichy Regime. See generally David Thompson, *Democracy in France Since 1870*, 5th ed. (London: Oxford University Press, 1969), 213–15.

4. In Weil's estimation, the courts of France had little if any meaningful power. For example, in her "Remarks on the Proposed New Constitution" she wrote: "It is untrue that in the current system the courts constitute a power. There is no judicial power. The judges only automatically put into effect, with a margin of personal evaluation which in reality is very weak, what they are commanded to do by an informal mixture of texts handed down by the kings, the two empires and parliament, and stripped of any relationship with the spirit or the letter of the Declaration of 1789" (EL 87).

5. What little Weil wrote about law dwelled on constitutive and criminal law matters largely to the exclusion of the civil law. So far as *law* is concerned, we find virtually nothing in her writings about civil liability, property, corporations, commercial transactions, etc. This is not to say that she did not have views on some of these topics, like her many observations on property. But those views never find any real legal expression in her works.

6. In *The Need for Roots* Weil noted: "Obligation is not based upon any *de facto* situation, nor upon jurisprudence, customs, social structure, relative state of forces, historical heritage, or presumed historical orientation; for no *de facto* situation is able to create an obligation" (NR 5).

7. In *Oppression and Liberty* Weil maintained: "True liberty is not defined by a relationship between desire and its satisfaction; but by a relationship between thought and action; the absolutely free man would be he whose every action proceeded from a preliminary judgment concerning the end which he set himself and the sequence of means suitable for attaining this end" (OL 85).

8. In her account of "hierarchism" in *The Need for Roots*, Weil noted: "Hier-

archism . . . is composed of a certain veneration, a certain devotion towards superiors, considered not as individuals, nor in relation to the powers they exercise, but as symbols. What they symbolize is that realm situated high above all men and whose expression in this world is made up of the obligations owed each man to his fellowmen. . . . The effect of true hierarchism is to bring each one to fit himself morally into the place he occupies" (NR 19).

9. See, e.g., Gabriella Fiori, *Simone Weil,* 361, n. 20 (discussing Weil's views on popular referenda, which—in the words of the biographer—are always "preceded by a long period of reflection and discussion").

10. See generally FLN 134 ("Contradiction is the lever of transcendence") and GG 89 ("The contradictions the mind comes up against—these are the only realities: they are the criterion of the real. There is no contradiction in what is imaginary. Contradiction is the test of necessity").

11. There remains as well the area of regulatory or administrative law.

12. See SP 507 ("they must always judge with equity. For them the law should only serve as a guide").

13. For Weil's comments on this matter, see, for example, N vol. II, 348.

14. See generally Finn Nielsen, "The Political Vision of Simone Weil," unpublished Ph.D. dissertation, University of California at Santa Barbara, 1976, 102 (Simone Weil rejected the idea that "rights and obligations are . . . on the same level and implicitly rejected recourse to the idea of a contract as an explanation of establishing a social or political order").

15. In her London notebook, Weil wrote: "Today, if a man sold himself as a slave to another, the contract would be juridically invalid, because liberty, being sacred, is inalienable" (FLN 346).

16. Stressing much the same point, Weil noted that "perfect liberty cannot be conceived as consisting merely in the disappearance of that necessity whose pressure weighs continually upon us" (OL 84). Obedience to just laws serves as a salutory reminder that liberty cannot be unlimited.

17. See generally PR 242 ("In a certain sense she may have reproduced the notion of natural law under a new name").

18. See, e.g., NR 243–44 (highly critical of Thomistic thought).

19. See also LTP 62 ("Complete liberty within its own sphere is essential to the intelligence").

20. In March 1943, Weil wrote to her parents: "I spend hours . . . watching people listen[ing] to orators. [Perhaps] this is the last remaining trace in . . . the world . . . of the discussions of the Athenian Agora" (SL 181).

21. See SE 154 ("When empty words are given capital letters, then, on the slightest pretext, men will begin shedding blood for them and piling up ruin in their name, without effectively grasping anything to which they refer. . . ." She continued: "To clarify thought, to discredit the intrinsically meaningless words,

and to define the use of others by precise analysis—to do this, strange though it may appear, might be a way of saving human lives").

22. Given Weil's strong reservations about public expressions that convey a conviction about some truth, it seems odd that she selected the phrase "freedom of *opinion*" rather than the phrase "freedom of *thought*," which she also used but less frequently.

23. She added: "What has been called freedom of association has been, in fact, up to now, freedom for associations. But associations have not got to be free; they are instruments, they must be held in bondage. Only the human being is fit to be free" (NR 33).

24. See also SP 507 (quoting Weil's "Essential Ideas for a New Constitution" report: "Judges must have much more of a spiritual, intellectual, historical, and social education than a juridical one").

25. See also "Remarks on the New Constitution" (EL 87): "There can only be judicial power if: 1. the judges receive a spiritual formation; 2. it is accepted that judgment in *equity*, inspired by the Fundamental Declaration, is the normal form of judgment."

26. See note 8 above.

27. See, e.g., NR 40 ("But, it will be objected, how can we guarantee the impartiality of the judges?"); Little, *Waiting on Truth*, 89 ("some of the distinctions she makes seem somewhat arbitrary").

28. "The Prime Minister, at the end of his five year term of office—if he has completed it without difficulty—would automatically pass before a High Court of Justice to give an account of his actions" ("Essential Ideas for a New Constitution," EL 97).

29. See also EL 157 ("*Judicial mission*. Remove a man from his surroundings, put him in a center or intensely spiritual atmosphere, have him judged 3, 5 years, return him home").

30. Little, *Waiting on Truth*, 90.

31. See also NR 20 ("Crime alone should place the individual who has committed it outside the social pale, and punishment should bring him back again inside it").

32. In an unpublished 1943 Free French report, Weil wrote: "Any punishment that is not, in regard to the culprit, a proof of respect is a worse crime than that committed by the criminal. It clearly follows that the punishment must aim, sooner or later, at evoking in the guilty man a movement of the soul that will lead him to recognize that the punishment is just and to submit to it freely" (Quoted in SP 508).

33. See generally N vol. I, 3 ("Punishment. If there is to be a cure for sin, punishment must not be considered an affliction. A painful experience, yes, certainly. A breaking in. What sort of a breaking in?"); see also FLN 332

("Criminals . . . should be cured by a hard and laborious but healthy and happy open-air life in unpopulated country, where they would be employed. . . . And only when cured, if they feel the need of it, should they be made to suffer").

34. See SE 32 ("All talk of chastisement, punishment, retribution, or punitive justice nowadays always refers solely to the basest kind of revenge").

35. Connor Cruise O'Brien, "The Anti-Politics of Simone Weil," *The New York Review of Books* 24, no. 8 (12 May 1977): 23; reprinted in *Simone Weil: Interpretations of a Life*, ed. George A. White (Amherst: University of Massachusetts Press, 1981), 96. For one response, see Dietz, *Between the Human and the Divine*, 181–85.

36. See generally Blum and Seidler, *A Truer Liberty*, 84–88 ("Liberty understood as freedom from any restriction—the core of the liberal conception of freedom—is a fantasy, for it has no connection with the real conditions of human existence and therefore, Weil insists, can have no value or meaning").

37. Of course, still other key concepts are relevant to this general inquiry, concepts such as Weil's notion of tradition.

38. See Plato, *The Laws* 632c in *Plato: The Collected Dialogues*, ed. Edith Hamilton and Huntington Cairns, dialogue trans. A. E. Taylor (Princeton: Princeton University Press, 1963), 1233 ("When the lawmaker has completed his discovery he will set over the whole system a body of guardians endowed some with wisdom, some with true beliefs, to the end that intelligence may knit the whole into one, and keep it in subjection to sobriety and justice, not to wealth or self-seeking"). See also Paul Friedländer, *The Dialogues: Second & Third Periods*, trans. Hans Meyerhoff, vol. 3 (Princeton: Princeton University Press, 1969), 440–43.

39. See Plato, *The Laws* 951d sq., 961a sq. See also Friedländer, *The Dialogues*, 441–43 and PR 251 (Weil's judges remind us of the nocturnal council).

40. Quoted in Max Lerner, *America as a Civilization*, 2nd ed. (New York: Henry Holt & Co., 1987), 1009–10.

41. To the best of our knowledge, based on her published writings, Weil never said exactly how and by whom her judges were to be selected. Our guess is that they would be selected by other judges. Cf. EL 88 ("The Supreme Court of Political Justice [why this adjective?] is badly composed. It is nominated by the President of the Assembly. Why?").

42. See generally N vol. II, 619 ("Through punishment the criminal ought to be made to feel himself reincorporated in the collectivity, not excluded from it").

SELECTED BIBLIOGRAPHY

Appiah, Kwame Anthony. *In My Father's House: Africa in the Philosophy of Culture*. Oxford: Oxford University Press, 1992.

Allen, Diogenes. "The Concept of Reading and the 'Book of Nature.' " In *Simone Weil's Philosophy of Culture*, edited by Richard H. Bell. Cambridge: Cambridge University Press, 1993.

Allen, Diogenes, and Eric O. Springsted. *Spirit, Nature and Community: Issues in the Thought of Simone Weil*. Albany: State University of New York Press, 1994.

Baier, Annette. "What Do Women Want in a Moral Theory?" In *Virtue Ethics*, edited by Roger Crisp and Michael Slote. Oxford Readings in Philosophy. Oxford: Oxford University Press, 1997.

Bell, Richard H. "Reading Simone Weil on Rights, Justice and Love." In *Simone Weil's Philosophy of Culture*, edited by Richard H. Bell. Cambridge: Cambridge University Press, 1993.

————. "Reading Simone Weil." Review of Peter Winch. *Simone Weil: The Just Balance. Religious Studies* 26, no. 1(March 1990).

————. "Simone Weil and Post-Holocaust Judaism." *Cahiers Simone Weil* 20, no. 1 (March 1997).

————. "Understanding African Philosophy from a Non-African Point of View: An Exercise in Cross-cultural Philosophy." In *Postcolonial African Philosophy, A Critical Reader*, edited by Emmanuel Chukwudi Eze. Oxford: Basil Blackwell, 1997.

Bell, Richard H., ed. *Simone Weil's Philosophy of Culture*. Cambridge: Cambridge University Press, 1993.

Bell, Richard H., with Barbara L. Battin. *Seeds of the Spirit: Wisdom of the Twentieth Century*. Louisville: Westminster John Knox Press, 1996.

Blum, Lawrence. *Moral Perception and Particularity*. Cambridge: Cambridge Unviersity Press, 1994.

Blum, Lawrence, and Victor Seidler. *A Truer Liberty: Simone Weil and Marxism.* London: Routledge & Kegan Paul, 1989.

Brenner, Rachel Feldhay. *Writing as Resistance: Four Women Confronting the Holocaust.* University Park: The Pennsylvania State University Press, 1997.

Camus, Albert. *The Rebel.* New York: Vantage Books, 1958.

Cohen, Mitchell, and Nicole Fermon, eds. *Princeton Readings in Political Thought.* Princeton: Princeton University Press, 1966.

Coles, Robert. *Children in Crisis.* Boston: Atlantic-Little, Brown, 1967, 1972, 1978.

———. *The Moral Life of Children.* Boston: The Atlantic Monthly Press, 1986.

———. *The Political Life of Children.* Boston: The Atlantic Monthly Press, 1986.

———. *Simone Weil: A Modern Pilgrimage.* Reading, Mass.: Addison-Wesley Publishers, 1987.

———. *The Spiritual Life of Children.* Boston: Houghton Mifflin Company, 1990.

Collins, Ronald K. L., and Finn E. Nielsen. "The Spirit of Simone Weil's Law." In *Simone Weil's Philosophy of Culture*, edited by Richard H. Bell. Cambridge: Cambridge University Press, 1993.

Devaux, André. "On the Right Use of Contradiction According to Simone Weil." In *Simone Weil's Philosophy of Culture*, edited by Richard H. Bell. Cambridge: Cambridge University Press, 1993.

Dietz, Mary G. *Between the Human and the Divine: The Political Thought of Simone Weil.* Totowa, N.J.: Rowman & Littlefield, 1988.

Doering, E. Jane. "Simone Weil: A Woman's Voice." Unpublished essay given at the 1992 American Weil Society Meetings.

Dunaway, John M., and Eric O. Springsted, eds. *The Beauty That Saves: Essays on Aesthetics and Language in Simone Weil.* Macon, Ga.: Mercer University Press, 1966.

Elshtain, Jean Bethke. "A Man for This Season: Václav Havel on Freedom and Responsibility." Unpublished essay.

———. "Politics Without Cliché." *Social Thought* 60, no. 3 (Fall 1993).

———. *Women and War.* New York: Basic Books, 1987.

Evans, Christine Ann. "The Power of Parabolic Reversal: The Example in Simone Weil's Notebooks." *Cahiers Simone Weil* 19, no. 3 (September 1996).

Ferguson, Harvie. *Melancholy and the Critique of Modernity: Søren Kierkegaard's Religious Psychology.* London and New York: Routledge, 1995.

Finch, H. L. "Simone Weil: Harbinger of a New Renaissance?" In *Simone Weil's Philosophy of Culture*, edited by Richard H. Bell. Cambridge: Cambridge University Press, 1993.

Fiori, Gabriella. *Simone Weil: An Intellectual Biography.* Translated by Joseph R. Berrigan. Athens and London: University of Georgia Press, 1989.

————. *Simone Weil: Une femme absolue*. Paris: Éditions du Félin, 1987.

Fingarette, Herbert. *Confucius: The Secular as Sacred*. New York: Harper and Row, 1972.

Fischer, Clare. "Simone Weil and the Civilization of Work." In *Simone Weil's Philosophy of Culture*, edited by Richard H. Bell. Cambridge: Cambridge University Press, 1993.

Foucault, Michel. *The Foucault Reader*. Edited by Paul Rabinow. London: Penguin Books, 1984.

Freire, Paulo. *Letters to Cristina: Reflections on My Life and Work*. Translated by Donaldo Macedo with Quilda Macedo and Alexandre Oliveira. New York: Routledge, 1996.

————. *Pedagogy of Hope*. Translated by Robert Barr. New York: Continuum, 1994.

————. *Pedagogy of the Oppressed*. Translated by Myra Bergman Ramos. New York: The Seabury Press, 1968.

Friedländer, Paul. *The Dialogues: Second & Third Periods*. Translated by Hans Meyerhoff, vol. 3. Princeton: Princeton University Press, 1969.

Gilligan, Carol. "In a Different Voice: Women's Conceptions of Self and of Morality." In *Women and Values: Readings in Recent Feminist Philosophy*, edited by Marilyn Pearsall. 2d ed. Belmont, Calif.: Wadsworth Publishing Co., 1993.

Gilman, Sander L. *Jewish Self-Hatred: Anti-Semitism and the Hidden Language of the Jews*. Baltimore: The Johns Hopkins University Press, 1986.

Hallie, Philip P. *Lest Innocent Blood Be Shed: The Story of the Village of Le Chambon and How Goodness Happened There*. San Francisco: Harper & Row, 1979.

————. "Scepticism, Narrative, and Holocaust Ethics." *Philosophical Forum* 16, nos. 1–2.

————. *Tales of Good and Evil, Help and Harm*. Introduction by John J. Compton and afterword by Doris A. Hallie. New York: HarperCollins Publishers, 1997.

Havel, Václav. "A Dream for Czechoslovakia." *The New York Review of Books*, (25 June 1992), 8–13.

————. "The Future of Hope: Observations On the Subject of Hope from Hiroshima, 'a city where we cannot help thinking of death.'" *Religion and Values in Public Life*. Harvard Divinity School 5, no. 2/3 (winter/spring 1997).

————. *Letters to Olga*. New York: Henry Holt & Co. 1989.

————. *Living in Truth*. Edited by Jan Vladislaw. London: Faber and Faber, 1989.

Illich, Ivan. *Deschooling Society*. New York: Harper Torchbook, 1988.

————. *Gender*. New York: Pantheon Books, 1982.

———. *Imprisoned in the Global Classroom.* London: Writers and Readers Publishing Cooperative, 1976.

Irigaray, Luce. *An Ethics of Sexual Difference.* Translated by Carolyn Burke and Gillian C. Gill. Ithaca, N.Y.: Cornell University Press, 1993.

———. *je, tu, nous: Toward a Culture of Difference.* Translated by Alison Martin. London: Routledge, 1993.

———. *Sexes and Genealogies.* Translated by Gillian C. Gill. New York: Columbia University Press, 1993.

Kerr, Fergus. *Immortal Longings: Versions of Transcending Humanity.* London: SPCK, 1997.

Kozol, Jonathan. *Amazing Grace: The Lives of Children and the Conscience of a Nation.* New York: HarperCollins, 1995.

———. *Death at an Early Age.* Boston: Houghton Mifflin, 1967.

———. *Illiterate America.* New York: New American Library, 1985.

Lerner, Max. *America as a Civilization,* 2d ed. New York: Henry Holt & Co., 1987.

Levinas, Emmanuel. "Simone Weil against the Bible." In *Difficult Freedom: Essays on Judaism.* Translated by Seán Hand. Baltimore: The Johns Hopkins University Press, 1990.

Little, J. P. *Simone Weil: Waiting on Truth.* Berg Women's Series. Oxford: St. Martin's Press, 1988.

———. "Simone Weil's Concept of Decreation." In *Simone Weil's Philosophy of Culture,* edited by Richard H. Bell. Cambridge: Cambridge University Press, 1993.

MacIntyre, Alasdair. *After Virtue.* Notre Dame: University of Notre Dame Press, 1981.

MacKinnon, Catherine A. "Rape: On Coercion and Consent." In *Women and Values: Readings in Recent Feminist Philosophy,* edited by Marilyn Pearsall. 2d ed. Belmont, Calif.: Wadsworth Publishing Co., 1993.

MacPherson, C. B. *The Political Theory of Possessive Individualism.* Oxford: Oxford University Press, 1962.

McLellan, David. *Simone Weil: Utopian Pessimist.* London: Macmillan, 1989.

———. "Simone Weil: Utopian Pessimist." A film documentary written by David McLellan and produced and directed by John Mair. A Mair Golden Moments Production for Channel 4, Great Britain, 1989.

Merton, Thomas. *The Way of Chuang Tzu.* New York: New Directions, 1969.

Meyerhoff, Hans. "Contra Simone Weil: 'The Voices of Demons for the Silences of God.' " In *Arguments and Doctrines: A Reader of Jewish Thinking in the Aftermath of the Holocaust,* edited by Arthur A. Cohen. New York: Harper and Row Publishers, 1970.

Miles, Sian, ed. *Simone Weil: An Anthology.* London: Virago Press Limited, 1986.

Moulakis, Athanasios. *Simone Weil and the Politics of Self-Denial.* Translated by Ruth Hein. Columbia: University of Missouri Press, 1998.

Murdoch, Iris. *Sovereignty of Good.* New York: Schocken Books, 1970.

Nevin, Thomas. *Simone Weil, Portrait of a Self-Exiled Jew.* Chapel Hill: University of North Carolina Press, 1991.

Nielsen, Finn. "The Political Vision of Simone Weil." Unpublished Ph.D. dissertation. University of California at Santa Barbara, 1976.

Noddings, Nel. *Caring: A Feminine Approach to Ethics and Moral Education.* Berkeley, Calif.: University of California Press, 1984.

————. "Ethics from the Standpoint of Women." In *Women and Values: Readings in Recent Feminist Philosophy,* edited by Marilyn Pearsall. 2d ed. Belmont, Calif.: Wadsworth Publishing Co., 1993.

Nye, Andrea. *Philosophia: The Thought of Rosa Luxemburg, Simone Weil, and Hannah Arendt.* New York: Routledge, 1994.

Nussbaum, Martha. *Love's Knowledge: Essays on Philosophy and Literature.* New York: Oxford University Press, 1990.

O'Brien, Connor Cruise. "The Anti-Politics of Simone Weil." *The New York Review of Books* 24, no. 8 (12 May 1977): 23; reprinted in *Simone Weil: Interpretations of a Life.* Edited by George A. White. Amherst: University of Massachusetts Press, 1981.

O'Connor, Flannery. *Letters of Flannery O'Connor: The Habit of Being.* Selected and edited by Sally Fitzgerald. New York: Vintage Books, 1980.

Panichas, George A., ed. *The Simone Weil Reader.* New York: The David McKay Co., 1977.

Pearsall, Marilyn, ed. *Women and Values: Readings in Recent Feminist Philosophy* 2d ed. Belmont, Calif.: Wadsworth Publishing Co., 1993.

Perrin, J. M., and Gustave Thibon. *Simone Weil as We Knew Her.* Translated by Emma Craufurd. London: Routledge & Kegan Paul, 1953.

Pétrement, Simone. *Simone Weil: A Life.* New York: Pantheon Books, 1976.

Phillips, D. Z. "God and Concept-formation in Simone Weil." In *Simone Weil's Philosophy of Culture,* edited by Richard H. Bell. Cambridge: Cambridge University Press, 1993

Plato. *The Laws* 632c, *The Laws* 951d sq., 961a sq. In *Plato: The Collected Dialogues.* Edited by Edith Hamilton and Huntington Cairns, dialogue translated by A. E. Taylor. Princeton: Princeton University Press, 1963.

Rawls, John. *A Theory of Justice.* Cambridge: Harvard University Press, 1971.

Rhees, Rush. *Discussions of Simone Weil.* Edited by D. Z. Phillips, assisted by Mario von der Ruhr. Albany: State University of New York Press, forthcoming 1998.

————. *Rush Rhees on Religion and Philosophy.* Edited by D. Z. Phillips. Cambridge: Cambridge University Press, 1997.

Rolland, Patrice. "Simone Weil et le Droit." *Cahiers Simone Weil* 13, no. 3 (September 1990).

Rorty, Richard. *Contingency, Irony, and Solidarity.* Cambridge: Cambridge University Press, 1989.

Rosenzweig, Franz. *Franz Rosenzweig: His Life and Thought.* Edited by Naham Glatzer. New York: Schocken Books, 1953.

Ruddick, Sara. "Maternal Thinking." In *Women and Values: Readings in Recent Feminist Philosophy.* Belmont, Calif.: Wadsworth Publishing Co., 1993.

Sandel, Michael. *Liberalism and the Limits of Justice.* Cambridge: Cambridge University Press, 1982.

Schell, Jonathan. *The Fate of the Earth.* New York: Alfred A. Knopf, 1982.

Shklar, Judith N. *The Faces of Injustice.* New Haven: Yale University Press, 1990.

Solomon, Robert C., and Mark C. Murphy, eds. *What Is Justice?* Oxford: Oxford University Press, 1990.

Soloveitchik, Joseph. *Halakhic Man.* Philadelphia: Jewish Publication Society of America, 1983.

Soyinka, Wole. *The Open Sore of the Continent: A Personal Narrative of the Nigerian Crisis.* New York: Oxford University Press, 1966.

Springsted, Eric O. "Of Tennis, Persons and Politics." *Philosophical Investigations* 16, no. 3 (July 1993).

———. "Rootedness: Culture and Value." In *Simone Weil's Philosophy of Culture*, edited by Richard H. Bell. Cambridge: Cambridge University Press, 1993.

———. *Simone Weil & The Suffering of Love.* Cambridge: Cowley Publications, 1986.

———. " 'Thou Hast Given Me Room': Simone Weil's Retheologization of the Political." *Cahiers Simone Weil* 20, no. 2 (June 1997).

Steiner, George. "The Self-hatred of Simone Weil." *Times Literary Supplement,* 4 June 1993.

Stringfellow, William. *The Politics of Spirituality.* Philadelphia: The Westminster Press, 1984.

Sullivan, William M. "A Public Philosophy for Civic Culture." In *Rooted in the Land: Essays on Community and Place*, edited by William Vitek and Wes Jackson. New Haven: Yale University Press, 1996.

Taylor, Charles. *Philosophical Arguments.* Cambridge: Harvard University Press, 1995.

———. *The Sources of the Self: The Making of the Modern Identity.* Cambridge: Harvard University Press, 1989.

Terry, Megan. *Approaching Simone.* Old Westbury: The Feminist Press, 1973.

Thompson, David. *Democracy in France since 1870.* 5th ed. London: Oxford University Press, 1969.

Tronto, Joan. "Beyond Gender Difference to a Theory of Care." *Signs* 12, no. 4 (1987).

Tung-chi, Lin. "The Chinese Mind: Its Taoist Substratum." *Journal of the History of Ideas* 8, no. 3 (June 1947).

Tzu, Lao. *Tao Te Ching.* Translated and introduction by D. C. Lau. London: Penguin Books, 1963.

van Beeck, S. J., Frans Jozef. *Loving the Torah More than God? Toward a Catholic Appreciation of Judaism.* Chicago: Loyola University Press, 1989.

Vetö, Miklos. *The Religious Metaphysics of Simone Weil.* Translated by Joan Dargan. Albany: State University of New York Press, 1994.

Vitek, William, and Wes Jackson, eds. *Rooted in the Land: Essays On Community and Place.* New Haven: Yale University Press, 1996.

Weil, Simone. The citations of her works referred to in this book are included in the abbreviations list at the beginning of the book.

White, James Boyd. *"This Book of Starres": Learning to Read George Herbert.* Ann Arbor: University of Michigan Press, 1994.

Williams, Rowan. "Critical Notice." *Philosophical Investigations* 14 (April 1991).

———. "The Necessary Non-Existence of God." In *Simone Weil's Philosophy of Culture,* edited by Richard H. Bell. Cambridge: Cambridge University Press, 1993.

Winch, Peter. *Simone Weil: "The Just Balance."* Cambridge: Cambridge University Press, 1989.

Wittgenstein, Ludwig. *Culture and Value.* Chicago: University of Chicago Press, 1980.

———. *Philosophical Investigations.* London: The Macmillan Co., 1953.

Wolgast, Elizabeth. *The Grammar of Justice.* Ithaca, N.Y.: Cornell University Press, 1987.

INDEX

abortion, 40–41, 42
affliction, 26–29, 45–46, 47, 63, 106, 170, 181–82; and the cross, 61, 62, 94, 98, 183
Africa, 43, 104, 124, 126, 127, 135, 142–43, 149, 201, 202. *See also* South Africa
America. *See* United States
anarcho-syndicalist, 9
Antigone, xv, 13, 45, 45n21, 87, 98, 138, 161, 229
Arendt, Hannah, xi, 25
Aristotle, 57, 225, 233
Assyrians, 172, 174. *See also* Nebuchadnezzar
Athenian democracy, 36, 65, 207. *See also* Greek thought (classical)
attention, xiv, 47–51, 54, 60–61, 92–93, 117–19, 147, 152–56, 233, 236, 237

balance. *See* equilibrium
Berlin, 4, 104
Bernanos, George, 123
Bhagavad-Gita, 16, 98, 173, 212, 213
Blum and Seidler, 28, 31, 37, 53, 96, 98
Book of the Dead, The Egyptian, 62, 87, 98

Brazil, 124, 148, 148n3, 151. *See also* Paulo Freire
Brenner, Rachel Feldhay, 168–171
Brion, M. Marcel, 92n17
Buddha, 87, 183, 199, 200
Buddhism, 16, 91, 92n17, 173, 199, 203, 212

Camus, Albert, xi, xii, xv, 10, 104
Catholic Church, xiii, 168, 169, 170, 176, 201, 211. *See also* Christianity
Central America. *See* Latin America
Charter of '77, The, 106n5
China, 10, 80, 87, 91, 92n17, 99, 105, 124, 126, 132, 167, 173, 174, 193. *See also* Confucius
Christ, 9n10, 94, 98, 134, 169, 183, 199, 200, 210. *See also* Jesus
Christianity, xiii, xiv, 6n6, 9n10, 24n6, 28, 40, 67, 92, 93, 135, 167, 169, 170, 172, 173, 175, 176, 199, 200, 201, 210–211, 212, 213. *See also* Catholic Church
Christology, 16, 183, 186
Chuang Tzu, 92n17, 133
Cold War, 3, 104–105
collective, 6n6, 9, 24–25, 137–138, 177, 194; favorable use of, 137–138
Collins and Nielsen, 114, 115, 118, 119

colonialism, 10, 126–127, 142, 195, 201

communism, 3–4, 9, 10, 105–106, 195, 209, 226

community, 78, 125–126, 130–144, 234–235; and politics, 143–144, 207–208, 234–235. *See also* society and politics

compassion: compassion-based morality, xiii, 13, 78, 84–87, 91, 98, 110, 115, 130, 184–185; and humility, 94–96, 204–205; the "Tao" of, 70, 91–96, 98–99, 92n17. *See also* justice as compassion

Confucius, 62, 92n17, 99, 131–137, 132n6

"conscientization," 150–151, 155–156

consent, 30, 41–42, 50–52, 54, 57–58, 65, 82, 198, 224, 233

Constitution, United States, 80, 129n4

country, 141–143, 209

Czech Republic, xiii, 119

Czechoslovakia, 104, 105, 106, 107, 107n7, 119

death, Simone Weil's, xiin1, 169–170, 175–176, 191

de Beauvoir, Simone, xi, xii, 12

de Gaulle, Charles, xii, 219, 229, 238

de Viau, Théophile, 130

decreation, 42, 169, 185

democracy, 4–5, 37, 149–150, 151–152, 193, 195, 207–208, 209. *See also* Athenian democracy

Descartes, 7, 13, 16, 208, 212

desire for the good, 71, 78–81, 92, 147, 183

Dietz, Mary, 6, 6n6, 25, 26

Eastern Europe, 10, 52, 104, 110, 127, 149, 168, 193

Eckhard, Meister, 15

education: for civilization, 30, 159–163; for liberation, 149–150, 155–156, 159; motives for, 156–158; values in, 126, 148, 157–158

Egypt, 10, 62, 68, 80, 87, 98, 167, 173, 199, 200, 203

Eliot, T.S., xii, 33

Elshtain, Jean Bethke, 111, 111n20

enlightenment, 8, 33, 37, 64, 67, 80–81, 106, 107, 171, 172, 196

equilibrium, 7, 21, 23, 25, 46, 58, 61, 117

Erikson, Erik, 6n6, 87

ethics: of care, 13, 88–91; communitarian, 26, 35, 36, 46n22, 88; of relativism, 37, 45, 233

Evans, Christine Ann, 3, 82n4

fascism, 3–4, 9, 10, 105–106, 148, 195, 209

Father Perrin, 48, 169, 211, 212

Faust, 72, 73

feminist/feminism, 12–13, 40–41, 66–67, 86–91, 87n6, 89n11, 148, 226; woman's point of view, 11–14, 12n15, 67n5, 71, 88–91, 168, 171, 213

Fingarette, Herbert, 132–134, 135

Fiori, Gabriella, 14

First Amendment, 116, 129n4

Fischer, Clare, 13

Foucault, Michel, 69, 70, 74

France, laws. *See* law, in France

Free French, 10, 191, 217–220, 236

free market capitalism, 9, 10, 36, 150, 226

freedom, 225–227, 233

Freire, Paolo, 149n3, 149–153, 155, 156, 159, 160

French Revolution, 67, 83, 84, 129, 219, 220
Freud, Anna, 172, 176
Freud, Sigmund, 87
friendship, 26, 64–69
Fulbright, William, 195

Germany, 4, 9, 107, 107n7, 148, 168, 193, 208
Gide, André, xii
Gilligan, Carol, 87
Gilman, Sander, 167
God: absence of, 27, 29, 61, 74, 85, 178, 180–183, 185–186, 185n48, 191, 191n1, 204–205; "draw God down," 7, 16, 54, 63–64, 82, 185, 197, 199; presence of, 29, 58, 63, 74, 84–85, 191n1, 204–205; as supernatural, 96–99
Goethe, 72
Gospel, 25–26, 62, 68, 86, 97, 199, 213
grace, 61–64
Grail, 16, 49–50, 93, 153
Great Beast, 22–23, 34n4
Greek thought (classical), xiv, 10, 11, 34, 45, 46, 65, 67, 68, 80, 83, 98, 161, 162, 167, 173, 174, 199, 200, 212, 213, 229. *See also* Plato, Socrates, *Symposium*

Hallie, Philip P., 72–73, 159
Havel, Olga, 107, 108, 110
Havel, Václav, xii, xv, 52, 104, 105–112, 119–120, 149, 196, 207
Hebrew culture. *See* Jewishness
Heidegger, Martin, xi, 13
Herbert, George, 8n8, 9n10, 210
Heschel, Abraham, 184
Hinduism, 10, 87, 174, 201, 202, 203. *See also* Krishna

Hiroshima, 120, 208
Hitler, Adolf, 124, 128, 159, 174, 181, 192. *See also* Nazis
Hobbes, Thomas, 34
Hull, Massachusetts, 73
humiliation, 25, 39, 45, 62, 106, 128
Hungary, 104
Husak, Dr. Gustav, 106

idealism, 16, 26
Iliad, The 11, 22, 45–46, 50, 62, 88, 89, 98, 181, 182, 184, 194, 200n7
incarnation: foreshadowing of the, 95–96, 198–199; of Christ, 61, 98; of ideas, 5, 16, 114
India, 68, 80, 167, 199. *See also* Hinduism
individualism, 6, 34–36, 82
Indochina, French, 201, 212
Irigaray, Luce, 66–67
Isaiah, 173, 175

James, Joshua, 73
Jesus, 64, 94, 175, 199. *See also* Christ
Jew. *See* Jewishness
"Jewish self-hatred." *See* Jewishness
Jewishness, xiii, 6n6, 12, 165–186, 212
Job, 27, 167, 173, 182
Joyce, James, 273
Judaism. *See* Jewishness
judges. *See* law and judicial system
judicial. *See* law and judicial system
justice: and attention, 47–51, 117–119; as compassion, xiv, 31, 72–75, 130, 148, 158, 183–185, 191, 192, 205, 210; grammar of, 39–40, 63, 196–197; and love, 45, 46, 48, 63; rights vs., 36–38, 43–46; struggling for, 8, 36, 43, 69, 71, 78, 129, 159,

163, 194, 197, 205, 213; supernatural virtue of, xiii, 54, 57–64.

Kant, Emmanuel, 81, 87, 88, 91, 114, 208
kavanah, 184
Kierkegaard, Søren, 15, 70, 74, 87n7, 126
Kolitz, Zvi, 165, 183
Kozol, Jonathan, 149, 149n4, 151
Krishna, 93, 199, 200

labor. *See* work
Languedoc, 65, 67–68, 87, 162, 201, 203, 211
language: conceptual analysis of, 2–6, 38–44, 104–105, 166n4; importance of, 2–7, 7n7, 42, 62, 110–111
Lao Tzu, xi, 62, 70, 92–93, 92n17, 94, 99, 132, 136, 174
Latin America, 98, 104, 126, 149, 202
law and judicial system, 112–119, 217–238; "eternal source" of, 113, 118; in France, 82n4, 113, 129, 218–220, 223, 230, 236; and judges, 117–119, 227–230, 235, 235n41; and punishment, 116–117, 230–232, 231n32, 237–238
Le Chambon-sur-Lignon, 72, 72n11, 73
Le Puy, 8, 161–162
Levinas, Emmanuel, 108, 174, 179–181
li, 132–134
liberal society, 33–38, 53
liberation theology, 91, 98
liberty, 6, 24–25, 27, 84, 207, 221–223
Little, J. P., 5, 41, 83, 84, 230
Locke, John, 34

London, 9, 10, 173, 176, 191, 218–220, 225
London writings, xiv, 24, 29, 69, 118, 117n26, 134, 147, 174, 228, 237
love: "madness of love," 52, 61, 69–75; of God, 49–50; of neighbor, 63, 64–65, 180–181; sexual, 65–66; unconditional, 53, 58, 60
Luxemburg, Rosa, 13, 148

MacKinnon, Catherine A., 51. *See also* rape
Mandela, Nelson, 105n3, 207
Maritain, Jacques, 270
Marseilles, 11, 92, 92n17, 170, 211n10, 223
Marx, Karl, xiv, 5, 21, 22, 29, 36, 67, 150, 223
Marxism, 21–23, 29, 37, 148
Maurras, 173
McLellan, David, xii, 10, 11, 34n2, 45n20, 146
Merleau-Ponty, Maurice, 13
Merton, Thomas, 133
Meyerhoff, Hans, 174n21
Minister of Education, letter to, 166
money, 59–60, 126, 197–198
morality: and governance, 128–130, 139–144; moral responsibility, 108–109, 111, 111n20; in politics, 30–31, 108–109, 138, 210. *See also* compassion-based morality and right-based morality
Moses, 173, 175
Murdoch, Iris, xii, xv, 46n22, 88, 89

Nagasaki, 208
Napoleonic Code, 236. *See also* laws, in France
Nazis, 4, 208. *See also* Hitler, Adolf
Nebuchadnezzar, 173, 174

neighborhoods, 139–141, 140n20
New York City, 9, 11, 77, 170, 173, 227
Nietzsche, Friedrich, 37, 87
Nigeria, 143
Noddings, Nel, 13, 89–90, 156
non-active action, 48, 92–94
Nozick, Robert, 34, 35
Nussbaum, Martha, 149–200
Nye, Andrea, 22, 40, 66, 71, 142, 144, 148, 157, 161

obedience, 129–130, 224
obligation: civic, 31, 234; to the law, 113–115, 233; moral, 82–84, 82n4, 90, 92; vs. rights, 83, 91–92
O'Brien, Connor Cruise, 232, 233
Old Testament, 87, 172, 173–175, 201. *See also* Torah
order, 138–139
"Oriental wisdom," xiv, 11, 92–96, 98–99, 131–137, 132n6, 170, 199

pacifism, 9
Paglia, Camille, 227
Paine, Thomas, 227
Paris, 9, 179
peace, 94, 130
Pétrement, Simone, xii, 9n10
Plato, 7, 10, 39, 65, 66, 92, 118, 173, 183, 208, 212, 235. *See also Symposium*
pluralism: cultural, 139–140, 141, 200–203, 210–213; religious, 167, 170, 173–174, 198–201, 210–213.
Poland, 104
political, 30–31, 38, 105, 131, 218–220, 238
politics, 25, 52–53, 127–130, 143–144, 206–207; and politicians, 127–130, 198

Pope John XXIII, xii
Pope Paul VI, xii
Portugal, 9, 29, 201, 210
power: abuse of, xiii, 22–24, 27, 46, 71, 94–95, 94n19, 110, 195; and responsibility, 142–144. God's, 93–94, 96
powerlessness, 93–96, 110; God's, 93–94, 96
pragmatism, 3, 16
Proudhon, Pierre Joseph, 21, 29
Psalms, 167, 173, 174
public sphere, 6, 25–26, 31, 105, 113, 125, 130–131
punishment. *See* law and judicial system

Rakover, Yossel, 165, 166, 177–186
rape (violated women), 13, 41, 51–52, 60
Rawls, John, xi, 34, 35, 43, 80–81, 88
reading, 14, 14n19, 39, 60, 150, 155–156, 236, 237
realpolitik, 3, 82
"rebel" and rebellion, xii, xv, 104, 149
religious experiences, 9, 9n10, 26, 28–29
Renaissance, true and false, 67, 171, 172
Rhees, Rush, 15, 15n23, 39, 140n20, 166, 174–175, 201, 210
Rich, Adrienne, xii, 11–12
rights: as contentious, 36, 40–46, 60; rights-based morality, 35–36, 47, 78, 82–83, 86, 91, 98, 185; social, 28, 44–45; women's, 40, 168
Rolland, Patrice, 114, 228, 238
Roman thought (classical), 59–60, 68, 68n4, 83, 172, 174
Rome, 172, 174, 201
rootedness, 29, 103–104, 112, 123, 125, 130, 136–137, 144, 162

Rousseau, Jean-Jacques, 21, 92
Ruddick, Sara, 88–89
Russia, 4, 67, 193. *See also* Soviet
    Union

Saint-Etienne, 8, 161
Saint Francis of Assisi, 201, 210
Saint John of the Cross, 15, 173, 210
Sandel, Michael, 35
Scheler, Max, 87n7
Schmäling, Julius, 72n11
Schumann, Maurice, xii, 9, 175
self-renunciation, 12, 48, 61, 73, 95–
    96, 169, 175–176
Slovak peoples, 119
Smith, Adam, 35, 224
society, 103–106. *See also* community
Socrates, xv, 1, 2, 6, 7, 39, 59, 62, 65,
    225
Socratic thinker, 1, 6, 7, 39–40, 59
Soloveitchik, Rabbi Joseph, 185
South Africa, 43, 104, 105n3, 124,
    142. *See also* Mandela, Nelson
South America. *See* Latin America
Soviet Union, 10, 104, 105, 106, 107,
    110, 124, 149. *See also* Russia *and*
    Stalin, Joseph
Soyinka, Wole, 143
Spain, 4
Spanish Civil War, 9, 29, 124
Spanish Popular Front, 9
spiritual: spirituality, 8, 68, 97–98,
    199, 210–213; vocation, 28, 162,
    203, 205–208; way of life, 10, 81,
    96–99, 106–107, 119–120, 192,
    206n9; writer, xii, xiii, xiiin7, 8,
    8n8, 11, 15, 15n23
Springsted, Eric, 38, 47, 54, 91–92,
    103, 196
Stalin, Joseph, 4, 105
Steiner, George, 167n7, 168

Sullivan, William M., 141
"supernatural realm," 96–99, 97n25,
    107–108, 111, 111n20
Sylvie (Weil's niece), 168n10
Symposium, 65, 66, 205. *See also* Plato

Taney, Chief Justice Roger, 235
Tao Te Ching, 92, 92n17, 94–95, 204
Taoism, xv, 16, 91–96, 92n17, 98, 99,
    132, 132n6, 133, 154, 173, 183,
    200, 203, 204, 212, 213. *See also*
    Lao Tzu
Taylor, Charles, 33, 34, 35, 38
"the state," 127
Thibon, Gustav, 210
time, 1–3
Torah, 179–86
Trocmé, André, 72
Trocmé, Magda, 72
Trotsky, Leon, 21
Troy, 3, 4, 200n7
Tzimtzum, 185

United States, 10, 36, 51, 73, 80, 83,
    105, 124, 127, 142, 202–203, 225,
    229, 235
Upanishads, 173
uprootedness, 29, 112, 123–125, 126–
    127, 162, 172, 197–198. *See also*
    war

Vichy, 218
Vigny, 183
violated women. *See* rape

Wahl, Jean, 173
waiting, 7, 48, 49, 154
war, 3, 123–125, 124n1, 124n2, 181
Warsaw Ghetto, 165, 177, 224
White, James Boyd, 8n8

Williams, Rowan, xiin5, 191n1
Winch, Peter, xii, 5, 7, 43, 47, 50–51, 96–98
Wittgenstein, Ludwig, 1, 15, 39, 74, 168
Wolgast, Elizabeth, 35, 39, 89
work, 21, 26–30, 126; civilization of, 28, 141; factory, 9, 12–13, 26–29, 44–45, 86; spirituality of, 28–30, 53, 141, 162, 206, 208; women's, 12–13, 13n16, 113
World War II, 40, 72, 104, 105, 124, 125, 165, 167, 171, 203, 209
"worthy civilization," 29–30, 193–194
wu wei, 94

yen, 134

ABOUT THE AUTHOR

Richard H. Bell is Frank Halliday Ferris Professor of Philosophy at The College of Wooster, Wooster, Ohio. He has published several articles on Simone Weil and edited *Simone Weil's Philosophy of Culture* (Cambridge University Press) stemming from a two-year consultation he directed with Simone Weil scholars from France, Great Britain, Ireland, Finland, and the United States. Professor Bell has also published widely on the philosophers Ludwig Wittgenstein and Søren Kierkegaard, and in the area of contemporary spirituality. His most recent research, besides this book, is focused in the area of African philosophy and cross-cultural studies.

ABOUT THE APPENDIX AUTHORS

Ronald K. L. Collins is a legal scholar at Catholic University of America and teaches law at the University of Seattle, Washington. He is the cofounder of the Center for the Study of Commercialism, a non-profit public interest group in Washington, D.C. He has recently co-authored with David M. Skover *The Death of Discourse*, Boulder and Oxford: Westview Press, 1996.

Finn E. Nielsen is Senior Lecturer, Department of English, Swedish School of Economics and Business Administration, Helsinki, Finland, as well as on the staff of the Department of Political Science at the University of Helsinki. His doctoral dissertation was entitled "The Political Vision of Simone Weil" (University of California at Santa Barbara, 1976).

		DATE DUE		